G I N

A TASTING COURSE

GIN
A TASTING COURSE

ANTHONY GLADMAN

CONTENTS

8   A FLAVOUR-FOCUSED APPROACH

10 WHAT IS GIN?

12   LEGAL DEFINITIONS OF GIN

16   GETTING TO KNOW JUNIPER

18   HISTORICAL USES OF JUNIPER

20   A SPECIES UNDER THREAT

22   A LITTLE NIP OF GIN'S HISTORY

24   THE GIN CRAZE

26   MUCH ADO ABOUT DRINKING

28   THE TIPPLING ACT

30   GIN PALACES

32   GIN COMES OF AGE

34   THE SHADOW OF EMPIRE

38   PUTTIN' ON THE RITZ

40   POSTWAR DOLDRUMS

42   GIN'S RENAISSANCE

44   GIN AND THE ENVIRONMENT

48   DISTILLATION

50   THE POT STILL

52   THE COLUMN STILL

54   CONDENSERS

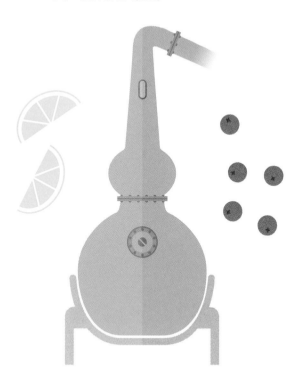

56 VAPOUR INFUSION

58 DISTILLATION FRACTONS AND FLAVOURS

60 WHY ARE STILLS MADE OF COPPER?

62 WHAT IS LOUCHING?

64 OTHER METHODS OF DISTILLATION

66 WHAT IS GIN MADE FROM?

68 BASE SPIRITS: MAKE OR BUY?

70 COMPOUNDED GINS

72 DIFFERENT STYLES OF GIN

76 SLOE GIN

78 FLAVOUR COMPOUNDS

80 THE MAIN BOTANICALS

86 MORE BOTANICALS

92 WHAT ABOUT BARRELS?

94 HOW FLAVOUR WORKS

96 THINKING ABOUT FLAVOUR

98 GET READY TO TASTE YOUR GIN

100 A SYSTEMATIC APPROACH TO TASTING

102 WRITING TASTING NOTES

104 DOES THE GLASS MATTER?

106 TYPES OF GLASSES

108 THE IMPORTANCE OF ICE

110 WAYS TO SERVE GIN

112 LET'S TALK TONIC

114 MAKING AN ICON: THE GIN AND TONIC

116 CLASSIC GIN COCKTAILS

118 COCKTAIL-MAKING EQUIPMENT

122 ARMY & NAVY/AVIATION

124 BEE'S KNEES/BIJOU

126 BRAMBLE/BRONX

128 CLOVER CLUB/CORPSE REVIVER NO. 2

130 DIRTY MARTINI/DRY MARTINI

132 ENGLISH GARDEN/FRENCH 75

134 GIBSON/GIMLET

136 GIN BASIL SMASH/GIN FIZZ

138 HANKY PANKY/JULIET AND ROMEO

140 LAST WORD/MARTINEZ

142 NEGRONI/OLD FRIEND

144 RED SNAPPER/SATAN'S WHISKERS

146 SOUTHSIDE RICKEY/20TH CENTURY

148 WHITE LADY/WHITE NEGRONI

150 THE GARNISHES

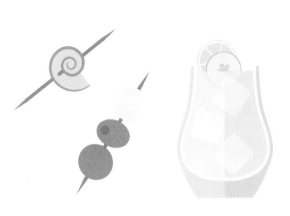

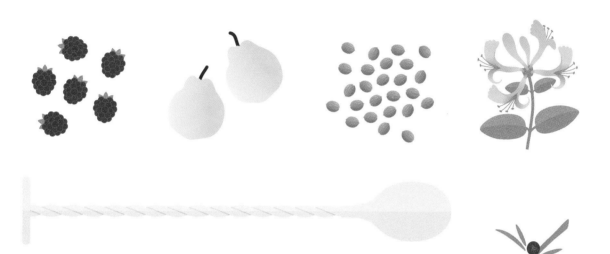

154 NAVIGATING GIN BY FLAVOUR

156 GINS THAT "TASTE OF GIN"

166 CITRUS-FORWARD GINS

174 HERBAL GINS

182 FLORAL GINS

190 FRUITY GINS

198 EARTHY AND AROMATIC GINS

206 MARITIME AND UMAMI GINS

214 SUGAR IN TONICS

216 GLOSSARY

218 INDEX

223 ACKNOWLEDGMENTS

A FLAVOUR-FOCUSED APPROACH

This book is all about the flavour of gin.

Flavour is what really matters, after all, when you're choosing a G to match with some T or deciding which cocktail to make. How's it going to taste? My aim is to give you the tools to answer that question, with at least some confidence, before you raise the glass to your lips.

I remember watching wine expert Oz Clarke on television back when I was barely old enough to drink. I was amazed by the colourful yet precise language he used to describe wine. It seemed to me that he must experience taste more vividly than I could ever hope to.

I was wrong. Your sense of taste isn't fixed at birth. It's not something you're stuck with. Tasting is a skill like any other, and with practice, you can improve. Together we will explore what flavour is and how it works, and discover how putting it into words can turn you into a better taster.

To take a step towards connoisseurship, you must move beyond recognizing what you taste; you must also understand it. This book guides your first steps on this path with a look at gin's history, its ingredients, and how it is made.

Most importantly, exploring this delicious spirit is about fun – and perhaps a little drop of escapism. Gin is alchemy. The best distillers capture the spirit of a place and suspend it in time, like a genie in its lamp, waiting for us to pull the stopper and release it again. Its flavours can transport us through time and space, even to places we've never been.

Before you settle down to read the rest, check my take on how to make the perfect gin and tonic and strategies for matching your garnish to your gin's flavour. Mix yourself a drink, sit back, then enjoy.

GIN'S FLAVOURS CAN TRANSPORT US THROUGH TIME AND SPACE, EVEN TO PLACES WE'VE NEVER BEEN.

ABOUT THE GINS IN THIS BOOK

I have reviewed more than 100 gins in this book and I've grouped them all by flavour. It might be interesting to learn where each one was made or discover which weird techniques the distiller employed, but, let's be honest, none of that matters if you don't enjoy drinking the end result.

Having said that, I've tried to give you a good selection of gins from around the world. Gin is a global spirit, and even though the UK still dominates, some of the most innovative gins right now come from elsewhere – places like Australia, France, India, and South Africa.

Gin is a complex drink. Some of the gins listed could have sat quite happily among two flavour groups or even three. I've always tried my best to reflect which characteristic is strongest within each gin, but people are sensitive to flavours to differing degrees. If I've said a gin is herbal, but to you it tastes more floral, that's fine. You're not wrong. Trust your own palate above all else. It won't let you down.

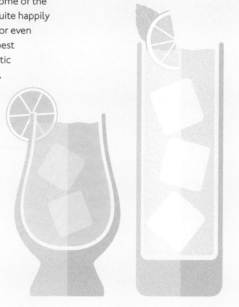

WHAT
IS
GIN?

WHAT MAKES A DRINK GIN? There are so many gins, it can be hard to imagine they are the same thing. This section will equip you with the tools to answer that question and others you may have about this delicious, complex spirit. We get to know juniper, gin's star attraction, in more depth. We also lift the lid on gin's other botanical ingredients that lend their wonderful aromas and flavours to the drink. We look at where gin came from and chart its history to the bloom of modern craft distilling. We learn how gin is made and how every choice the distiller makes can be tasted in the glass. Then we see how our senses combine to create uniquely personal impressions of flavour, and plot our way to improve as tasters. Finally, there are practical tips for perfecting your G&T.

LEGAL DEFINITIONS OF GIN

Understanding the laws that govern what gin is, which ingredients can go into it, and how it is made leads to a greater understanding of gin as a whole. And as a nice little side benefit, it also helps you decode the labels when you're choosing which gin to buy.

ALL GIN IN THE EU AND
THE UK MUST HAVE A
"PREDOMINANT TASTE"
OF JUNIPER.

UK AND EU MINIMUM STRENGTH FOR BOTTLED GIN

37.5%

ABV

GIN IN THE EU AND UK

All gin in the European Union (EU) and UK must be made from ethyl alcohol at 96% alcohol by volume (ABV) or more and have a "predominant taste" of juniper. There is no test to determine whether juniper's taste is predominant, so this is open to interpretation. The minimum strength for bottled gin in the EU and the UK is 37.5% ABV.

WHICH TYPE OF JUNIPER?

Distillers in the EU and the UK must use common juniper (*Juniperus communis*; see pp16–17), although there's nothing to stop them using other species alongside it as long as they're safe to consume – not all are.

US law does not restrict gin makers to any particular juniper species, although most use common juniper. The law in Australia and New Zealand doesn't mention juniper at all (see p14).

TYPES OF GIN DEFINED BY EU AND UK LAW

There are three separate types of gin defined by law in the EU and UK, plus a fourth in the EU.

GIN

The broadest definition of gin is a spirit made by adding natural or approved artificial flavouring to alcohol. Colouring or sweetening the gin is also permitted at this point. Compounded gins (see pp70–71) fall into this category.

DISTILLED GIN

Distilled gin is made by redistilling neutral alcohol with approved flavourings, which may be natural or artificial. After distillation, it may be diluted with more alcohol of the same composition, purity, and alcoholic strength as was initially used. Additional flavouring and sweetening are also permitted.

LONDON GIN

London gin (often called London Dry gin) must be made by redistilling ethyl alcohol, in the presence of only approved natural flavourings, to a minimum of 70% ABV. London gin requires a higher quality base spirit than other types of gin, which must contain less than 5g of methanol per hectolitre (22 gallons) of 100% ABV alcohol. After distillation, further colouring is forbidden and sweetening is limited to 0.1g of sugars per litre (1¾ pints). Distillers may also add water or further alcohol of the same composition, purity, and strength as was used in the initial distillation. The "London" part of the designation refers only to how the gin is made, not where.

GIN DE MAHÓN

EU law also mentions one further type of gin. Gin de Mahón comes from the Spanish island of Menorca and is covered by an EU protected geographical indication (PGI). There are just three permitted ingredients: ethyl alcohol of agricultural origin, distilled water, and common juniper berries with 7 to 9 per cent essential oil content by weight. No further flavourings may be added. It must be made in copper pot stills heated over an open wood fire, with the juniper berries in the pot. The final distillate is filtered. Xoriguer Mahón Gin (see p181) is the only example of this style.

GIN DE MAHÓN
This gin from Menorca is made with just three permitted ingredients.

DISTILLED WATER + **ETHYL ALCOHOL** + **COMMON JUNIPER BERRIES** = **GIN DE MAHÓN**

US MINIMUM STRENGTH FOR BOTTLED GIN

40%

ABV

GIN IN THE UNITED STATES

US law defines gin as a spirit displaying "a main characteristic flavour derived from juniper berries produced by distillation or mixing of spirits with juniper berries and other aromatics or extracts derived from these materials and bottled at not less than 40% ABV (or 80 proof)". In the United States, proof is the percentage of alcohol multiplied by two.

GIN IN AUSTRALIA AND NEW ZEALAND

Gin in Australia and New Zealand has no legal definition. Instead, it is lumped in under a catch-all definition for "spirit", which is defined as "a potable alcoholic distillate, including whisky, brandy, rum, gin, vodka and tequila, produced by distillation of fermented liquor derived from food sources, so as to have the taste, aroma and other characteristics generally attributable to that particular spirit".

TYPES OF GIN DEFINED BY US LAW

DISTILLED GIN

Distilled gin is made by the "original distillation of mash with or over juniper berries and other aromatics or their extracts, essences or flavours". No further flavouring is permitted after distillation.

REDISTILLED AND COMPOUNDED GIN

This gin is made by the redistillation of distilled spirits with the same flavourings stipulated for distilled gin, and compounded gin (see pp70–71) is made by mixing neutral spirits with them. Compounded gins may be further flavoured by essences made from approved natural or artificial ingredients. None of these gins may be coloured.

SLOE GIN

Sloe gin (see pp76–77) must contain at least 2.5 per cent sugar by weight and derive its main flavour from sloe berries (the law says nothing on juniper here). Sloe gins may be coloured as long as this is disclosed on the label.

GIN LIQUEUR OR GIN CORDIAL

These must display the "predominant characteristic flavour of gin". They must be made with gin as the exclusive distilled spirits base and bottled at or above 30% ABV. They may contain wine up to a maximum of 2.5 per cent by volume.

FLAVOURED GIN

This is defined as "gin flavoured with natural flavouring materials, with or without the addition of sugar, bottled at not less than 30% ABV". The predominant flavour must be declared on the label. Wine may also be added and, beyond a certain threshold, must also feature on the label. Flavoured gins may be coloured as long as this is disclosed on the label.

AGED GIN

There are also laws governing the labelling of aged gin that mirror those of other spirits, under which "statements regarding age or maturity […] are permitted only when the distilled spirits are stored in an oak barrel and, once dumped from the barrel, subjected to no treatment besides mixing with water, filtering, and bottling. If batches are made from barrels of spirits of different ages, the label may only state the age of the youngest spirits."

SLOE GIN
In the US, sloe gin is defined as a type of liqueur or cordial.

Sloe gin must contain at least 2.5 per cent sugar by weight

Sloe berries are the main flavour component

WILLIAM OF ORANGE
William of Orange is depicted in this painting landing with the Anglo-Dutch fleet for the invasion of England in 1688.

typically distilled from wine or beer in which juniper or other botanicals had been infused.

What we do know is that genever gave us the word "gin". Its first written use comes from 1714. In a pamphlet called "The Fable of the Bees: or, Private Vices, Publick Benefits", Anglo-Dutch philosopher Bernard Mandeville wrote: "The infamous liquor, the name of which deriv'd from juniper berries in Dutch, is now, by frequent use […] shrunk into a Monosyllable, intoxicating Gin."

DEFINITIONS OF GENEVER

Genever is made with ethyl alcohol, grain spirit, or grain distillate flavoured with juniper, which need not be the dominant flavour. It can either be "*jonge*" (young) or "*oude*" (old). These are not age statements but indicate whether the spirit was made using the newer distillation process or the older traditional style. Beyond that, there are a few defined subtypes (see box below).

A HISTORY OF GENEVER

Genever is a Dutch spirit closely related to gin that is also flavoured with juniper. Many historical accounts put genever as gin's precursor. The English supposedly developed a taste for it while fighting alongside the Dutch in European wars of the late 1500s and early 1600s, coining the term "Dutch courage" along the way. They took the spirit home with them, so the story goes, and began to make their own versions – especially after the Dutch William of Orange took England's throne in 1689. Their rotgut genever copies slowly evolved into today's gin.

Some historians doubt this is how things actually went down. They point out the English were distilling in the 1200s and 1300s, so didn't need to learn how from the Dutch. Also, distilling books from the mid-1400s onwards feature recipes for juniper-flavoured spirits and would have been available in England. Importantly, some of these early English recipes began with an already-distilled base spirit to which juniper berries and other botanicals were added, which mirrors how gin is made today. Genever, on the other hand, was

TYPE OF GENEVER	DESCRIPTION
JONGE GENEVER	Made with at most 15 per cent malt wine and 10g (¼oz) of sugar per litre (1¾ pints).
OUDE GENEVER	Made with 15 per cent or more malt wine and at most 20g (¾oz) of sugar per litre (1¾ pints).
GRAANGENEVER	Made entirely from grain.
OUDE GRAANGENEVER	Made entirely from grain and aged for at least one year.
KORENWIJN	Made with 51 per cent or more malt wine; it need not contain any juniper.

GETTING TO KNOW JUNIPER

Juniper is essential for gin. It is the one botanical gin *must* contain in order to fit the legal definition. If you look at all the classic and perhaps best-known gins – Beefeater, Gordon's, Tanqueray, and so on – juniper is the dominant flavour note.

THE ROLE OF JUNIPER

In recent years, the gin market has become very crowded. Some distillers, looking for a way to make their gin stand out, have dialled back juniper's leading role and placed other botanicals to the fore. This risks muddying the waters of what is and isn't gin. Without a strong juniper lead, gin can lose its distinctive edge and become just another flavoured spirit. Let's take a closer look at this plant, without which we wouldn't have gin today.

FLAVOURS OF JUNIPER

The juniper berry (actually a small, seed-bearing cone) is the main component of gin. The essential oils found within these berries contain a large range of volatile flavour compounds, particularly a group of chemicals called monoterpenes, which contribute to gin's characteristic flavour (see also "Flavour Compounds", pp78–79).

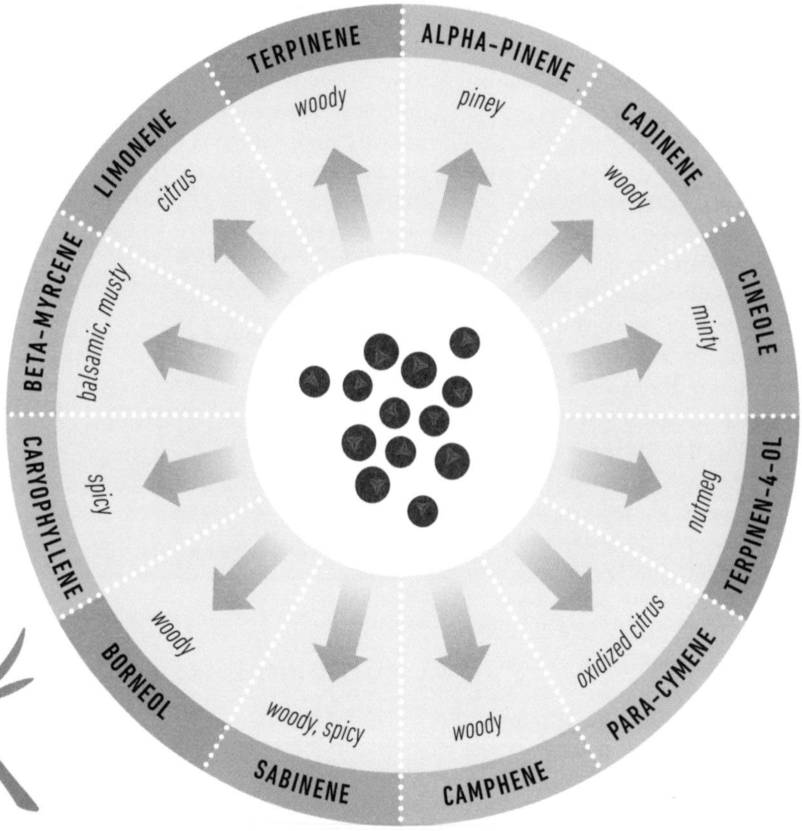

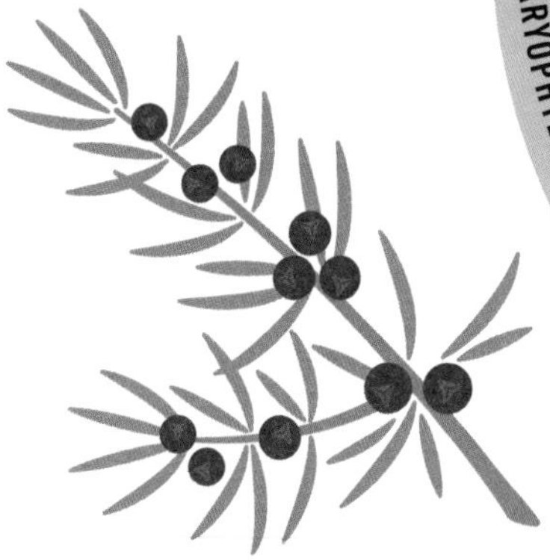

TERPINENE — woody
ALPHA-PINENE — piney
LIMONENE — citrus
CADINENE — woody
BETA-MYRCENE — balsamic, musty
CINEOLE — minty
CARYOPHYLLENE — spicy
TERPINEN-4-OL — nutmeg
BORNEOL — woody
PARA-CYMENE — oxidized citrus
SABINENE — woody, spicy
CAMPHENE — woody

COMMON JUNIPER

Common juniper (*Juniperus communis*) is an evergreen conifer that is native to cool, temperate parts of the northern hemisphere, including northern areas of North America, Europe, and northern Asia. It has greyish, brownish bark that peels with age, and reddish-brown twigs that sprout grey-green needles in thick, spiky clumps. It most often grows as a low, rather scruffy-looking shrub that spreads along the ground, although some mature trees can grow up to 10m (33ft) tall in the right conditions.

The species is dioecious, meaning the male and female reproductive organs in flowers grow on separate plants. It can take around 15 years for a tree's sex to become apparent. The flowers of male trees don't produce fruit. Female trees bear fruit in the form of berries, which resemble blueberries when ripe. It takes around 18 months for the berries to mature from green to purple-black.

Juniper grows on moorland, chalk lowland, in rocky areas, and in old native pine woodland. A plant can live for up to 200 years, and you'll sometimes see mature plants that have been bent and gnarled into fantastic shapes by long decades spent exposed to the prevailing winds.

Juniper often grows alongside old droving routes, where farmers moved their cattle. The cattle would rub up against the juniper to scratch their various itches on the plant's needles. In so doing, the cattle knocked the seed-bearing berries to the ground, and their heavy hooves broke up the soil. In this way, new juniper plants were propagated.

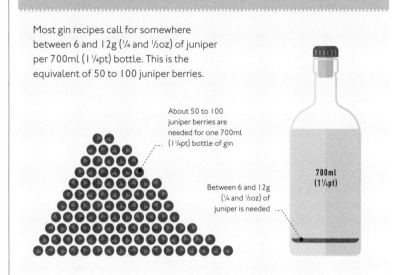

HOW MUCH JUNIPER IS IN MY GIN?

Most gin recipes call for somewhere between 6 and 12g (¼ and ½oz) of juniper per 700ml (1¼pt) bottle. This is the equivalent of 50 to 100 juniper berries.

About 50 to 100 juniper berries are needed for one 700ml (1¼pt) bottle of gin

Between 6 and 12g (¼ and ½oz) of juniper is needed

700ml (1¼pt)

HARVESTING JUNIPER

It's hard to believe, but the truth is no one has yet managed to cultivate juniper commercially. This means all the juniper used to make gin comes from wild plants. Because juniper grows in such inaccessible areas, the harvesting must be done by hand. The process takes place between October and February and goes something like this:

- Take a long walk, usually uphill, to some remote spot where the juniper grows.
- Find your female fruiting juniper bush and place a tub underneath it.
- Whack the branches with a stick to knock the berries into the tub.
- Take another long walk back down the hill, this time carrying a tub full of berries.

Although the UK is the leading manufacturer of gin, very little native juniper is used in British gins.

Even those brands that do use it tend to do so alongside juniper from elsewhere – typically Italy, North Macedonia, and Croatia. The juniper in those countries is more abundant and offers a different composition in flavour compounds, such as alpha-pinene and sabinene (see opposite), that consumers generally prefer. Juniper is also harvested in Serbia, Bulgaria, and India. European juniper berries tend to be small and dark, while Asian ones are larger (and cheaper).

Most distillers in the United States import their juniper from Europe, as the locally grown berries are often too strongly flavoured. Distillers in Australia and New Zealand use European juniper too, as it doesn't grow well in the southern hemisphere.

Distillers buy juniper by weight and often store it for a number of years. During that time, the berries become dry and shrivelled, but although they lose moisture, they don't lose their essential oils.

HISTORICAL USES OF JUNIPER

People have long turned to juniper for more than its flavour. Evidence of humans using the essential oils in juniper for medicine stretches back through the ages and encompasses all sorts of ailments from coughs to cancer.

ANCIENT USES OF JUNIPER

Juniper appears in one of the oldest medical texts we know, the ancient Egyptian *Ebers Papyrus*. These were written around 1500 BCE, although some parts may be significantly older. Even back then, the use of juniper for tapeworms was already long established.

The Romans used juniper to aid digestion, and Greek athletes ate it to to increase their stamina. Indigenous peoples in North America used juniper to help heal cuts and wounds.

NICHOLAS CULPEPER

The English herbalist Nicholas Culpeper wrote in the 1600s that juniper is "scarce to be paralleled for its virtues". Its berries, he wrote, were potent against poison and therefore "excellent good against the biting of venomous beasts". He also claimed that they were "as great a resister of the pestilence as any growing", and that juniper "is so powerful a remedy against the dropsy, that the very lye made of the ashes of the herb being drank, cures the disease".

DE MATERIA MEDICA
Pedanius Dioscorides, a Greek physician in the Roman army, wrote his *De Materia Medica* between 50 and 70 CE. It lists the medicinal uses of more than 600 plants, including juniper, shown here

A UNIVERSAL PANACEA

If you had diarrhoea, juniper could stop it. If you had piles, juniper would soothe them. If you had pains in the belly, ruptures, cramps, or convulsions, juniper would be your remedy. It was good for a cough, shortness of breath, or consumption. People used its berries as a diuretic to ease urinary tract infections, kidney stones, and bladder stones. They sought it out to soothe their indigestion, dampen their heartburn, restore their appetite, reduce their bloating, flush out their intestinal worms, and calm their flatulence.

Women took juniper during childbirth to speed their ordeal along – its berries contain a chemical that can stimulate contraction of the uterine muscles. Others took the berries somewhat earlier, hoping to hasten unwanted pregnancies to an end. "Giving birth under the juniper tree" was a common euphemism for miscarriage induced by juniper.

USES IN MAGIC

Some uses of juniper were more magical than medical. Lovelorn souls cooked juniper in potions to ensnare their as-yet-uninterested

IT WAS SAID THAT IF YOU DREAMT OF GATHERING JUNIPER BERRIES, IT WAS AN OMEN OF PROSPERITY.

JUNIPER WREATH
People used juniper branches to ward off evil spirits and to commune with the dead.

mate. If the interest was already satisfactorily mutual, another use was to enhance male potency. Herbal viagra, if you like.

It was said that if you dreamt of gathering juniper berries in winter, it was an omen of prosperity to come. People also believed the berries signified honour in dreams or presaged the birth of a boy.

Juniper's branches came in handy, too. In parts of Europe, people used them to deter witches and the devil. During Beltane (May Day), when people believed the veil between the spirit world and ours was thin, they hung its branches over doorways to ward off fairies (these were mischievous trouble-makers rather than Tinker Bell).

People used juniper branches at Samhain (Halloween) to discourage visits from the bothersome dead. They believed juniper could aid clairvoyance, and burnt it when they wanted to commune with the departed. They also used its aromatic smoke for ritual purification.

WHAT DOES JUNIPER TASTE LIKE?

Juniper would once have been a very familiar flavour, but these days, few of us ever get to taste it in isolation. We usually encounter it alongside lots of other flavours crowding the picture.

On its own, juniper has a piney and resinous taste with hint of citrus. It's a fragrant, bittersweet taste. Sometimes it gives notes of lavender, camphor, and black pepper.

Once distilled, ripe juniper tastes fresh, piney, grassy, and a little bit herbal. Some gins also make use of green, unripe juniper. After being distilled, this is more earthy and woody than ripe juniper, with flavours of cedar and sandalwood, and pine again on the finish.

The primary aromatic molecule in juniper is alpha-pinene, which smells strongly of pine and spruce. The amount contained in the juniper varies greatly depending on where it grows. In gin, the flavour of angelica root is often confused with juniper owing to its similar scent, though angelica is a little more musky and woody. Angelica contains both alpha-pinene (like juniper) and beta-pinene.

ANGELICA

LAVENDER

CITRUS

SANDALWOOD

BLACK PEPPER

A SPECIES UNDER THREAT

Common juniper is not having a great time at the moment. The number of natural sites where it grows is at an all-time low. Within those sites, the population of trees is shrinking. Mature trees are less fertile than they once were and are having trouble reproducing. In the UK, it has become one of the rarest native trees. No one really knows why.

INFECTED PLANTS

One theory puts the blame on the soil-borne pathogen *Phytophthora austrocedri* – a fungus-like organism that infects and kills cypress and juniper trees. It damages the plant's root and stem, affecting its ability to take water and nutrients from the soil. Signs of infection are the browning of foliage and the progressive death of twigs, branches, shoots, or roots.

To date, *P. austrocedri* has been discovered in the wild only in Argentina and the UK. In Argentina, it infects the Chilean cedar tree. It was first identified in the UK in 2011 but had probably been there for a while already. *P. austrocedri* may have been introduced in the late 1990s, during a campaign to bolster the UK's juniper populations by growing wild seeds in nurseries and replanting the new trees in the wild. Infected and healthy plants may have mixed

AFFECTED AREAS

These charts show sites in England and Scotland where juniper is showing signs of poor growth or dieback due to *Phytophthora austrocedri*.

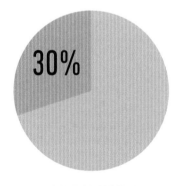

SCOTTISH SPECIAL AREAS OF CONSERVATION (SACs)
30% of areas affected

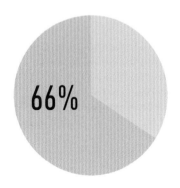

ENGLISH SITES OF SPECIAL SCIENTIFIC INTEREST (SSSIs)
66% of sites affected

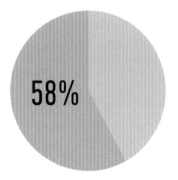

SCOTTISH SITES OF SPECIAL SCIENTIFIC INTEREST (SSSIs)
58% of sites affected

PLANT DESTROYER

The gin-bothering *Phytophthora austrocedri* bug belongs to the same genus as the species that was responsible for the potato blight and famine in Ireland in the 1840s.

in the nurseries, allowing the pathogen to spread. The discovery of *P. austrocedri* in plant nurseries across Europe supports this theory. Since 2011, *P. austrocedri* has been found in 100 sites around the UK, mostly in Scotland and northern England, some of which are known to contain trees grown in nurseries.

Organisms in the *Phytophthora* genus live in the soil, and they transfer through the movement of water and the movement of infected soil by animals and people.

CONTROLLING THE THREAT

There are few ways of controlling *P. austrocedri* infection. We don't yet have any chemical means of fighting it. All we can do is ensure good drainage where juniper grows, and try to slow the spread of infection by cutting and burning out infected trees. Some trees seem to display a natural resistance to infection, but research has yet to confirm this.

The European Union (EU) has legislated to protect juniper, requiring that member states manage and maintain populations. It is likely this legislation will continue to be observed in the UK, but the responsibility now falls to landowners.

THE FIGHTBACK

Some gin distillers are fighting back by replanting juniper stocks. The makers of Hepple Gin in Northumberland, England, for instance, hope to build up enough stocks to supply all of the juniper for their stills, although they say this may take at least 20 years. Until then, they operate a strict soil quarantine and only plant juniper propagated on their own estate.

Likewise, the distiller of Rock Rose Gin in Caithness, Scotland, began planting juniper on its site in 2018. It hopes to be able to produce gin using 100 per cent Scottish botanicals by 2028. In the meantime, the distillery continues to import juniper from Bulgaria and Italy.

OTHER JUNIPER SPECIES

Juniperus communis is not the only juniper species – there are 60 or so species around the world. Although most legal definitions for gin still specify common juniper, distillers are starting to experiment with other types of juniper to convey a sense of connection to their roots.

TEXAS OR REDBERRY JUNIPER

(*J. pinchotii*) grows in the United States. Its fruit is copper to copper-red in colour and is juicy and sweet rather than resinous. Think of dried cranberry and you won't be too far away.

GREEK AND PHOENICIAN JUNIPER

Distillers in Lebanon have Greek (*J. excelsa*) and Phoenician juniper (*J. phoenicea*) to contend with. These produce berries so rich in oils and so potent in flavour that they are hard to tame.

AFRICAN PENCIL CEDAR

In Kenya, distillers use berries from the African pencil cedar (*J. procera*). It is the only juniper species native to the southern hemisphere and gives distinctive earthy flavours.

A LITTLE NIP OF GIN'S HISTORY

Gin has a long and sometimes rather murky past. It wasn't always the carefree spirit we enjoy today. Let's take a tour through some edited highlights and low points from its history.

DISTILLATION IN THE ANCIENT WORLD

Spirits have been around for a long time. There's evidence that people in China were distilling spirits from rice beer since at least 800 BCE. People in the East Indies and the ancient empires of Greece and Egypt produced spirits too, more than 2,000 years ago.

Alchemists in the city of Alexandria, in Egypt, developed alembic stills as far back as the 1st or 2nd century CE. They used "hydraulic" distillation – based on water rather than wine – not to get drunk but to live forever. Alchemy may have produced some pleasant-smelling perfumes and floral essences, but its real goals were to turn base metal into gold and discover the "elixir of life" that would grant immortality.

THE SPREAD OF DISTILLATION

From Alexandria, with its school of alchemy, knowledge of distilling spread over the following centuries throughout the Middle East to Byzantine Greece and Persia. As it spread, so it was improved. By the 6th century, alembic stills had developed from two crude vessels connected by a tube to stills made of glass.

In the 7th century, Arabs conquered Alexandria and Persia, and in so doing, learned about hydraulic distillation. Arab scientists continued to improve upon the technology, eventually discovering how to distil grapes and then wine – for which they (mostly) had little other use.

ISLAMIC SCHOLARS REFINE DISTILLATION

It was an Islamic alchemist-philosopher named Abu Musa Jabir ibn Hayyan (721–815) who left the earliest-known written reference to distillation, which dates back to the 8th century. He wrote about the flammable vapours he found at the mouths of bottles in which wine and salt were boiled.

Over the following decades, other Muslim scientists wrote about their use of alcohol as a solvent for making inks, lacquers, medicines, and cosmetics. The first to produce alcohol in any volume was an Arab Andalusian chemist and surgeon named Abu al-Qasim al-Zahrawi (c.936–1013). To

THE PROCESS OF DISTILLATION
An illustration from *Book of the Seven Climes* shows the process of distillation. It is from an 18th-century copy of the book on alchemy by the 13th-century Islamic scholar Abu al-Qasim al-Iraqi.

produce alcohol in volume, vapours must be rapidly cooled using water, and it was al-Zahrawi who dreamt up the necessary improvements in cooling technology to do this.

KNOWLEDGE SPREADS FROM SALERNO

The Christian and Muslim worlds met just south of Naples, in Italy, at Salerno. There the world's oldest medical school had amassed texts in Latin, Greek, Hebrew, and Arabic. Its tutors were drawn from the best physicians in the world. Salerno was a melting pot where Muslims and Christians shared ideas. They also translated medical books written in Arabic, Hebrew, and Greek into Latin – including those of Jabir (known to Western scholars as Geber).

In Europe, literacy and medicine were concentrated in the hands of the Catholic Church, and so it was from cathedrals and monasteries throughout Christendom that scholars came to Salerno, and then returned with their new-found knowledge of distillation.

Salerno was not the only place where Christians learned the secrets of distillation from Arabs. There were Christian monasteries and convents in Egypt, Iraq, and Syria, which was particularly noted for its wine and arak (distilled wine). In large cities such as Baghdad, non-Muslims ran wine shops. The wine trade was also important in Muslim-ruled Andalusia (al-Andalus).

SCHOLA MEDICA SALERNITANA
The medical school at Salerno was founded in the 9th century and is considered to be the oldest medical school of modern civilization.

CHRISTIAN SCHOLARS RETURNING FROM SALERNO SPREAD THEIR NEW-FOUND KNOWLEDGE OF DISTILLATION.

THE GIN CRAZE

Hopping forward a few hundred years, London in the early 18th century was a time when gin drinking went through its awkward, rebellious teenage years.

THE ANGLO-DUTCH ANGLE

In the late 1600s, with the memory of the English Civil War (1642–51) still fresh in the national psyche, England was a country split between Protestants and Catholics. James II, a Catholic, and, moreover, Scottish, held the throne but was deeply unpopular among the country's Protestant nobles. They eventually deposed him in the Glorious Revolution of 1688–89, and invited the Protestant Dutch Prince William of Orange to rule in his place.

William ascended the English throne in 1689 (becoming William III) and ruled as co-monarch with his wife, Mary II (who was James's daughter). William brought with him a taste for drinking genever (see p15), a Dutch gin-alike spirit.

In 1690, Parliament introduced laws designed to encourage the distillation of spirits from corn (wheat), so that homegrown English spirits might replace the imported French brandy that had hitherto been popular. Another law enacted in 1694 introduced new taxes on beer, and the stage was set for gin to become the cheaper of the two drinks.

William died in 1702 and was succeeded by Queen Anne. In that same year, the Worshipful Company of Distillers, which had until that point enjoyed a monopoly over distilling in London, lost its charter. Very quickly people began to make, and drink, more gin.

A series of good harvests saw workers' wages rise and food costs fall, meaning people had a little money to spend on drink. Annual consumption had been a little over 4.5 million litres (1 million gallons) in 1700; by 1714, this had doubled, and it would continue to grow even more rapidly for the next few decades.

LONDON'S GROWING HANGOVER

In the early 1700s, Britain's population was shifting. Parliament had introduced a large number of Inclosure Acts that saw open fields and common land pass into private ownership. Dispossessed of what little land they had, and facing crippling work for little reward, rural labourers moved to the cities, and particularly London, to seek a better life. Most did not find one.

Class-based British society kept the workers poor and dependent upon their employers, with a sprinkling of snobbery that implied this was the natural order of things. Demand for unskilled labourers in cities was low, and with more arriving every day, wages were also low. Hunger and grinding poverty made people's lives a misery.

With little else to do, many of the urban poor turned to drink. Gin, being cheapest, is what they sought out.

LONDON SLUMS
People lived in appalling squalor in parts of London in the 1700s. Little wonder, then, that they turned to drink.

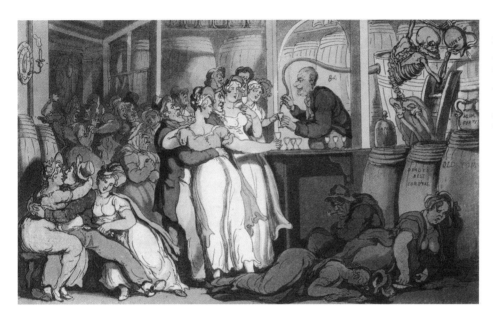

DANCE OF DEATH
An illustration by Thomas Rowlandson depicts people drinking in a "dram shop". It is captioned: "Some find their death by sword and bullet and some by fluids down the gullet."

MOTHER'S RUIN

With its short history in Britain, gin lacked beer's long-established ties to alehouses and taverns, which were traditionally male spaces. Women took to gin with just as much enthusiasm as their menfolk, but were often treated more harshly for it. They were blamed for neglecting their babies or using gin to quieten them, and thus gin became known as "Mother's Ruin".

In 1723, the death rate in London exceeded the birth rate. It would remain higher for the next decade. Around this time, some 23 million litres (5 million gallons) of gin were distilled each year in London alone, and the number of shops and houses selling "strong waters" grew to 6,000 or more. This meant that about a quarter of all dwellings in London were gin shops.

Little wonder, then, that many babies in the city were born with foetal alcohol syndrome. As many as three in four children born in London died before they reached the age of five.

DEFOE BLAMES GIN

In 1728, the English writer Daniel Defoe blamed gin for many of London's problems and denounced drinking among women, especially mothers. He wrote, "in less than an Age, we may expect a fine, Spindle-shank'd Generation". Many among the upper classes shared this fear of an enfeebled nation. What might England become without fresh bodies to feed its mills and foreign wars?

MUCH ADO ABOUT DRINKING

To put the Gin Craze into context, it's important to understand that drinking was common among people of all ages, sexes, and classes. Any "concern" expressed by the wealthy upper classes that the "lower orders" were drinking to excess was hypocritical at best.

THE GIN ACTS

The upper classes felt not compassion but disapproval: the wrong sort of people were having the wrong sort of good time, drinking the wrong sort of booze. They felt the poor were becoming "luxurious" and accustomed to ideas and pastimes above their station, which threatened to upset the prevailing social order.

Successive governments tried and failed to control gin drinking through a number of laws known as the Gin Acts. The first, in 1729, sought to restrict gin sales by licensing retailers and taxing spirits to which juniper berries or other ingredients were added. It was widely flouted (people just took the juniper out), and the big distillers lobbied hard to have it repealed.

The second Gin Act, in 1733, attempted to promote gin drinking in taverns but instead drove it into thousands of underground gin shops. The third, in 1736, imposed eye-watering taxes, unworkable minimum measures of sale, and even costlier licences on retailers, driving many respectable taverns out of business.

SATIRICAL PRINT
A print by an anonymous artist shows the "funeral of Madame Genever", a satire on the Gin Acts.

GIN LANE
William Hogarth's print from 1751 depicts the debauchery and drunkenness that were said to follow from drinking gin.

GIN THE SCAPEGOAT

The government employed informers to help prosecute unlicensed gin sellers. These informers were deeply unpopular figures and were often attacked or even killed. People protested in the streets, and gin sales continued to rise. The unrest was more likely driven by the unbearable conditions the poor were forced to endure, rather than the gin they drank to escape, but gin was a useful scapegoat for the rich to blame for society's ills.

GIN LANE: THE CRAZE REACHES ITS PEAK

London's gin swilling reached its peak in 1743, when annual consumption reached 36 million litres (8 million gallons). By then, the government, embroiled in European wars again, needed to raise funds and finally introduced a Gin Act that reduced consumption.

This time, it went after the distillers rather than the sellers. It forbade distillers to sell directly to the public and raised the excise duty they had to pay. Retail licences were lowered to £1, which allowed respectable publicans to get back into business, thus ending the need for informers.

Despite the fall in consumption, the complaints and hand-wringing about gin's terrible influence continued. Gin was blamed for farm labourers, freshly arrived in London, dropping dead after drinking too much. Gin was the culprit for women spontaneously bursting into flames after drinking too much. Gin was blamed when Mary Estwick passed out in a chair and let the baby she was minding fall into the fire and burn to death. Gin was responsible when Judith Dufour killed her infant daughter and sold her clothes for money with which to get drunk.

By 1749, although gin's peak had passed, Londoners in want of a dram could still choose from more than 17,000 gin shops. William Hogarth's *Gin Lane* print was published soon after, in 1751. This was essentially propaganda on behalf of beer brewers, and leaned heavily on the more lurid fears whipped up around gin drinking in order to contrast them with beer's image as wholesome, natural, and, above all, British. (Of course, people could and did get just as drunk on beer as they did on gin.)

THE TIPPLING ACT

In 1751, magistrate Henry Fielding published *An Enquiry into the Causes of the Late Increase in Robbers*. Gin and crime were, by now, intimately linked in the public imagination.

THE BEGINNING OF THE END

Although crime did increase in London during the Gin Craze, so did the city's population. The crime rate was actually rather stable. The growth of newspapers and increasing public literacy meant the fear of crime spread, and gin's critics used this to their own ends.

In 1751, the government felt compelled to act against gin once more and introduced a law known as the Tippling Act. This was the last Gin Act and is often seen as marking the beginning of the end of the Gin Craze. It included a small rise in the duty paid on spirits, and doubled the price of a retail licence, which was now available only to alehouses, taverns, and inns.

This dramatically curtailed the availability of gin and put an end to

ST CRISPIN'S DAY
An engraving by British caricaturist George Cruikshank depicts a gin court scuffle during St Crispin's Day celebration in Petty France, London.

THE TIPPLING ACT PUT AN END TO BACK-STREET GIN HAWKERS AS SALES MOVED INTO ALEHOUSES, TAVERNS, AND INNS.

its sale in the back streets and gin shops. By 1752, the volume of spirits produced (legitimately) fell by more than one-third.

GIN'S RESET BUTTON

A poor harvest in 1757 led to fears of a bread shortage. The government banned the distillation of grains, and halted the export of corn and malt, so that the little wheat and barley there was could be used to feed the nation. These measures were extended when the harvest failed again in 1758.

Spirit production didn't halt completely. Some distillers switched to making alcohol from imported molasses, but in nothing like the volume at which gin had poured from the stills. Importers also sought out rum to fill the gap that gin had left. Even so, Londoners were drinking much less.

The harvest in 1759 was a good one, and farmers and distillers called for the ban on distilling to be lifted. Despite the arguments of the church and moral reformers, who supported a total ban on alcohol, the government restored corn distilling early in 1760. (It was, after all, a nice earner for the state.) Excise duty on spirits was doubled, and the government offered subsidies on all spirits exported abroad.

AFTER THE CRAZE

The urban poor continued to drink themselves silly, but moved back to beer, which was again cheaper than spirits. Gin began to attain a sheen of respectability, and the regulation of distilling eventually resulted in a small number of distillers dominating the industry. Gin began to improve in quality too, becoming more like the drink we enjoy today.

It was during the second half of the 18th century, following the reintroduction of grain distilling in 1760, that many famous gin brands were established, including Greenall's (1761), Gordon's (1769), and Plymouth (1793). By 1794, gin production was a well-established industry, with more than 40 distillers operating in London alone in the districts of Westminster, the City of London, and Southwark.

NIGHT
William Hogarth's satirical engraving entitled *Night*, part of which is shown here, shows a drunken man being supported home by his servant.

GIN PALACES

Pubs in England in the early 1800s were rather drab and dingy. Picture dark bricks, wooden shutters, and shadows where candlelight couldn't reach. There wasn't a huge difference, architecturally speaking, between the public house and any other house. But all that was about to change.

THE ORIGINS

England was awash with illegally imported gin. So much was smuggled ashore that villagers in Kent supposedly used it to clean their windows. The government wasn't keen on all this untaxed

LONDON GIN PALACE
An illustration from 1821 depicts people of different classes and states of inebriation drinking "blue ruin", or gin, in a London gin palace.

alcohol sloshing around, so, in 1825, it cut taxes on the legal stuff almost in half, to 6 shillings per gallon (almost £6 per litre in today's money).

The result was, predictably, another boom in gin drinking. Consumption shot up from 16.8 million litres (3.7 million gallons) in 1825 to 33.6 million litres (7.4 million gallons) in 1826. It wasn't long before a new kind of drinking establishment came along to cater for drinkers' renewed thirst for gin.

The new gin palaces were a thrilling, modern assault on the senses with high ceilings, double-height windows, etched and frosted mirrors to bounce the light around, and the new modern miracle: gas lights, everywhere, gleaming off the polished mahogany bar and illuminating the ornate mouldings. It must have felt like drinking in the future, a Victorian Las Vegas.

What gin palaces lacked, though, was seating. They weren't

THE BRIEF REIGN OF THE GIN PALACE LEFT A LASTING LEGACY.

places to linger with friends, passing a pleasant evening in conversation. They were machines for the efficient separation of drinkers from their money and their sobriety.

DRINK MORE GIN!

Gin palaces offered no food, no private meeting rooms, no newspapers or distractions. There was nothing to do but drink your fill – the quicker the better – and move on, making room for more customers to come and do the same.

And come they did, a great tide of people thirsty for gin. More than half a million every week poured through the doors of London's 14 largest gin palaces alone. The customers were poor and the gin was cheap, but still, a well-placed establishment might make as much

as a guinea, about £100 in today's money, every minute.

The poor old pubs saw their trade drop away. Many simply closed, while others remade themselves in the new gin palace model. This wasn't an easy option. Refurbishing a pub to match the gin palace's splendour might cost as much as £3,000, which was an enormous sum for the time.

BEER FIGHTS BACK

In 1830, parliament was at the tax levers again, this time swinging the pendulum back towards beer. It removed duty on British beer and eased restrictions on who was allowed to brew and sell it. This led to an explosion of new public houses and breweries throughout the country, particularly in the rapidly expanding industrial

centres in the north of England. In the first six months alone, 25,000 new licences were granted. Working-class drinkers could once again return to an affordable pint and comfortable seating.

The brief reign of the gin palace was at an end, but they left behind a lasting legacy, not least in the look and feel of the classic Victorian pub that you can still see today. Less obviously, we have gin palaces to thank for the flowering of Victorian philanthropic public works – its parks, public libraries, and the current site of the National Gallery in London. These arose (at least partly) to provide London's poor with something better to do than drinking themselves to death.

COATES & CO. PLYMOUTH GIN
Coates & Co. made their Plymouth Gin at the Black Friars distillery in the naval town of Plymouth from 1793. Much of Coates & Co.'s gin was purchased by the Royal Navy for its officers.

GIN COMES OF AGE

During the 1800s, gin escaped for good from its rough-and-ready roots and became the drink we know today. While Britain was its spiritual home, this was the period when it first began to spread around the world.

LONDON DRY EMERGES

In 1831, Irish inventor Aeneas Coffey patented a design for a new type of still (see p52) that could run continuously and produce alcohol in excess of 90% ABV. Before this, he had worked for more than two decades as a distillery excise tax collector, and so had plenty of opportunity to become familiar with earlier types of stills and their limitations. His new design improved upon one from 1826 that used two linked columns rather than a pot.

Coffey's new still was able to produce purer alcohol much more efficiently and cost-effectively than distillers could manage before, and it became popular very quickly. By the middle of the 1800s, the quality of gin, made using these stills, had improved greatly and was much closer to the gin we enjoy today. Distillers had previously added sugar to their gins to soften the harsh alcohol, but this was no longer needed, so they began to leave it out. The new style of gin became known as dry gin, and then as London Dry gin (see p73).

GLOBAL TRADE

By the mid-1800s, Britain was becoming the most powerful trading nation in the world (see p35), with a growing empire and a vast fleet of ships to transport its goods around the globe. Parliament removed export duties on gin in 1850, and gin began to spread from London into new markets. Gin went to sea on British Navy ships and into new lands with British soldiers. It was during this time that people started to mix gin with tonic, bitters, and lime (see p37).

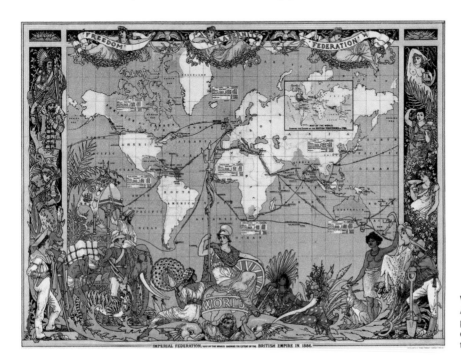

WORLDWIDE EMPIRE
A global map by Walter Crane, published in 1886, shows the extent of the British Empire in the 19th century.

GIN BENEFITED GREATLY FROM THE LACK OF COMPETITION FROM WINE.

GIN DISTILLERS
Many of gin's most famous distillers were established during the latter part of the 1800s, such as Beefeater, Hayman's (both 1863), and Seagram's (1883).

MARTINI TIME

The Martini was invented in 1888. Probably – it's not 100 per cent clear. What we do know is that hazy memories of Martini-like drinks start appearing around California during the Gold Rush (1848–55). These mixtures of Old Tom gins (see pp74–75) and sweet vermouth, perhaps with orange curaçao and bitters, most likely form the basis of the Martinez (see p141), from which the Martini evolved over the next few decades. We're not quite at the Dry Martini (see p131) yet, but it's notable that gin had improved so much that drinking it in this way was starting to sound like a good idea.

GIN GETS A BOOST

In the 1860s, gin got a boost thanks to phylloxera. This tiny parasitic insect found its way across the Atlantic and onto French vines, where it caused the Great French Wine Blight. Many vineyards were destroyed by the disease these aphids spread, and the country's mighty wine industry was almost wiped out. Supplies of French wine, and the brandy made from it, all but disappeared for more than a decade, and people turned to other drinks instead. Gin benefited greatly from this lack of competition.

Many of gin's most famous distillers got their start during the latter part of the 1800s, such as Beefeater and Hayman's (both 1863), and Seagram's (1883). America's first dry gin appeared in 1868 when the Fleischmann Brothers established their distillery in Cincinnati, Ohio.

Improvements in glass-making during the 1890s meant that clear glass became more common. Until then, gin was sold in wooden casks or earthenware crocks. The new, clear glass bottles were a perfect showcase for the clarity of the spirit within.

MARTINI
By the 1880s, gin had improved to the extent that Martinis were now on the table.

THE SHADOW OF EMPIRE

Gin's history is intimately wrapped up with that of tonic, and both are steeped in colonization and empire. This history is most often shaped to serve the interests of the colonizers, not the colonized, and washes away untold injustices and suffering.

THE SPICE TRADE

Europeans had enjoyed spices such as cloves, nutmeg, and mace for centuries but remained ignorant of their origin until the early 1500s. Spices came from the tiny Spice Islands, today known as the Moluccas (or Maluku Islands), in the Indonesian archipelago.

Europeans' hunger for spices helped set the template for colonization and imperial expansion. Soon after Portuguese explorer Vasco da Gama discovered a sea route to India in 1497–99, Portugal took over the majority of the world's spice trade. It retained its dominance for almost a century, but was eventually supplanted by the Dutch, who formed the Dutch East India Company (Vereenigde Oostindische Compagnie, or VOC) in 1602. The VOC was permitted to govern territories in the East and could run its own shipyards, build its own forts, raise its own armies, and make treaties in its own name.

Portugal, England, and the Netherlands fought for control over the Spice Islands for many years. During these struggles, local populations on the islands also fought with the colonizing powers. Their reward was bloody oppression: their cities were burned to the ground, and they were massacred in their thousands, deported, or enslaved. Until recently, history has tended to ignore the suffering of the Indigenous peoples.

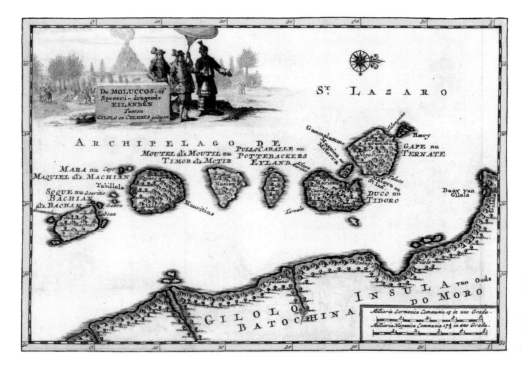

SPICE ISLANDS
A Dutch map from 1707 shows the tiny Spice Islands in the East Indies.

EAST INDIA COMPANY'S YARD
East India Company ships are shown moored at Deptford, on the Thames, in this painting from the 1680s.

PLUNDERING WEALTH

The success of early European voyages to the Indian Ocean in the late 1500s inspired English traders to set up their own East India Company (EIC). The British Empire may eventually have spanned the globe, but the source for much of its fabulous wealth lay in India.

When the EIC landed on the Indian subcontinent in the early 1600s, England produced about 3 per cent of global manufacturing. India was home to 25 per cent and produced about 35 per cent of the world's gross domestic product (GDP).

The EIC, with its own private army, soon seized Bengal and forced local rulers to trade with it. From there, it expanded throughout the subcontinent, bribing local rulers, installing puppet regimes, and plundering as it went.

Britain was soon busy establishing colonies elsewhere, and by the 1760s, it had control over most of North America and the Caribbean. Thanks to these colonies, and India, Britain had access to all the ingredients it needed to flavour gin. Ships brought these back to Britain and up the Thames into London. The capital also had plentiful access to grain and fresh water from springs in Bloomsbury and Clerkenwell, making it an ideal hub for distilling gin.

By the early 1800s, the British EIC's army was twice as large as the British Army and its annual revenues in India were around £300 million in today's value. The first governor of the Bengal Presidency was Robert Clive, who was also the British EIC's major-general. He was so rich, it is said his wife's pet ferret had a diamond necklace worth £262,000 in today's money.

The EIC amassed power in Britain too. It spent prodigiously – for instance, building the London docks through which the wealth and goods of the empire flowed. Some of its profits saw its stockholders elected to Parliament through rotten boroughs (constituencies that had very few voters but were able to elect a member of Parliament); the EIC controlled one quarter of the legislature. It was autonomous on paper, but in reality, the EIC was another, often corrupt arm of the British state.

THE EAST INDIA COMPANY'S ARMY WAS TWICE AS LARGE AS THE BRITISH ARMY.

TONIC'S SUPPORTING ROLE

It's doubtful the troops of the EIC and later British armies would have had such success without the quinine that kept malaria at bay. This bitter alkaloid, which gives tonic water its distinctive flavour, is extracted from the bark of the Andean fever tree (*Cinchona* species). This tree is native to the cloud forests of the eastern Andes, spanning what is now Ecuador, Bolivia, and Peru.

Europeans first learned of its curative properties in the early 1600s from the Quechua, the Cañari, and the Chimú Indigenous peoples, who had long used it to fight fevers. Spanish missionaries brought it back to Europe, earning it the name "Jesuit's bark". Ironically, the deadliest form of malaria, which Europeans needed quinine to cure, did not exist in the eastern Andes until colonial expansion spread the disease to the Americas.

For the next 300 years, quinine extracted from this bark was the only effective treatment for malaria, which was common across Europe as recently as the early 1900s. But it could do more than cure malaria – it could also prevent it (see box right).

Quinine eventually became a vital tool for imperial control and expansion. Its discovery opened the interior of Africa – hitherto known as the "white man's grave"

PREVENTING MALARIA

Some historians credit quinine's first use in preventing malaria to a Scottish physician, William Balfour Baikie, during an expedition along the Niger River in 1854. However, there is evidence that it was being used this way almost a century earlier. In 1768, James Lind (above), a British naval surgeon, recommended a daily ration of cinchona powder to sailors in tropical ports, where malaria was rife.

owing to a particularly fatal strain of malaria – to European exploration and colonization. It also enabled the British to maintain the personnel they needed to enforce imperial dominance in India.

When taken as a medicine, powdered quinine was sometimes mixed with sugar and soda water to mask its awful, bitter taste. However, it was most often mixed with alcohol – usually wine, gin, or rum. The first ready-made tonic water was patented by Erasmus Bond in 1858. This was marketed not as a fever medication but as a digestive and general tonic, and was not immediately popular.

During the 1860s, Britain stole cinchona seedlings from Peru to

Rubiaceae.

Cinchona Calisaya Wedd.

ANDEAN FEVER TREE
An illustration from *Köhler's Medicinal Plants* (19th century) shows *Cinchona calisaya*. The bark of several cinchona species contains quinine.

THE FIRST WRITTEN RECORD OF A "GIN AND TONIC" COMES FROM THE *ORIENTAL SPORTING MAGAZINE* IN 1868.

PITT'S AERATED TONIC WATER
Erasmus Bond, owner of Pitt & Co., marketed his tonic water as a digestive and general tonic.

establish its own plantations in India, thereby securing its own supply of quinine. The Dutch also took seedlings to Java. The Spanish, who still controlled Peru, had permitted this, although it went against the wishes of the local population, who knew their livelihoods would be stolen.

These new plantations relied upon indentured workers who grew, harvested, and processed cinchona bark into quinine and other alkaloids. The workers were mostly local people, sometimes whole families, who were promised land in return for the labour. Non-local workers and even prisoners were drafted in to supplement their numbers.

One account from 1878 of the bark harvest in Ecuador told how some workers would "fall victims to the deadly fevers while bearing upon their backs the very specific intended for the relief of the sick in distant lands", and were "...now made human sacrifices to furnish health to the white foreigners".

By 1863, adverts for quinine tonic waters appeared across the British colonies, still marketing the drinks as general tonics but by now also mentioning their role in fighting fevers. However, it's not clear whether these tonics were effective in this role, or whether this was just some clever marketing.

The first written record of a "gin and tonic" comes from the *Oriental Sporting Magazine* in 1868, which reports people calling for it at the end of a horse race. This suggests the British in India enjoyed their G&T as a refreshing drink in hot weather rather than medicine.

POST-COLONIAL G&TS

While some modern gins, notably Bombay Sapphire (see p158), still trade on the imagery of empire, most no longer play on such associations. Instead of exoticism, gin brands generally prefer to highlight their use of local botanicals as a selling point.

Indian producers now make their own tonic and their own gin using locally grown botanicals (apart from the juniper, which is largely imported). Indian tonic producers include Svami, a "progressive drinks company" from Mumbai, and Jade Forest, Bengal Bay, and Sepoy and Co., all based in Delhi. Some examples of Indian gin are Stranger & Sons Gin, Greater Than Gin (see p159), and Hapusā (see p203).

PUTTIN' ON THE RITZ

Gin became popular again in the early 1900s thanks largely to the rise of the cocktail, which gave it an air of glamour and sophistication.

MIXED DRINKS

Cocktails as we know them today became popular around the 1920s, but people were enjoying "mixed drinks" long before. In the mid-1800s, these were mostly punches, cups, and cobblers – mixes of brandy, wine, fruit, and sugar prepared in large bowls for communal drinking.

Gin was mostly absent from these, but did feature in a hot, sweetened, and spiced drink called Rumfustian, in which it was mixed with egg yolks, strong beer, citrus, and wine. Gin Twists, made with gin, lemon juice, sugar, and boiling water, were popular, as was the Gin Flip, made with egg, sugar, gin, nutmeg, and heated beer.

AMERICAN COOL

By the late 1800s, "American bars" were beginning to appear in England. They brought with them innovations that would shake up the culture of mixed drinks.

One was a level of showmanship hitherto unseen – the best-known example being perhaps Jerry Thomas, a "genuine Yankee professor" of booze, who toured the English cities of London, Southampton, and Liverpool mixing drinks with solid-silver bar tools worth £1,000.

The other innovation was the use of ice in drinks. This had long been an expensive luxury, and was only slowly becoming more widespread following the invention of refrigeration. Thomas's

JERRY THOMAS
American bartender and mixologist Jerry Thomas was known for his flamboyant style when mixing cocktails.

"sensation-drinks" included Gin Slings (with ice) and Ladies' Blushes, which are made with Old Tom gin, noyau (a French liqueur made with fruit stones), and absinthe.

EARLY MIXED DRINKS

Gin featured in a few early mixed drinks, which were the forerunners of modern-day cocktails.

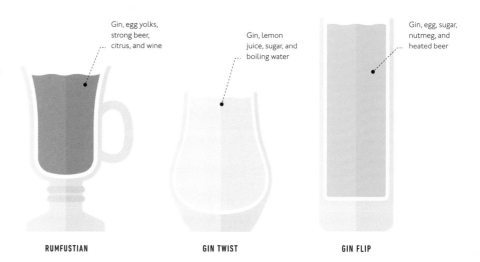

Gin, egg yolks, strong beer, citrus, and wine

Gin, lemon juice, sugar, and boiling water

Gin, egg, sugar, nutmeg, and heated beer

RUMFUSTIAN

GIN TWIST

GIN FLIP

PROHIBITION

Ironically it was prohibition – a ban on making, importing, transporting, or selling alcohol in the United States from 1920 to 1933 – that spurred on gin's popularity on both sides of the Atlantic.

In the United States, some drinkers got around the ban by distilling their own bathtub gin. This was pretty awful stuff, cheap bootleg spirit adulterated with juniper oil and other flavourings, but it did at least get you drunk. Gin cocktails developed to make the hooch more palatable while it did its work.

They were popular also in the speakeasies that emerged to replace the nation's now-closed bars as places to enjoy alcohol sociably. These ran on bootlegged, low-quality gin and other liquors that also needed to be gussied up into something more appealing.

INTERWAR GLITZ

Prohibition also drove some of America's bartenders into Europe's open arms. The most famous among them was arguably Harry Craddock, who wrote *The Savoy Cocktail Book* (first published in 1930). Craddock was well known for his "anti-fogmatics", hangover cures including the Corpse Reviver No. 2 (see p129), to be taken "before 11am, or whenever steam and energy are needed".

GLAMOROUS GIN
An advertisement for Seagers Gin from the 1930s depicts it as the choice for the glamorous and sophisticated.

Gin had by now shaken off its image as Mother's Ruin, a drink for the poor. It was instead the tipple of choice for aristocratic socialites dubbed the "Bright Young Things" – particularly the women who took great pleasure in a Gin and It (see p111). And in the 1930s, it was most likely Craddock who gave us the dictum that any cocktail made for the British monarchy should contain gin.

COMMERCIAL SUCCESS

Britain's big gin distillers naturally wanted to cash in on gin's new-found popularity, and even the most staid and steady brands began to introduce new products. Gordon's released new orange and lemon gins, which proved popular. It also had a range of "ready-to-serve" cocktails, as did Beefeater. Fortnum & Mason, a department store on London's Piccadilly, sold gin cocktails by the bottle.

Britain's empire played its role still in London's interwar cocktail culture, with drinks like the Singapore Sling and the Pegu Club lending exoticism and glamour from the colonies to the rainy motherland.

GIN WAS THE TIPPLE OF CHOICE FOR THE "BRIGHT YOUNG THINGS".

POSTWAR DOLDRUMS

While the early years of the 1900s were kind to gin, the 1940s onwards saw the spirit's fortunes decline in the face of a changing world and increasing competition from other drinks. Gin's image became outdated and stale, as younger drinkers turned away from their parents' history of war and empire.

WAR SPOILS THE PARTY

The Second World War (1939–45) knocked the shine off gin's good times. Many of the largest distilleries were based in London and suffered bomb damage during the Blitz – the German bombing campaign targeting the capital and other UK cities in 1940–41. Bombs hit distilleries outside London too; the Plymouth Gin distillery offices and archives were almost completely destroyed. Many distilleries also lost staff to military service.

More importantly, grain was in short supply owing to German attacks on the merchant shipping on which Britain relied for its food imports. The government imposed strict grain quotas for spirits, forcing distilleries across the nation to curb their production. Some gin makers got around this by distilling gin from molasses, but many did not recover to their previous production levels until the end of rationing in the 1950s.

IMPERIAL HANGOVER

Before the war, gin's rise had been, at least in part, linked to the rise of the British Empire (see pp34–37). As the empire began to dissolve – a process

The Colonel says "Now that's a winner— it's Gilbey's...."

GILBEY'S GIN
YOU'LL BE GLAD YOU GOT GILBEY'S

STAID OLD GIN
By the 1950s, gin had become associated with a stuffy and old-fashioned kind of Englishness.

hastened by the war – gin's fortunes withered with it. Gin was no longer fresh and frivolous. Instead, it became associated with a stuffy and old-fashioned kind of Englishness that was out of step with the modern world, in which Britain had "lost an empire and not yet found a role".

The counter-cultural upheaval of the 1960s deepened the divide between gin and the young drinkers it needed to attract in order to survive. Gin was a drink for older generations and the establishment. It didn't fit with sex and drugs and rock and roll.

GIN WAS A DRINK FOR OLDER GENERATIONS AND DIDN'T FIT WITH SEX AND DRUGS AND ROCK AND ROLL.

OTHER WHITE SPIRITS

Vodka had been creeping into British glasses since the 1930s, but in the 1960s, its popularity took off. It lacked gin's ties to Britain's fading past, and was an easy-going spirit that mixed well with cola or fruit juice – perfect for young drinkers who found the cocktails of their parents' generation too fussy.

This is not to say drinkers abandoned cocktails altogether, but even in the nation's bars, vodka had become the spirit of choice. In the 1970s and 80s, further competition came from rum, with the rise of tiki cocktails like the Mai Tai and the Jungle Bird.

CUTTING BACK

Some gin distillers sought to ride out gin's decline by cutting costs. For many, this meant making their gin weaker, thereby getting more bottles to sell each time they ran their still. This was bad news for drinkers as it weakened the gin's flavour. Some gins were bottled as low as 28% ABV. Gins featuring long lists of botanicals, such as The Botanist (see p181) or Monkey 47 (see p188), would have been unthinkable, and wildly unprofitable.

THE RISE OF VODKA
In the 1960s and 70s, vodka acquired a fresh and fun-loving image that appealed to younger drinkers.

GIN'S RENAISSANCE

Luckily for us, gin's decline was not terminal. The early years of the 21st century saw a renewed interest in the spirit, driven by consumers' increased focus on provenance and flavour for all sorts of food and drink.

UK SUPER-PREMIUM LEADS

The launch of Bombay Sapphire in 1987 marked a turn in gin's fortunes. It was the first successful launch of a new gin in decades. Its move away from strong juniper to a lighter, more floral approach offered a template that could lure drinkers away from vodka to fuel gin's modern renaissance. Bombay Sapphire was a luxury version of Bombay Dry, with cubeb and grains of paradise added to bring new flavour notes.

Tanqueray No. Ten followed in 2000, again a premium version of an existing gin with the addition of grapefruit, fresh limes, and camomile. This was joined by Hendrick's (launched in 2000 in the United States and 2003 in the UK),

establishing a new category of super-premium gins. Beefeater added Beefeater 24 in 2008, which had a higher ABV and blended Chinese green tea and Japanese sencha tea. In the same year, Hayman's and Jensen's brought Old Tom gins (see pp74–75) back to the market to fuel the growing demand for cocktails based on the style.

England's new gin boom really took off in 2009 and 2010 with the repeal of two obscure laws that forbade brewers from distilling on the same site, and limited distillers to a minimum pot size of 18 hectolitres (396 gallons). This allowed the Sipsmith and Chase distilleries to begin production, with Adnams following soon after.

In their wake came a wave of small craft distillers. In 2010, there

were 116 distilleries in the UK, mostly in Scotland, making whisky. By 2020, this had increased to 563, with the majority now in England and making gin.

US NEW WESTERN DRY

In the United States, too, distilling was getting interesting. American craft distilling began in the early 1980s, but for many years, it remained small scale and focused on other spirits. Around 2000, the US gin market was still dominated by the big British brands. However, a new appetite for cocktails was driving interest in the spirit.

In 1998, Anchor Brewing and Distilling released its Junipero Gin (see p162), arguably the USA's first craft gin. When Bluecoat American

**BOMBAY SAPPHIRE
LAUNCHED IN 1987**

**TANQUERAY TEN
LAUNCHED IN 2000**

**HENDRICK'S
LAUNCHED IN 2003**

**BEEFEATER 24
LAUNCHED IN 2008**

**HAYMAN'S AND JENSEN'S OLD
TOM, LAUNCHED IN 2008**

UK GINS
Established brands paved the way with super-premium versions of existing gins. Smaller distillers added innovation and variety.

Dry Gin (see p157) launched in 2005, its distillery was the first built in Pennsylvania since prohibition (1920–33). This gin marked a trend in US distillers doing things their own way rather than copying British tradition, which included opting for a softer juniper profile to suit the American palate. Ryan Magarian introduced Aviation Gin (see p183) in 2006, and with it the concept of New Western Dry gins (see p74) that put juniper into a supporting role for other botanicals.

AUSTRALIA'S UNIQUE GINS

Rum reigned in Australia for many years, and the country's gin industry is very young compared to those in other countries. Its roots lie in the

AUSTRALIAN GINS
Australian gin distilling began in the 1990s, but took off during the 2010s. Native botanicals give Australian gins distinct flavours.

KANGAROO ISLAND
SPIRITS O GIN
LAUNCHED IN 2006

MANLY SPIRITS
COASTAL CITRUS GIN
LAUNCHED IN 2017

FOUR PILLARS
OLIVE LEAF GIN
LAUNCHED IN 2020

1990s with Tasmanian distiller Bill Lark, who overturned a historical ban on small-pot distilling so that he could make whisky. Bill's success inspired his brother Jon and Jon's wife, Sarah, to set up Kangaroo Island Spirits, Australia's first dedicated gin distillery.

The Larks' aim was to make gin using native Australian botanicals – something that has helped

Australian gins carve out their own unique place in the global market. Ingredients such as lemon myrtle and Tasmanian pepperberry have become the distinctive profile of gins from down under.

In 2013, Australia produced around 10 gins, with distilleries like West Winds and Four Pillars dominating the scene. By 2020, this figure had increased to about 700.

FRANCE'S WINE AND PERFUME KNOW-HOW

French gin has taken influences from its wine, Cognac, and Calvados producers and also from its perfume industry. The country's distillers have demonstrated high levels of skill in distilling, blending, and sometimes also aging their gins in wooden casks. Gins like Mediterranean Gin by Léoube (see p179) and 44°N (see p183) demonstrate the distinctive results these approaches can achieve.

JUNIPERO LAUNCHED
IN 1998

BLUECOAT AMERICAN
DRY LAUNCHED IN 2005

AVIATION GIN
LAUNCHED IN 2006

US GINS
Craft distilling began in the 1980s. By 2000, US distillers were reimagining gin's flavours to suit the American palate.

GIN AND THE ENVIRONMENT

Distilling spirits is an energy-intensive business, but there are many ways in which its impact on our environment can be reduced.

ENERGY IN THE DISTILLERY

Want to emit less carbon dioxide (CO_2) while you make your gin? The simple way is to use less energy heating your still by using multi-shot distillation (see p65) rather than single-shot. This produces more bottles of gin each time you fire the still, meaning you can heat it less often.

Some gin makers claim this method produces inferior gin. But no matter, there are still choices. Instead of heating the still less often, you can heat it to a lower temperature by using vacuum distillation (see p64). It is possible to create a vacuum inside a traditional still, and while there's always some tradeoff between the energy used to create the vacuum and the thermal energy saved, this method can cut CO_2 emissions by about 40 per cent.

You can take this further and use a dedicated rotary evaporator, which distils at even lower temperatures – room temperature sometimes – and can use up to 90 per cent less energy than a traditional pot still.

You could even forgo distillation altogether and compound your gin (see pp70–71). We're likely to see distillers adopting combinations of all of these approaches as they look for ways to produce their gins more sustainably.

Where the energy comes from matters too. Switching to green energy suppliers and installing solar panels are already increasingly popular options for suppliers. Some brewer-distillers, such as Adnams and Ramsbury, also have the option of using steam from the brewery to run their stills, which can bring down their overall CO_2 emissions.

SINGLE-ESTATE GIN

A big question for distillers has always been which alcohol base to use. Sustainability now adds a new angle to this decision. The base spirit typically accounts for the largest chunk of the CO_2 emissions from each bottle of gin, in some cases up to 50 per cent. For some distillers, making their own base spirit is the greener option.

Ramsbury (see p196), for instance, is a single-estate gin. Its distillers grow their own grain, source their own water, make their own base spirit, and distil the gin all on the same site. This only works if distillers are able to produce a base spirit more efficiently than the big producers. For other, smaller distillers, buying alcohol remains the more sustainable option.

GROW GRAINS ON SITE

SOURCE WATER ON SITE

MAKE OWN BASE SPIRIT

DISTIL ON SITE

GOING GREEN IN THE DISTILLERY

Distillers can use various methods, or a combination of them, to reduce carbon emissions in the process of gin making.

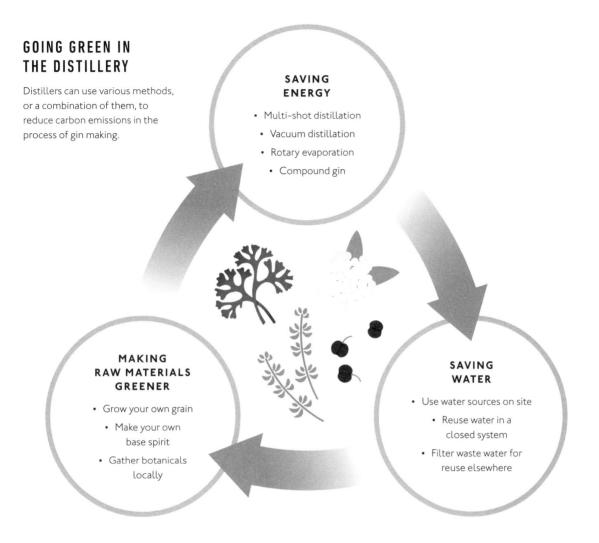

SAVING ENERGY

- Multi-shot distillation
- Vacuum distillation
- Rotary evaporation
- Compound gin

SAVING WATER

- Use water sources on site
- Reuse water in a closed system
- Filter waste water for reuse elsewhere

MAKING RAW MATERIALS GREENER

- Grow your own grain
- Make your own base spirit
- Gather botanicals locally

THE BOTANICALS

Botanicals are another important contributor to gin's carbon emissions. Many distilleries gather ingredients that grow locally by hand. This has the double benefit of giving their spirit distinct flavours tied to the place it was made, while also reducing carbon emissions. There is no blanket rule here, and for some ingredients, for some distilleries, buying botanicals from specialist suppliers remains the more efficient and sustainable choice.

WATER USE

Distillers need water to go into their stills. They also need water to dilute their spirit to bottling strength. Even more important, from a sustainability viewpoint, are the steam for heating and water for cooling. Some distillers are able to create closed systems where this water is reused, rather than letting it drain away. Ramsbury Distillery takes water from wells on its estate, and funnels waste water through a series of reed beds for natural filtration into a pond that supports wildlife on the estate.

MORE WAYS TO GO GREEN

Once they've made their gin, distillers can reduce carbon emissions further by using refills and recyclable packaging, and shipping in bulk.

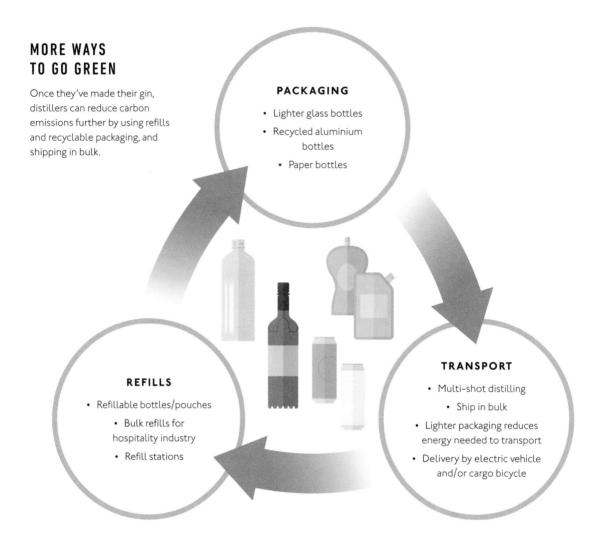

PACKAGING
- Lighter glass bottles
- Recycled aluminium bottles
- Paper bottles

TRANSPORT
- Multi-shot distilling
- Ship in bulk
- Lighter packaging reduces energy needed to transport
- Delivery by electric vehicle and/or cargo bicycle

REFILLS
- Refillable bottles/pouches
- Bulk refills for hospitality industry
- Refill stations

PACKAGING

Gin may come in easy-to-recycle glass bottles, but that doesn't mean its packaging gets a free pass. It's still a large contributor to the industry's carbon emissions, and an area where much can be done to improve matters.

For a start, glass bottles are heavy. Cutting the weight of a gin's bottle by even a small amount can lead to huge CO_2 savings in the long run, as it means less energy and fewer raw materials used to make the bottle, and less energy for shipping the bottles. When Plymouth Gin reduced the weight of its bottles by 15 per cent in 2021, the brand's owners, Pernod Ricard, calculated this would save 60 tonnes (59 tons) of carbon a year.

While glass is recyclable, not all glass is equally so. Most gin comes in clear bottles to reveal how clear the gin is, but these cannot be made with as much recycled material as coloured glass.

Some distilleries are ditching the glass altogether. Gins such as Silent Pool's Green Man and Lowlander Gin come in paper bottles that are 94 per cent

TRANSPORT IS AN IMPORTANT AREA FOR REDUCING GIN'S EMISSIONS.

recyclable, have a carbon footprint 85 per cent lower than regular glass bottles, and use four times less water to produce. They are also much lighter (so save energy during transport) and thermally stable (so take less energy to keep cool).

In 2023, Penrhos Spirits switched to using 100 per cent recycled aluminium bottles for its gins, which it believes to be the most sustainable option. It is estimated that 75 per cent of all aluminium ever produced is still in use today.

REFILLABLE PACKAGING

Another way to make packaging greener is to enable consumers to use it again and again. Over the last few years, many producers have started offering ways for drinkers to refill their empty gin bottles.

The Isle of Harris Distillery sells refills of its gin in aluminium bottles, which can then be recycled at home or reused as lightweight water bottles. Wye Valley Distillery sells gin refills in aluminium cans, and Dunnet Bay Distillers sells refills for its ceramic bottles of Rock Rose Gin in fully recyclable plastic pouches. Other distillers offer refill stations where drinkers can take their empties back to be topped up with more delicious gin. Silent Pool offers this service, but this is limited to refilling their own branded bottles. The East London Liquor Co. will put its gin into any empty 700ml (1¼-pint) bottle, no matter where it originally came from. In their words, the world already has enough bottles.

Pubs and bars get through even more bottles than we do at home, and there are improvements to be made there too. The East London Liquor Co. delivers gin in bulk to its hospitality industry customers to refill their empty bottles. This reduces associated carbon emissions by 88 per cent.

Hepple offers bars the option of serving its gin from an ornate etched glass balloon. This holds 10 litres (2 gallons) and can be refilled from gin delivered in 10- or 25-litre (2- or 5½-gallon) drums. A larger drum is equivalent to removing 36 standard bottles from its value chain each time it is used, which saves around 34kg (75lb) of carbon. In 2023, Hepple added the option to receive gin in 5-litre (1-gallon) pouches, which can be posted back to be used again.

TRANSPORT

Transport is an important area for reducing gin's emissions, and many other parts of the gin jigsaw intersect with it: bottle weight, for instance, or shipping in bulk. This can be taken further by combining bulk shipping with the multi-shot method (see p65). On a smaller scale, many gin companies make local deliveries by electric vehicle and cargo bicycle to cut their carbon emissions.

DISTILLATION

Distillation is the basic process by which all spirits are made. It begins with an alcoholic liquid that is then concentrated, resulting in a drink that is stronger in alcohol and sometimes flavour, too.

FERMENTATION

The first step is to create some alcohol to distil, which means fermenting a sugary liquid. Most of the time, it's one made from grains like wheat or barley. These contain starches that can be turned into sugar, which can, in turn, be fermented to create alcohol.

Wheat or barley must first be malted to unlock the starches deep inside the grains. Maltsters do this by soaking grains in water until they start to germinate. They then dry them to halt the process in its tracks.

Next, distillers grind the malted grains in a mill and steep them in hot water, like a porridge. This extracts the starch from inside the grains into the liquid, now called wort, where the enzyme amylase converts it into simple sugars. Barley contains amylase, so distillers will often add a little to the grain mixture even if they're mostly using wheat.

Once the wort has been strained to remove the grains, distillers add yeast to it. Yeast converts simple

THE DISTILLATION PROCESS

The aim of distilling alcohol is to concentrate it and make it stronger. The wash that goes into a still is heated and vaporizes. The vapour is collected in the still and recondenses into a stronger liquid.

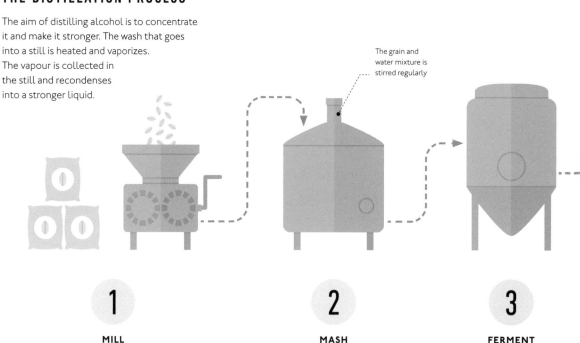

The grain and water mixture is stirred regularly

1

MILL
The malted grains, such as wheat or barley, are ground in a mill.

2

MASH
The grains are steeped in hot water, which extracts the starch into the liquid, called wort.

3

FERMENT
The wort is transferred to a fermentation tank, where yeast is added.

sugars into alcohol and carbon dioxide. There are many types of yeast, including wild ones that live all around us, but distillers add a known, cultivated strain of *Saccharomyces cerevisiae* that behaves in a predictable manner.

Once the fermentation is complete, you have an alcoholic liquid, called a wash, that is ready to distil.

THE DISTILLATION PROCESS

Distillation is the process by which ethanol is separated from water in the wash. It exploits two interesting properties of alcohol: its low boiling point and its ability to dissolve other substances (see box above). Ethanol has a boiling

ALCOHOL IS A SOLVENT

The two ends of an ethanol compound behave in different ways. One end is polar – it behaves like water and dissolves hydrophilic (water-loving) compounds such as sugar and salt. The other, nonpolar end acts on hydrophobic (water-hating) compounds, such as oils and fats. As most substances on Earth fall into one of these two camps, alcohol is an almost universal solvent. During distillation, alcohol carries off some of the botanicals' flavour-bearing essential oils as it vaporizes (see p50). These flavours will still be present when the vapour condenses back into the final spirit. Tasty!

point of 78°C (173°F), so it will vaporize in the heated still long before the still reaches water's boiling point of 100°C (212°F). Distillation works by collecting these ethanol vapours, cooling them, and allowing them to condense back into a liquid again. This strips away the water and any other impurities and leaves what we're interested in: the hearts, or the spirit, of the drink.

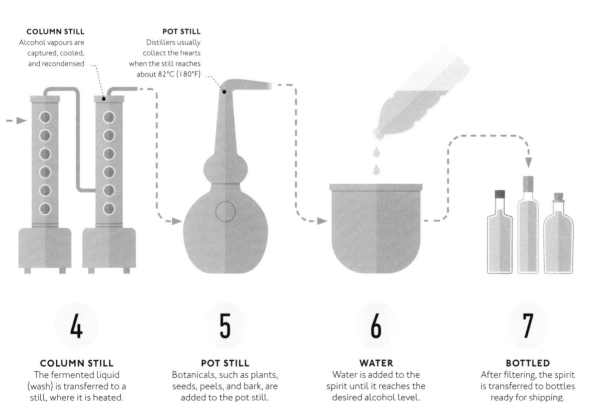

COLUMN STILL
Alcohol vapours are captured, cooled, and recondensed

POT STILL
Distillers usually collect the hearts when the still reaches about 82°C (180°F)

4
COLUMN STILL
The fermented liquid (wash) is transferred to a still, where it is heated.

5
POT STILL
Botanicals, such as plants, seeds, peels, and bark, are added to the pot still.

6
WATER
Water is added to the spirit until it reaches the desired alcohol level.

7
BOTTLED
After filtering, the spirit is transferred to bottles ready for shipping.

THE POT STILL

This is the simplest form of distillation, and is the main method used to produce all sorts of spirits from rum to whisky. Gin producers use a pot still to rectify (redistil) an already-distilled base spirit along with botanicals to add flavour. The base spirit is made in a column still (see p52).

VOLATILITY

Volatility is the capacity for a substance to turn into a vapour. The higher a substance's volatility is, the more likely it is to evaporate.

THE METHOD

To make gin, distillers fill the pot with a charge – a mixture of base spirit, water, and botanicals. They will often leave this to macerate for anywhere between 12 and 48 hours to extract more flavour from the botanicals before they run the still.

When the charge is ready, distillers gradually heat the still to its target temperature. In the past, distillers heated the pot over an open fire, but very few distillers do this today. Instead, there is usually a heating element, which may be made of coils inside the pot itself,

or a steam jacket that wraps the lower part of the pot.

The distillate comes through in fractions, which are called foreshots, heads, hearts, and tails (see pp58-59). Distillers want to keep the hearts portion for their gin as this is the fraction that contains the best flavours.

MONITORING THE SPIRIT

As the still heats, distillers monitor its temperature. They usually do this at a few points on the still, including the pot, neck, and condenser. They also record the

alcohol by volume (ABV) of the spirit as it emerges from the spirit safe after condensing.

JUDGING FRACTIONS

Together, the temperature and ABV of the spirit indicate which fraction of distillate is passing through the still. Distillers can also smell and taste the spirit to aid them in judging when to start collecting the spirit and when to stop.

SHAPE OF THE STILL

The shape of the still affects the flavour of the finished spirit. Many will have a "helmet" section above the pot, which encourages the alcohol vapours to condense and fall back into the pot to be distilled over and over again, until they are pure enough to pass through into the neck and lyne arm.

The angle of the lyne arm also impacts flavour: if it points downwards, it allows heavier, less volatile flavour compounds to pass through into the condenser. If it points upwards, only compounds with higher volatility can pass through, which makes a lighter, more delicate spirit.

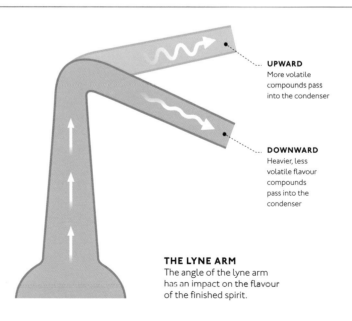

UPWARD
More volatile compounds pass into the condenser

DOWNWARD
Heavier, less volatile flavour compounds pass into the condenser

THE LYNE ARM
The angle of the lyne arm has an impact on the flavour of the finished spirit.

THE POT STILL

A pot still consists of a pot, neck, head, swan neck, and lyne arm, which carries vapours to the condenser.

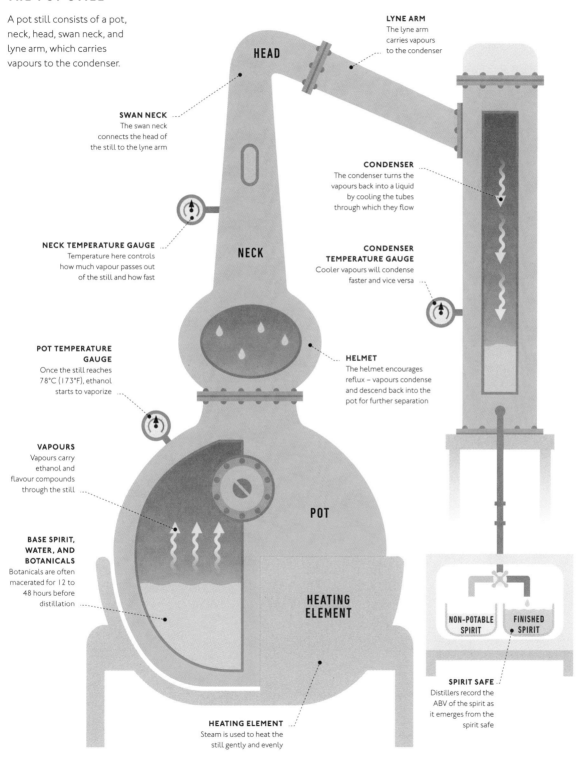

HEAD

LYNE ARM
The lyne arm carries vapours to the condenser

SWAN NECK
The swan neck connects the head of the still to the lyne arm

CONDENSER
The condenser turns the vapours back into a liquid by cooling the tubes through which they flow

NECK TEMPERATURE GAUGE
Temperature here controls how much vapour passes out of the still and how fast

NECK

CONDENSER TEMPERATURE GAUGE
Cooler vapours will condense faster and vice versa

POT TEMPERATURE GAUGE
Once the still reaches 78°C (173°F), ethanol starts to vaporize

HELMET
The helmet encourages reflux – vapours condense and descend back into the pot for further separation

VAPOURS
Vapours carry ethanol and flavour compounds through the still

POT

BASE SPIRIT, WATER, AND BOTANICALS
Botanicals are often macerated for 12 to 48 hours before distillation

HEATING ELEMENT

NON-POTABLE SPIRIT   **FINISHED SPIRIT**

HEATING ELEMENT
Steam is used to heat the still gently and evenly

SPIRIT SAFE
Distillers record the ABV of the spirit as it emerges from the spirit safe

THE COLUMN STILL

Unlike pot stills, which must be run in batches and be emptied and cleaned in between each distillation, column stills are capable of continuous distillation. They can run without interruption for days or even weeks at a time.

THE METHOD

A column still is composed of a column that houses a series of perforated copper plates. Each plate has its own sight glass, like a little porthole in the side of the still, which allows distillers to check what's going on inside.

The preheated alcoholic wash enters the column at the feed. As the wash vaporizes, the less volatile vapours pass downwards towards the bottom, where they will be heated again, while the more volatile vapours pass upwards to the plates above.

In the stripping section below the feed, volatile compounds escape from the liquid (stripping). In the rectification section, less volatile compounds are removed by liquid descending from above (rectification; see also p69).

At each plate, the vapour condenses back into a liquid that is heated by yet more vapours rising from below, as well as by the column's heat source. Any elements volatile enough to escape will evaporate again and continue their upwards journey, leaving the less volatile liquid to descend through the downcomer to the plate below.

In this manner, each plate purifies the vapours passing through it. The concentration of alcohol in the vapours increases as the vapours rise up the column and the concentration of flavour compounds decreases.

TAKING THE VAPOURS

Instead of making cuts to isolate the hearts (see p58), distillers using a column still can draw the vapours off at one or more of its plates – usually near the top of the column, where the best balance of alcoholic strength and flavour is found.

COLUMN VS POT STILLS

Column stills are able to produce spirit at a much higher alcoholic strength than pot stills. With enough plates, distillers can reach strengths above 96% ABV. This requires a column containing around 40 plates. For practical purposes, these stills are usually split into pairs of interconnected columns.

THE COFFEY STILL

The modern column still is based on the Coffey still, which was patented by Irish inventor and distiller Aeneas Coffey (1780–1839) in 1831. It revolutionized distilling, allowing distillers to make higher-quality alcohol at much lower prices.

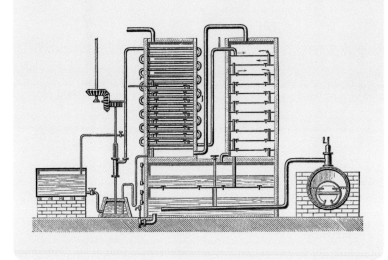

COLUMN STILL

Each plate in a column still purifies the vapours passing through it. As it rises, the vapour increases in alcohol strength and decreases in flavour compounds.

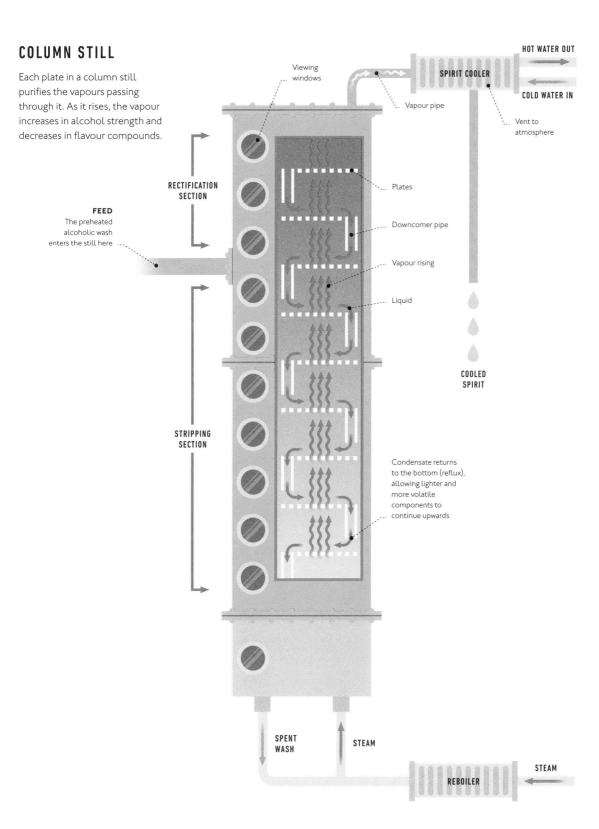

Viewing windows

Vapour pipe

HOT WATER OUT

SPIRIT COOLER

COLD WATER IN

Vent to atmosphere

RECTIFICATION SECTION

Plates

Downcomer pipe

FEED
The preheated alcoholic wash enters the still here

Vapour rising

Liquid

COOLED SPIRIT

STRIPPING SECTION

Condensate returns to the bottom (reflux), allowing lighter and more volatile components to continue upwards

SPENT WASH

STEAM

STEAM

REBOILER

THE CONDENSER

Once the vapours have made their way through the still and across the lyne arm, they reach the condenser. Here, they cool and condense, turning back into a liquid. This stage of distillation can affect the taste of the spirit in a number of ways.

CONDENSING THE SPIRIT

The size and shape of the condenser, the material it is made from, and the temperature it runs at can all affect the taste of the finished spirit. The size and shape both affect the surface area available for the vapours to condense on. They also affect the pressure inside the condenser, which can, in turn, influence the rate at which vapours flow through the system.

Temperature affects the rate at which the vapours condense, which affects the spirit's flavour. A colder condenser acts faster on the vapours and results in a "heavier" spirit (one with more of the less volatile flavour compounds still present). A warmer one condenses more slowly, resulting in a lighter spirit. The slower condensation affects the vapours' progress through the entire still, so heavier flavour compounds spend more time in the neck of the still and are more likely to condense there and return to the pot.

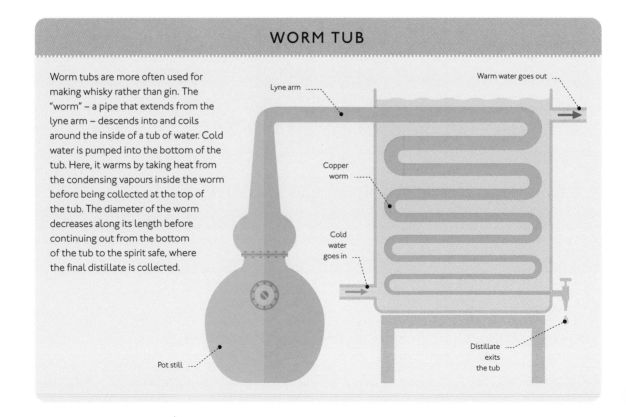

WORM TUB

Worm tubs are more often used for making whisky rather than gin. The "worm" – a pipe that extends from the lyne arm – descends into and coils around the inside of a tub of water. Cold water is pumped into the bottom of the tub. Here, it warms by taking heat from the condensing vapours inside the worm before being collected at the top of the tub. The diameter of the worm decreases along its length before continuing out from the bottom of the tub to the spirit safe, where the final distillate is collected.

Lyne arm

Warm water goes out

Copper worm

Cold water goes in

Pot still

Distillate exits the tub

Mostly, it all boils down to the amount and duration of copper contact the vapours achieve inside the condenser. The greater these are, the lighter and purer the spirit will be because of the reaction with any sulphides (see p61). Most condensers are made from copper, but some are stainless steel. Steel condensers will not "clean" the vapours as copper would.

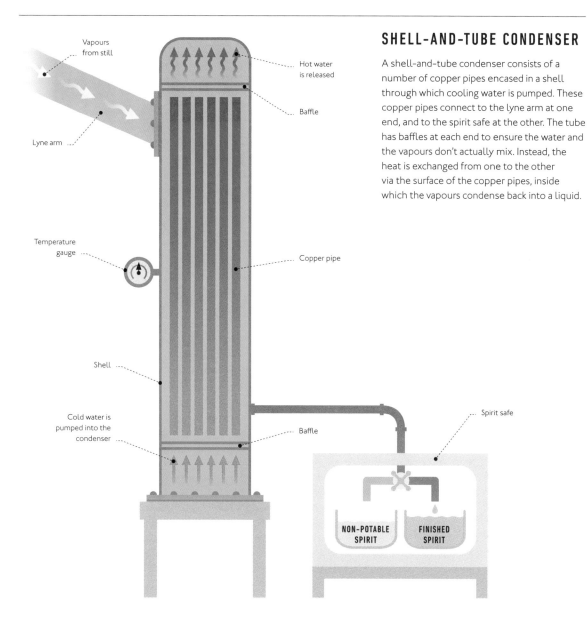

Vapours from still

Hot water is released

Baffle

Lyne arm

Temperature gauge

Copper pipe

Shell

Cold water is pumped into the condenser

Baffle

Spirit safe

NON-POTABLE SPIRIT

FINISHED SPIRIT

SHELL-AND-TUBE CONDENSER

A shell-and-tube condenser consists of a number of copper pipes encased in a shell through which cooling water is pumped. These copper pipes connect to the lyne arm at one end, and to the spirit safe at the other. The tube has baffles at each end to ensure the water and the vapours don't actually mix. Instead, the heat is exchanged from one to the other via the surface of the copper pipes, inside which the vapours condense back into a liquid.

VAPOUR INFUSION

Most of the time, distillers put their botanicals right into the still along with the base spirit and water. There are times, though, when this isn't ideal. If a particular botanical is too potent, for instance, it might dominate the flavour of the gin. In this case, distillers may turn to vapour infusion to solve their problem.

THE VAPOUR PATH

Vapour infusion occurs when a botanical is placed not in the pot but higher up the still in the path of the rising ethanol vapours. This might be a basket suspended in the head of the still, or it might be a separate chamber placed between the still and the condenser.

As the rising vapours pass through the botanical, they pick up some of its flavour compounds. Because this happens farther away from the still's heat source, the temperature is lower, and so vapour infusion captures only the lighter, more volatile flavours. The botanical's flavour is less "cooked" compared to when it is placed directly into the pot.

THE PROS AND CONS

Vapour infusion is a less efficient method of extraction than macerating in the pot, and the flavours extracted in this way are often less intense. This can be a plus when dealing with ingredients whose flavours would otherwise be too strong. But it can also mean distillers need more of a botanical in order to capture enough of its flavour. They must take care not to overcrowd the basket, which would block the still and mean some of the botanicals are not used as the vapour cannot reach them.

Vapour infusion can also be used for more delicate botanicals that may not withstand the distillation process as well in the pot. Floral and citrus botanicals can work well with this method.

Another advantage of vapour infusion is that it allows distillers to add or remove botanicals partway through the distillation. This can result in a finer control over the finished gin's flavour.

BOTANICALS FOR VAPOUR INFUSION

LAVENDER

CARDAMOM

Often, fresh citrus peels are used for vapour infusion, rather than dried, which usually go in the pot. Lavender often goes in the basket, and some distillers use cardamom, various peppers, juniper, and angelica to vapour infuse their gins.

Some gins that use vapour infusion include:
- Aval Dor Cornish Dry Gin (citrus peel)

- An Dúlamán Irish Maritime Gin (carrageen seaweed)
- Death's Door Gin (juniper, coriander, fennel)
- Lind & Lime Gin (citrus peel)
- Silent Pool Rare Citrus Gin (lavender, citrus peel, three kinds of pepper)
- The Botanist Islay Dry Gin (22 botanicals, mainly herbs and flowers).

ANGELICA

FENNEL SEEDS

JUNIPER

VAPOUR INFUSION

Rising vapours pass through
the botanicals in the chamber
and pick up some of their
flavour compounds.

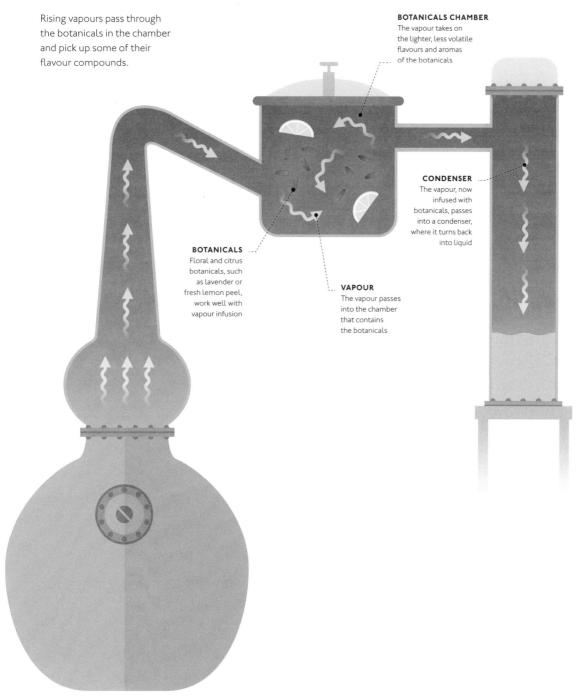

BOTANICALS CHAMBER
The vapour takes on
the lighter, less volatile
flavours and aromas
of the botanicals

CONDENSER
The vapour, now
infused with
botanicals, passes
into a condenser,
where it turns back
into liquid

BOTANICALS
Floral and citrus
botanicals, such
as lavender or
fresh lemon peel,
work well with
vapour infusion

VAPOUR
The vapour passes
into the chamber
that contains
the botanicals

DISTILLATION FRACTIONS AND FLAVOURS

When distillers run their still, it's not as simple as turning on a tap and having gin pour out. The spirit is produced in stages, or fractions: the foreshots, the heads, the hearts, and the tails.

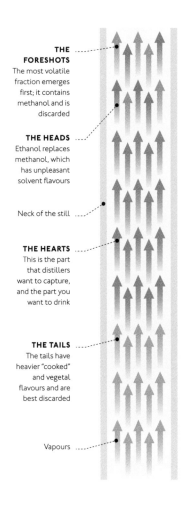

THE FORESHOTS
The most volatile fraction emerges first; it contains methanol and is discarded

THE HEADS
Ethanol replaces methanol, which has unpleasant solvent flavours

Neck of the still

THE HEARTS
This is the part that distillers want to capture, and the part you want to drink

THE TAILS
The tails have heavier "cooked" and vegetal flavours and are best discarded

Vapours

FRACTIONAL STAGES
The distillate passes out of the still in stages, called fractions.

THE FORESHOTS

The most volatile parts of the distillate, the foreshots, come through first. These contain methanol, a poisonous form of alcohol with a boiling point even lower than that of ethanol, as well as acetone and various aldehyde compounds. The foreshots must be discarded, but luckily for gin, most will have been removed when the base spirit was made.

THE HEADS

As the heat in the still rises, less volatile flavour compounds evaporate and make their way through to the condenser. Those found in the heads fraction are still among the lighter and more volatile, giving unpleasant solvent and astringent flavours.

THE HEARTS

Distillers must judge when to start collecting the spirit and when to stop in order to collect only the hearts, which is where we find all the best flavours that make up a gin. This usually begins when the spirit passing through the still is close to 82% ABV, and the temperature in the pot reaches around 82°C (180°F). As the pot temperature continues to rise, the spirit's ABV falls. The flavours in the spirit change during this time, from lighter floral and citrus notes all the way to earthy and spicy notes.

THE TAILS

At some point, the flavours coming through start to veer into less pleasant "cooked" and vegetal notes. This usually occurs when the ABV has fallen to about 60% and the pot has reached a temperature of 88°C (190°F). The tails can be collected and distilled again, with or without the heads, but are sometimes sold for non-beverage uses, such as for lighter fluid.

THE STILLAGE

The stillage is the material left in the pot once distillation has been completed. It includes any liquid that did not evaporate, as well as any botanicals that were placed in the pot. As it contains protein, some of the stillage can be repurposed as animal feed.

FRACTIONAL FLAVOURS

This graph shows the temperature, ABV, and flavours of each fraction of the distillate as it runs through the still. All fractions are present in the distillate at all times, but the relative proportions differ over time. Each fraction dominates in turn in the order set out below.

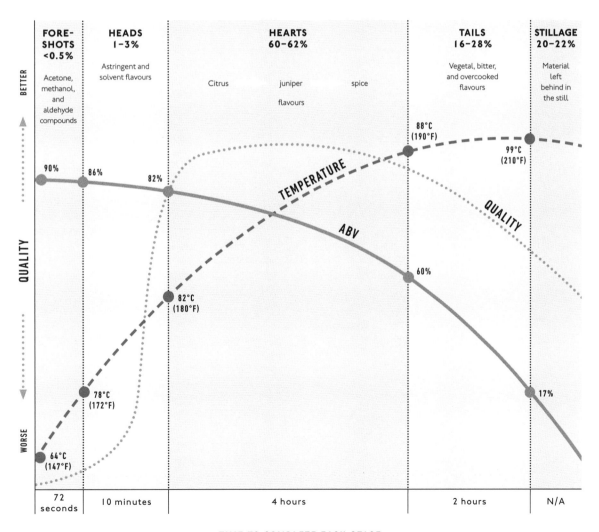

FORE-SHOTS <0.5%	HEADS 1–3%	HEARTS 60–62%	TAILS 16–28%	STILLAGE 20–22%
Acetone, methanol, and aldehyde compounds	Astringent and solvent flavours	Citrus juniper spice flavours	Vegetal, bitter, and overcooked flavours	Material left behind in the still

BETTER — QUALITY — WORSE

TEMPERATURE

ABV

QUALITY

90%   86%   82%

88°C (190°F)

99°C (210°F)

82°C (180°F)

60%

78°C (172°F)

17%

64°C (147°F)

| 72 seconds | 10 minutes | 4 hours | 2 hours | N/A |

TIME TO COMPLETE EACH STAGE

WHY ARE STILLS MADE OF COPPER?

Distillers like to use stills made of copper – not just because it looks good, but also because it has a number of practical advantages, such as its malleability and ability to conduct heat, that can result in a better spirit.

COPPER POT STILL
The Cotswold Distillery in Stourton, Warwickshire, in the UK, uses a 500-litre (110-gallon) copper pot still in the process of making its craft gin. The still was manufactured by coppersmith Arnold Holstein in Germany.

SHAPING

The size and shape of a still are both important to the quality and flavour of the alcohol it produces. Copper is a soft, malleable metal that can easily be formed into all sorts of shapes. The rounded pot stills, the bulbous or onion-shaped helmet on pot stills, the delicately tapering heads, and elegant swan necks, even the gently narrowing tubes found inside some condensers – all are precisely shaped to optimize their impact on the alcoholic vapours passing through them.

HEATING

A large part of distilling involves heating and cooling. Distillers transfer heat into the still and take it out again at the condenser, and they are careful to control it at every stage in between. Copper is a very good conductor of heat, which makes the distillers' job much easier. It takes less energy to heat the still than it would with a less conductive material, and distillers can remove the heat more easily in the condenser. Copper also gives distillers finer control over the rate of heating and cooling, which can directly affect the flavour of the finished spirit.

CLEANING

Copper performs another vital function during distillation: it removes sulphuric compounds from the vapours. These compounds occur naturally during fermentation and will always be present to some degree. If left in the spirit, they can give notes of raw meat, overcooked vegetables, rotten eggs, or struck matches (see box below).

When the vapours come into contact with the copper sides of the stills, they undergo a chemical reaction and form copper salts. These salts fall back down into the bottom of the still and are thereby removed from the vapours, which leads to a cleaner-tasting spirit at the end of the process.

ESTERS

Copper also acts as a catalyst for chemical reactions that create esters in the finished spirit. Esters are a very important category of flavour compounds that can contribute a huge amount to spirits like rum or whisky. This is less important for gin, where the main flavours come from the botanicals used.

CLEANING COPPER

Copper reacts with sulphur to form copper salts, which fall back into the still and are removed from the vapours.

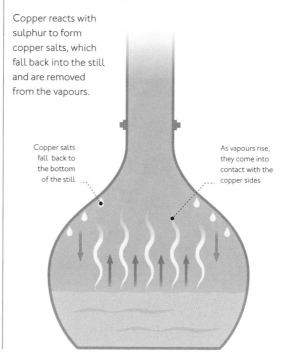

Copper salts fall back to the bottom of the still

As vapours rise, they come into contact with the copper sides

COPPER AND SULPHURIC COMPOUNDS

HYDROGEN SULPHIDE (H$_2$S)
Hydrogen sulphide smells of rotten eggs. It has a very low threshold for detection, so even tiny amounts can spoil a spirit. Fortunately, it is volatile enough to evaporate from the "new-make" spirit on its own in the right conditions.

DIMETHYL SULPHIDE (DMS; C$_2$H$_6$S)
Dimethyl sulphide smells of sweetcorn or tinned tomatoes. Like hydrogen sulphide, it is quite volatile and may evaporate on its own, but it's better to remove it from the spirit.

DIMETHYL TRISULPHIDE (DMTS; C$_2$H$_6$S$_3$)
Dimethyl trisulphide can smell rotten, meaty, or like overcooked cabbage. Thankfully, copper can be very efficient at removing this compound from the finished spirit.

WHAT IS LOUCHING?

Some gins can exhibit louching. The term "louching" describes the process by which a clear spirit or liqueur turns cloudy when it is diluted with water or another mixer. It's most often seen in drinks like pastis, absinthe, and ouzo, from which it takes its other common name: the ouzo effect.

HOW LOUCHING OCCURS

Arak, raki, and sambuca all louche, as does Cointreau. What these all have in common is that they contain hydrophobic (water-hating) essential oils from the botanical ingredients used to flavour them. The oils are dissolved within the spirit, which is largely a mixture of ethanol and water. Diluting the spirit lowers the concentration of ethanol in this mixture and, at a certain point, causes the dissolved oils to come out of solution and form tiny, oily droplets. These droplets scatter any light passing through the liquid, making it appear cloudy.

IS IT A FAULT?

You might well feel a little hesitant if something you were about to drink suddenly went from clear to hazy. Is it safe to drink?

Fret not. There is nothing wrong with your drink. The louching is just a sign that your drink contains a high concentration of essential oils, or, in other words, lots of flavour.

It's true that some gin distillers consider louching a fault and maintain the spirit should always be crystal clear. However, there is nothing in gin's various legal definitions to support this view.

HOW LOUCHING OCCURS

When certain drinks are diluted, essential oils come out of solution and form tiny droplets. These scatter light, making the drink appear cloudy.

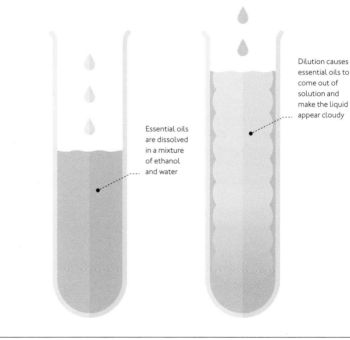

Essential oils are dissolved in a mixture of ethanol and water

Dilution causes essential oils to come out of solution and make the liquid appear cloudy

It is, these days, becoming rather outdated in any case. Many drinkers are perfectly happy to consume gins that louche, and feel that removing oils by chill filtering a spirit (see opposite) will also strip away too much of its texture and flavour.

LOUCHING IN THE GIN DISTILLERY

Even if distillers don't mind their gin louching in the glass, most want it to start off clear in the bottle. Gin comes off the still at around 80% ABV but needs to be closer to 40% ABV for bottling, so distillers will dilute the newly made spirit with water. This can lead to louching, especially if it's done soon after distillation.

Part of the reason for this is varying concentrations of oils and alcohol in different parts of the holding vessel. The spirit has not yet become homogeneous. Louching at this stage can sometimes be resolved simply by mixing and waiting.

BIGGER HEADS CUT

Distillers can avoid their gin louching by taking a bigger heads cut (see p58). As the still warms up, the first vapours to rise from the charge will hit cold parts of the still and reflux over and over until the whole still is warm enough for them to pass through. This means the first fraction to be collected will have been distilled many times and may have an overconcentration of juniper and other essential oils.

EARLY TAILS

Another option is to take out the tails (see p58) earlier so as not to collect as many of the heavier oils that come through towards the end of the distillation.

LESS DILUTION

Yet another choice open to distillers is to dilute the spirit with less water and bottle the gin at a higher ABV.

MORE NEUTRAL SPIRIT

If a gin has already louched, the distiller can sometimes fix it by adding more neutral spirit. This redresses the balance of ethanol to water, increases the solvency power of the spirit, and encourages the oils to go back into solution.

CHILL FILTERING

Finally, distillers may chill filter their gin to remove the oils. The gin is cooled to 0°C (32°F) and passed through an absorption filter, which removes the haze. However, the oils that cause louching are also responsible for the gin's flavour and texture, so this solution is not always ideal.

DEALING WITH LOUCHING

Often, simply mixing the distillate and giving it time to rest will resolve any issues. If that doesn't work, distillers have a number of options to avoid (or correct) their gin louching.

CHILL FILTERING

Chilling a gin to 0°C (32°F) and then filtering it remove the oils but may affect the gin's flavour and texture.

ADD NEUTRAL SPIRIT

Adding neutral spirit to a gin that has already louched encourages the oils to go back into solution.

Taking a bigger heads cut avoids the high concentration of juniper and other essential oils created as the still heats up.

TAKE A BIGGER HEADS CUT

DISTILLERS' METHODS

TAKE OUT THE TAILS EARLIER

Cutting the tails earlier excludes many of the heavier oils that come through towards the end of the distillation.

DILUTE WITH LESS WATER

Diluting with less water keeps the ethanol concentration higher and preserves more of the gin's solvency power.

OTHER METHODS OF DISTILLATION

Some distillers want even more control over the flavours they extract from their ingredients, and so turn to other distillation methods, some of which are borrowed from the science laboratory or the perfumer's toolkit.

HYBRID STILLS

Many distillers make use of hybrid pot-and-column stills. These are less expensive to run than full column stills, but also more efficient than pot stills and able to produce spirit at a higher alcoholic strength. In some hybrid stills, the column sits directly on top of the pot. In more advanced systems, the various parts are linked with piping and diverter valves. The distiller can then choose to send the vapours on different paths depending on the spirit being made.

SUPERCRITICAL EXTRACTION

A 100ml (3½fl oz) vial of absolute of juniper, produced by supercritical extraction, is sufficient to flavour 6,000 bottles of gin.

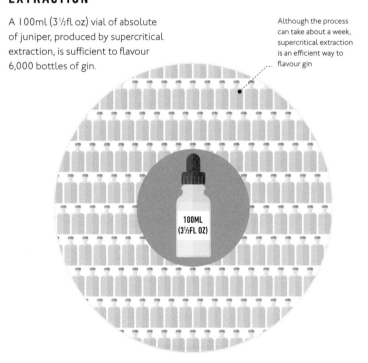

Although the process can take about a week, supercritical extraction is an efficient way to flavour gin

100ML
(3½FL OZ)

VACUUM DISTILLATION

Higher temperatures accelerate flavour extraction. (Just picture making tea with cold water instead of hot and you'll see what I mean.) Lowering the pressure inside the still also lowers the temperature at which the ethanol and flavour compounds evaporate, which can allow different flavours to come to the fore. By using vacuum distillation, a distiller can capture flavours that would be altered or even ruined at higher temperatures. It can lead to much lighter and more delicate flavours in the finished gin.

SUPERCRITICAL EXTRACTION

This is what happens when a distiller raids a perfumer's lab. Rather than lowering pressure, as with vacuum distillation, the supercritical extraction method ramps it up even higher. The machine compresses carbon dioxide (CO_2) until it reaches a "supercritical state", in which it behaves as a liquid and a gas at the same time. The compressed CO_2 then rushes through a bed of botanicals, where it acts as a solvent and strips out all the essential oils to produce what perfumers call an absolute.

VACUUM DISTILLATION ALLOWS DISTILLERS TO CAPTURE FLAVOURS THAT WOULD BE RUINED AT HIGHER TEMPERATURES.

Hepple uses this technique to produce an absolute of juniper. It looks like a small vial of neon-yellow salad dressing, and smells like you're inhaling every last bit of the juniper bush from the roots to the tips of the needles. Just 100ml (3½fl oz) take about a week to collect but will be enough to flavour 6,000 bottles of gin.

MULTI-SHOT DISTILLING

The pot-still distillation process (see pp50–51) is known as single-shot distillation. It's how gin always used to be made: one batch of botanicals, one distillation, one crate of bottles going to one bunch of happy customers.

The multi-shot (or concentrate) method adds enough botanicals to flavour many batches of bottles at once. The intense botanical concentrate is first diluted with more base spirit to bring the flavour back into balance, and then diluted again with water to bring the gin down to bottling strength. Supporters say multi-shot is more efficient, takes less time, uses less energy, and offers commercial benefits around managing supply and demand. Its detractors say it makes worse gin, though in blind tastings no one

CONTINENTAL METHOD

In this method, separately distilled botanicals are blended together at the end to make the finished gin.

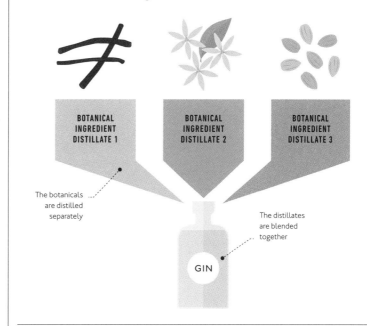

BOTANICAL INGREDIENT DISTILLATE 1

BOTANICAL INGREDIENT DISTILLATE 2

BOTANICAL INGREDIENT DISTILLATE 3

The botanicals are distilled separately

The distillates are blended together

GIN

has yet been able to prove this conclusively, and many well-established brands use multi-shot.

CONTINENTAL METHOD

With the so-called continental method, each botanical ingredient is distilled separately, and the resulting distillates are blended afterwards to create the finished gin. This method is rarely used in the UK but is more common in continental Europe (hence its name). Supporters of this method of distillation claim it can lead to a better quality and clarity of aromas in the finished gin.

WHAT IS GIN MADE FROM?

The legal definitions that govern some spirits dictate which agricultural ingredients may be used to form their base alcohol. Scotch whisky, for example, must be made from barley, while bourbon must be at least 51 per cent maize (corn). Not so with gin. As long as you can ferment it, you're good to go. As a result, you can find gins made from all sorts of things.

GRAINS

Even with the freedom to use other spirit bases, nearly all gin makers gravitate towards those made from grains. Price and quality are two main drivers: the big distillers producing grain spirit make a lot of it and have done so for a long time, so they know how to do it well and have grown so efficient that it need not break the bank. You can get barley or rye spirit, some of which you'll see used for gin, but the vast majority is made from wheat. If you see the letters "NGS" (for neutral grain spirit) or "GNS" (same words, different order), then chances are the spirit was made from wheat.

SUGARS

Everything listed on these pages is technically sugar in one form or another (whether it be glucose, fructose, lactose, or maltose), but here we're talking specifically about sucrose, which is found in sugar cane, molasses, and sugar beet. The first two are more commonly

THE SPIRIT BASE OF GIN

Most spirit bases in gin are made from grains, particularly wheat, but other ingredients that distillers might use include grapes, sugar, potatoes, or whey.

turned into rum, where the flavour is more evident, but even when distilled to 96% ABV and above, the "neutral" spirit retains a ghost of sucrose's gentle, warming sweetness. Once the French lost access to sugar from the West Indies during the Napoleonic Wars (1803–15), distillers in France turned to the sugar beet instead, the root of which contains sucrose.

GRAPES

We're all familiar with alcohol from grapes, so it's no surprise to see wine being distilled as well. Often, this becomes brandy, but if it's distilled to a base spirit, most of the grape character is stripped away – most, but not all. Grape spirit can be a little harsh but, with dilution, becomes more floral. Some producers use it to make very successful gins, such as G'Vine Floraison (see p185), Geometric Gin (see p202), London to Lima Gin (see p203), and Sandy Gray Gin (see p205).

POTATOES

Potatoes make terrible wine but good spirits. They give a smooth, creamy texture to the finished spirit and the tiniest whisp of flavour, a bit like mashed potato. Some gin makers say this viscosity means that a gin made from potato spirit will "carry" its botanical flavours better. Certainly, the creaminess can add a very pleasant textural element.

OTHER GIN BASES

Some Japanese producers make gin from a base of *shōchū* – a distilled spirit that is usually made from fermented rice, grain (barley or buckwheat), brown sugar, or sweet potatoes. The *shōchū* is evident in the finished gin, contributing both flavour and texture.

Some Japanese gins use a rice-based neutral spirit, for example, the Ki No Bi gins made in the Kyoto Distillery. The 135° East Hyōgo Gin (see p175), made by the Kaikyō Distillery, uses a splash of saké distillate from the Akashi Saké Brewery to aromatize its base spirit.

French Calvados producers Maison Drouin make Le Gin de Christian Drouin (see p195) from neutral spirit aromatized with distilled apple cider. The cider is made from more than 30 different kinds of apple, including bitter, bitter-sweet, sweet, and sharp varieties.

WHEY

Ireland, with its very large dairy industry, turns a lot of milk into butter and more still into cheese. That means there's a lot of leftover whey (the liquid left as a byproduct of cheese-making). It must have been a happy day indeed when some bright spark came up with the idea of fermenting whey (the lactose in milk being a sugar), distilling it, and turning it into gin.

Ireland now has quite a few "milk gins" and even more that use whey spirit without declaring it on the label. (Lactose is an allergen, but fermentation and distillation remove it all.)

BASE SPIRITS: MAKE OR BUY?

Very few gin makers distil their own base spirit. In the UK, which is the world's largest manufacturer of gin and home to around 563 distillers, just a handful go all the way from grain to glass – or potato to glass in some cases. Why don't more of them bother? And does it mean the gin from those who do is better?

AGRICULTURAL DISTILLERS

When knowledge of distillation first spread throughout the world, farmers adopted it as a means of dealing with surplus crops, particularly grains. Before distilling, their only option was to sell surplus grain before it spoiled. As more and more grain came into the markets, the price fell and farmers got less reward for their efforts.

By distilling their excess grain, farmers were able to turn it into a valuable and stable resource they could store almost indefinitely and sell during lean years to supplement their income. It was also much easier to store and transport a few barrels of distilled spirits than cartloads of grain.

So, alcohol was made where the raw materials grew. But gin was often made in the cities, near the ports where the botanical ingredients arrived from around the world. The distinction wasn't always necessarily as clear-cut as that, but generally speaking, it was true enough.

Even today, when we use the terms "agricultural distiller" or "farm distillery", we mean one where the raw materials are turned into spirit alcohol.

HOW PURE IS PURE?

In the UK and the European Union (EU), the legal definition of gin (see pp12–13) stipulates it must be made from ethyl alcohol of agricultural origin (itself a legally defined term), with an initial alcoholic strength of at least 96% alcohol by volume (ABV). In the United States, the minimum ABV is 95% (see p14).

Distilling to 95% ABV is no mean feat. It requires a column still (see pp52–53) with about 40 plates, which is expensive to buy and run, and requires a distillery with ceilings high enough to house it. It also means the distillery needs the space and equipment to house the raw materials (grain and so on), and ferment them into wash to feed the still.

Distilling to 96% ABV may not seem like a big step up, but it is a significant challenge. As the alcoholic wash in the still reaches this concentration, it comes to its azeotropic point – in other words, the point at which the mixture acts as if it were a single pure liquid with a constant boiling point. No further separation is possible at this stage without using a different method of distillation.

UK & EU BASE SPIRIT 96% ABV

US BASE SPIRIT 95% ABV

LEGAL GIN
Legal definitions of the alcoholic strength of the base spirit in gin vary around the globe, but not by much.

ECONOMIES OF SCALE

Those distillers who do make neutral spirit have distilleries designed to maximize efficiency for this task, rather than chopping and changing between making base spirit and making gin. Plus, they buy their ingredients in bulk, with the favourable contracts this allows. Put simply, it's almost impossible to match them for price. Making base spirit can add £5 onto the cost of a bottle of gin that may cost £30, while base alcohol can be bought in at a few pence per litre. And while the price may be low, the quality is high. So given all of that, would you bother to make your own?

WHERE DOES THE ARTISTRY LIE ANYWAY?

Picture the world of gin as an art gallery and all the different gins as paintings on its walls. Making the base spirit is like making the canvas. Do you go to a gallery to look at the canvas? No! You're more interested in what's painted on it.

Gin makers who make their own base spirit often like to talk about the sense of *terroir* this gives to their gin. But if you're distilling to 96% ABV, how much is this *terroir* going to express itself through flavour in the finished gin? Not much, I'd say. And while it might be a nice idea to have everything in a gin come from one place, that's more down to it making a pleasing story than anything else.

DISTILLING VS RECTIFYING

Any chemistry student can tell you that, technically speaking, there is no difference between distilling something and rectifying it. In practical terms, however, the term "distillation" is usually reserved for the first time a fermented liquid is turned into a spirit.

Rectification means running an already-distilled spirit through the still again. The process it undergoes doesn't change, but the purpose for sending it through the still is different. It might be to increase the spirit's alcoholic strength, further remove impurities, or infuse the spirit with other flavours – as is the case with gin.

In many countries, the government issues separate and distinct licences for each of these activities. This gives authorities greater control over distillers and allows authorities to raise more tax revenue from the duty paid on spirits.

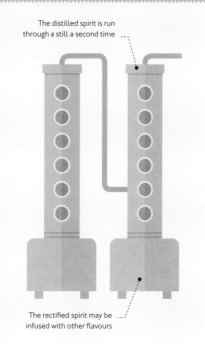

The distilled spirit is run through a still a second time

The rectified spirit may be infused with other flavours

There's certainly no reason to look down on any gin brand for buying in its base spirit. The vast majority of the industry does this, and plenty of producers are able to make excellent gins using bought-in base spirit.

The real artistry lies in the distillers' selection and combination of the botanicals, and in seeing that their chosen flavour profile expresses itself well in the finished spirit. This asks a lot of distillers. They must have a good palate and be able to imagine flavour in creative ways. They must understand how the still acts on the botanicals, and control their exposure to heat and alcohol. Distillers must also understand how changing the ABV of the finished gin will either hold on to or release specific flavours in the spirit.

COMPOUNDED GINS

If all this distillation business sounds like a bit of a bother, there is an alternative. You can flavour a base spirit with botanicals simply by mixing them together and waiting a while. Then you fish out any solids, dilute to strength, and bottle your spirit as normal. But does your spirit count as gin if it's made this way? Not everyone thinks so.

COLD COMPOUNDING

Compounding works by extracting flavour compounds from the botanicals into a mixture of alcohol and water. The ethanol in this mixture is a solvent (see p49), and will act to dissolve some of the essential oils from the botanicals. Other flavour compounds dissolve better in water, which is why compounders don't use pure spirit for the job. Some of the colour from the botanicals is usually extracted along with the flavour, so often a compounded gin may have a slight hue that reflects its ingredients.

Compounded gins, sometimes called bathtub gins (see p39), don't have a great reputation. Partly this stems from the prohibition era (1920–33) in the United States, when compounding was used to disguise the flavour of some terrible bootlegged spirits. It's also partly down to the fact that compounded gins have more robust, funkier flavours, are sometimes coloured, and can contain a higher concentration of essential oils, which makes them more liable to louche (see pp62–63).

COLD COMPOUNDING

Botanicals are left to infuse in a mixture of alcohol and water at room temperature (hence the term "cold compounding"). The ethanol dissolves some of the essential oils in the botanicals, extracting flavour compounds into the mixture.

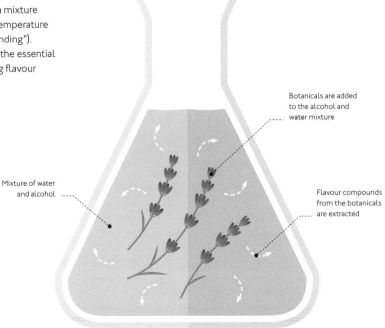

Botanicals are added to the alcohol and water mixture

Mixture of water and alcohol

Flavour compounds from the botanicals are extracted

APPLES

PEARS

QUINCE

SEASONAL FRUIT

FRUITS USED IN COLD COMPOUNDING

Fruits that contain flavour in their flesh rather than their peel work well in compounding. These include orchard fruits, such as apples, pears, and quinces, and seasonal fruits, such as blackberries, plums, strawberries, and sloes.

COMING IN FROM THE COLD

Modern drinkers are more accepting of all of these perceived "faults". Lots of us have more adventurous palates these days, and are more open-minded about how a drink looks if the taste is there to back it up. This allows compounded gins like Four Pillars Bloody Shiraz (see p193) to find a market – this gin sits on grapes for eight weeks post-distillation to take on some extra colour and flavour.

Compounded gins can work particularly well with fruits, especially those where the flavour comes from the flesh rather than the peel. These don't stand up well to the heat of distillation, but can come across well in compounding. It is a good way to feature seasonal fruits or orchard fruits like apples, pears, and quinces.

Because of their up-front flavours, compounded gins can be used with great success in cocktails, such as a Negroni (see p142). Try them anywhere the other ingredients risk overpowering a more delicate gin's botanicals.

GINS MADE FROM EXTRACTS

There is an even easier way to make a compound gin by mixing a neutral base spirit with pre-prepared botanical extracts or essences. They are less common in the UK and the United States, but many examples can be found for sale in Belgium and Spain.

These gins look completely clear and often do not mention on the label that they are compounded. Many people don't find the idea of gin made in this manner very appetizing. If you don't either, look for gins that state on the label they have been distilled, or that carry the designation "London Dry" (see p73), which must also be distilled.

DIFFERENT STYLES OF GIN

Gin is a complex drink. Its styles are not necessarily indicative of how a gin tastes; often they have more to do with how it was made. Yet there are important differences between the styles to keep in mind.

AGED OR BARREL-RESTED GINS

All gins would once have been aged in wood. Time in the barrel mellows out any bitter compounds and imparts flavours of vanilla, coconut, and baking spices (such as cloves, cinnamon, or nutmeg), plus flavours from any previous contents (see pp92–93). Some gin makers are aging gins in wood again, although this remains a vanishingly small part of the market and a niche interest among drinkers.

COASTAL GINS

A subset of New Western Dry-style gins (see p74) is emerging that makes particular use of maritime ingredients not usually seen elsewhere in gin. They have popped up all around Great Britain and Ireland (both islands with plenty of coastline) but seem to be particularly prominent in the "Celtic fringe" (along the coasts of Cornwall, Wales, and Scotland) and outlying islands, such as the

GIN STYLES

The style of a gin is related more to its manufacturing process rather than being an indication of taste.

AGED OR BARREL-RESTED GINS

COASTAL GINS

COLD-COMPOUNDED OR BATHTUB GIN

FLAVOURED GIN

Isles of Scilly and the Hebrides. These gins have a deliciously saline, umami, herbal-vegetal character. Some good examples are Lussa Gin (see p210), Isle of Harris Gin (see p210), and Rock Rose Coastal Citrus Gin (see p213).

COLD-COMPOUNDED OR BATHTUB GIN

Cold-compounded (bathtub) gin is a very loose style that describes the method of making the gin rather than how it tastes (see "Compounded Gins", pp70–71). Steeping the botanicals in the spirit without distillation can lead to funkier flavours and allows producers to include ingredients that may not survive distillation.

FLAVOURED GIN

This is another very loose category that includes all the pink gins (not to be confused with the cocktail of the same name), lemon gins, strawberry gins, and so on. The only thing they have in common is that they feature a distinct signature botanical that dominates the flavour, sometimes to the point that it overshadows the juniper – in which case, one might ask, is it even gin?

LONDON DRY

This is the best-known category gin has to offer. The gin doesn't have to be made in London, it's just that London is where this method of making gin arose. London Dry gins are made by redistilling ethyl alcohol with botanicals to at least 70% ABV (see p13). Importantly, nothing may be added after distillation except more ethyl alcohol (of the same source, strength, and composition) and water. Any colouring or flavouring is forbidden, as is sweetening, hence the "dry" part of the name.

Other than being juniper-led, these gins don't have to adopt any given flavour profile, yet many do adhere to the "classic London Dry" taste as exemplified by Tanqueray (see p164) or Jensen's Bermondsey Dry Gin (see p161). They often display a balanced and well-rounded flavour with citrus (often orange), coriander, orris root, and angelica.

LONDON DRY

NAVY STRENGTH

NEW WESTERN DRY

OLD TOM

PLYMOUTH GIN

NAVY STRENGTH

The Royal Navy used to store rum (for the men) and gin (for the officers) on board their ships. It was essential that, in the event of a spillage, the alcohol was sufficiently flammable so it wouldn't spoil the ships' gunpowder. Only spirits of 57.15% ABV or higher contain enough alcohol to burn when mixed with gunpowder, so this is the ABV we now call navy strength.

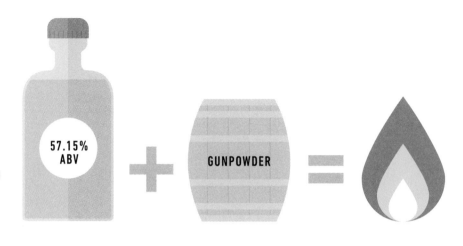

NAVY STRENGTH

Any gin that wants to test its strength against the navy must reach 57% ABV in order to prove itself worthy (see box above). There's no single flavour associated with navy strength gin. However, they do all share a degree of potency and botanical oomph driven along by all that alcohol. Good examples warm but do not burn or sting; in spirits-geek terms, this means the alcohol is "well integrated". Try Sweden's Hernö Navy Strength (see p160). Although strong gin and the navy go way back, the term "navy strength gin" may be a more recent invention. Apparently, we have marketing for Plymouth Gin in the 1990s to thank for it.

NEW WESTERN DRY

Ryan Magarian, one of the creators of Aviation Gin (see p183), came up with this term to describe a more contemporary gin, where juniper takes its foot off the gas a little and allows the other botanicals to shine. Importantly, the juniper should still remain dominant, otherwise what you have is no longer gin. The idea is for the other botanicals to "just about" share centre stage. One theory is these gins – also called "contemporary gins" or "new age gins" – were made to steal market share back from vodka. Many are lighter and more approachable than classic gins, but this doesn't mean they lack flavour. Tanqueray No. Ten (see p173), Bombay Sapphire (see p158), Hendrick's (see p186), and Roku (see p180) are all good examples.

OLD TOM

Old Tom is a sweeter style that was popular in the 18th and 19th centuries, then fell out of favour as London Dry rose in prominence. Many of the oldest cocktail recipes were written with Old Tom gins in mind. In the past, these gins were often sweetened with sugar or honey. Some distillers today are returning to the style and making "botanically sweetened" versions that use liquorice to achieve an impression of sweetness without adding sucrose.

MANY OF THE OLDEST COCKTAIL
RECIPES WERE WRITTEN WITH
OLD TOM GINS IN MIND.

Some makers (particularly in the US) like to age their Old Tom gins in barrels. This has never been a legal requirement for the style, and Old Tom gins do not generally carry age statements like whisky does. Other than sweetness and juniper, there's no particular flavour profile that ties these gins together. The sweetness should be in balance with the rest of the botanicals rather than overpowering them. Hayman's Old Tom is a good one to try.

PLYMOUTH GIN

How does a single gin become considered a style all of its own? It's probably a case of being in the right place at the right time. Plymouth Gin became the supplier to the British Navy as it was busy spanning the globe, so that certainly helped. It is also a little different from other gins: softer than a London Dry, smooth and full-bodied. It has a rootier, earthier botanical base and is off dry rather than bone dry.

At one point, Plymouth Gin could be made only in the English naval city of Plymouth, as the style was protected under European Union (EU) law. However, a change to the law meant brand owners Pernod Ricard would have had to reveal the recipe in order to maintain its protected status. They decided instead to let this "protection" lapse in 2014.

If you want to try this style, there is only one place to go: Plymouth Gin (see p163). It's great in almost any cocktail. Plymouth Gin also makes a navy strength version of its gin, which is where the idea of gin styles begins to get confusing. Which style is it, Plymouth or navy strength?

LOW(ER)-ALCOHOL GINS

Low-alcohol gin does not exist, indeed cannot exist, because gin has a legally defined minimum ABV of 37.5% in the UK and the EU, and 40% in the US (see pp12–14). That said, there are some countries, such as Australia and New Zealand, that don't have legal definitions for gin (see p14).

However, that does not mean that gin cannot offer a lower-alcohol option to drinkers who want to moderate their intake. Gin essences, or concentrates, are bottled at 40% to 50% ABV but are made with a massive overload of botanicals. This makes them so intensely flavoured that you only need a tiny amount (about 2.5ml/½ tsp) in your glass. When you dilute this with 200ml (7fl oz) of tonic, you bring the flavour back into balance so that it tastes like a normal G&T – but at something like 0.6% ABV. Examples are Hayman's Small Gin, Adnam's Smidgin Gin, and Chase Distillery's Dry Gin Essence. These are sold in 200ml (7fl oz) bottles and come with a measuring spoon, thimble, or built-in pipette to help measure out the right amount.

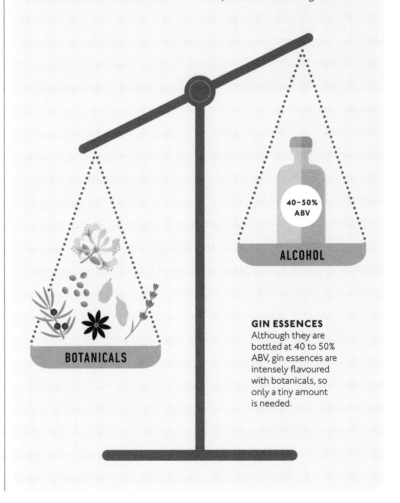

40–50% ABV

ALCOHOL

BOTANICALS

GIN ESSENCES
Although they are bottled at 40 to 50% ABV, gin essences are intensely flavoured with botanicals, so only a tiny amount is needed.

SLOE GIN

Sloes are the small, plum-like fruit of the blackthorn tree (*Prunus spinosa*). Most birds find them inedible, which means, come early autumn, they're still available for humans to soak in gin and sugar. This doesn't necessarily make the sloes any tastier, but it certainly does wonders for the gin.

FRUITY LIQUEUR

Sloe gin is technically a liqueur (because of the added sugar). It's a fruity, tart, and earthy concoction that's particularly good taken neat in the colder months as a fireside sipper, or glugged from a hip flask on a bracing hike through open country. But it's not only a winter drink – it also works well lengthened into a summery highball, mixed with bitter lemon or alongside sherry. Plenty of gin-based cocktails take on an extra dimension when you go sloe.

HARVESTING

Tradition says to harvest your sloes after the first frost, as the cold ripens them. You'll hear, too, about pricking your sloes with a pin – or even a thorn from the tree they grew on. My advice is to stick them in the freezer, which both ripens

MAKING SLOE GIN

It's a matter of taste whether you add sugar at the outset or wait till the gin has matured. If all that's too much fuss, you can, of course, just buy it ready-made.

1

CLEAN AND FREEZE
Rinse your sloes, and then put them into the freezer to ripen and rupture them.

2

FILL A JAR
Fill a large jar halfway with sloes and top up with gin.

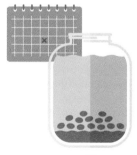

3

STORE
Store the jar in a cool, dark place for up to six months. Shake it gently from time to time.

PLENTY OF GIN-BASED COCKTAILS TAKE ON AN EXTRA DIMENSION WHEN YOU GO SLOE.

and ruptures your sloes at the same time. You can even buy your sloes online if you don't want to bother with all that ferreting about in thorny bushes.

WHAT'S THE RECIPE?

There's no set recipe for sloe gin. Harvest your sloes, just fill a jar or bottle roughly halfway with them, top it up with gin, and then wait as long as you can before drinking it.

Two to three months is the usual waiting time. Six is better if you can manage it.

Lots of people say to add sugar from the outset. Nine times out of 10, they're wrong. The fruit's natural sugar levels vary from one year to another, so it's better to leave your sloe gin to mature, then sweeten it with sugar, syrup, or honey to taste. And the 10th time? If you need sweetened sloes for baking, add the sugar early.

GOOD EXAMPLES OF SLOE GIN

HEPPLE SLOE & HAWTHORN GIN (see p194) is unusual for the addition of haws, the fruit of the hawthorn tree (*Crataegus*). These balance out the deep fruity flavour with a dry finish, through which comes the big piney thwack of juniper characteristic of a Hepple gin. My top tip: add a slug of this to your Guinness.

HAYMAN'S SLOE GIN (see p193) is tart and plummy with a delicious almond background flavour and a bone-dry finish. This one's good mixed with Aperol and lengthened with blood-orange soda into a wintry spritz.

ELEPHANT SLOE GIN If you fancy something a little different, Elephant Sloe Gin has a slightly higher ABV and leans a little more on the spicy side, with almost menthol, cracked black pepper notes behind the berry-tart sloes. It's unfiltered, too, giving it a hazier appearance than most.

Strain through clean muslin

4

SWEET OR NOT?
Leave it to mature and sweeten with sugar, syrup, or honey to taste.

5

FILTER AND DRINK
Filter your bounty through some clean muslin into a clean bottle, and off you go.

FLAVOUR COMPOUNDS

What does juniper share with citrus or lavender with liquorice? You can uncover links between gin's botanical ingredients if you look at the building blocks of its flavours. These aromatic compounds, often monoterpenoids, can explain why the peels, seeds, and herbs distillers use work together to make the flavours we love.

AROMATIC COMPOUNDS

This is just a small selection of the many thousands of volatile compounds that we know about thanks to the work of organic chemists.

PINEY AND WOODY

Juniper contains **pinene**, a monoterpenoid also found in many herbs, spices, and some citrus. It tastes piney, resinous, and "terpy" – think turpentine, solvents, and liquid fuels. Angelica is sweet, musky, and woody thanks to pinene alongside **carene** and other compounds. Woody notes also come from **cadinene**, which is found in juniper, marigolds, and avocados. **Myrcene**, commonly found in citrus peels (notably bitter orange), black pepper, and juniper, imparts woody, resinous flavours. These peels also contain **menthatriene**, which adds terpy and camphor flavours. Lime peel can be woody, terpy, and citric thanks to **terpinolene**, which is also in ginger and other spices.

CITRIC

The first compound you may hear of here is **limonene**. Despite its name, it is not especially lemony. Still, it is most commonly found in citrus fruits, and provides a fresh citrus, herbal, and terpy background note. Juniper also contains limonene. The aroma most of us associate with lemons actually comes from **geranial** and **neral**, which are also found in lemongrass, citrus peels, lemon verbena, eucalyptus, and ginger. **Citronellal**, found in lychees, citronella, makrut lime, and citrus peels, gives citrus notes but also floral and rose aromas.

FLORAL

Linalool tastes floral, sweet-citrus and lavender-woody. It exists in more than 200 plant species, notably mint, citrus, laurels, cinnamon, birch trees, coriander seeds, liquorice, lavender, basil, mugwort, hops, and cannabis. **Geranyl acetate** (fruity, floral, rose) is found in citrus, orange blossom, lemongrass, citronella, geranium, and eucalyptus. Sweet, floral, rose, and citrus notes also come from **geraniol** and **nerol**, found in roses and geraniums, but also lemon, citronella, and citrus. Rose notes also come from **rose oxide**. Orris root has a form of **irones** with woody-floral aromas described as warm, sweet, and violet. Meadowsweet gets its sweet, vanilla-like taste partly from **anisaldehyde**, which is also in anise, star anise, and basil flowers.

HERBAL

The source of most minty and cooling notes is one you may be familiar with: **menthol**. There's also **menthone**, which is found in mints and some geraniums. Two closely related volatiles are **mint carvone** (spearmint notes, found in mints, lavender, citrus) and **caraway carvone** (caraway and dill notes, found in both of those plus field mint and lavender). **Anethole** is responsible for the anise and medicinal notes of aniseed, star anise, liquorice, and fennel. **Estragole** gives notes that are anise, green, and herbal and is found in tarragon, basil, liquorice, and fennel.

WARMING AND SPICED

Camphor (medicinal, woody, and warming or cooling) is found in cinnamon, lavender, and many citrus, herbs, and spices. **Borneol** is also woody and warming and is found in pine and cypress trees, ginger, lavender, citrus peels, and spices. Citrus, rosemary, and lavender can also provide **cineole**, which tastes minty, piney, and warming. **Vanillin** (from vanilla) is also in oak, liquorice, and cherries. Cloves' warming taste – also found in cinnamon, basil, and bananas – comes from **eugenol**. Liquorice's complex aroma covers "green", thyme, floral, beany, anise, clove, sweet fenugreek, caramel, butter, smoky, and vanilla. Its flavour compounds not already named here include **nonadienal**, **carvacrol**, **thymol**, **sotolon**, **diacetyl**, and **guaiacol**.

FRUITY

The sweet berry notes (with a floral edge) that you might encounter in raspberries and loganberries come from a volatile called **hydroxyphenyl butanone**. It's also known as **raspberry ketone**, which is much easier to remember. An important part of the aroma of strawberries is **furaneol**. Its fruity and sometimes caramel notes also arise in pineapple, raspberry, mangos, some grapes, liquorice, and even tomatoes.

SAVOURY

Gin distillers always use different flavours for their gins. In recent years, many have looked to savoury, umami, or maritime notes. Seaweeds like dulse and carrageen can impart sweet and fresh iodine flavours thanks to **bromoform** and **hexanal** – an aldehyde with six carbon atoms – or its closely related forms with seven, eight, or nine carbon atoms. This aldehyde also crops up in olives, alongside the closely related but subtly different **hexenal**.

THE MAIN BOTANICALS

The beating heart of any gin is the combination of seeds, leaves, peels, roots, or bark that make up its flavour profile. Every gin maker will try to do something to make their gin unique, but it still has to taste similar enough to other gins to be accepted into the family. The "big three" botanicals are juniper berries, coriander seed, and angelica.

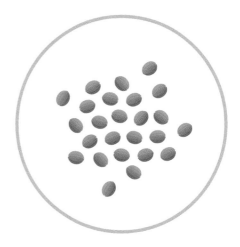

JUNIPER BERRIES

Juniperus communis, member of the Cupressaceae (cypress family)

Juniper is the *sine qua non* botanical; a spirit can't call itself gin without juniper. Specifically, common juniper, which (in most of the world at least) must be predominant among the botanicals employed. Few of us these days are familiar with its flavour in isolation. Its purple-blue berries (actually tiny cones) are rich in alpha-pinene, which gives a pine-rosemary-turpentine flavour. They also contain myrcene – which it shares with wild thyme, hops, and even cannabis – and limonene (think citrus and some herbs).

CORIANDER SEED

Coriandrum sativum, member of the Apiaceae (carrot family)

Coriander is perhaps the most important botanical in gin after juniper. Its dried seeds smell dusty and musty, with hints of a hay barn warmed in the late summer sun. But crush them, and a vibrant green citrus-spice aroma erupts at once. The essential oils within the seeds are rich in thymol, geranyl, and linalool. These compounds give, in turn, aromas and flavours of woody thyme, rich geranium, and bright, floral citrus. Coriander lends body and intensity to a gin.

OTHER COMMONLY USED BOTANICALS

As well as the "big three" of juniper, coriander, and angelica, there are other commonly used botanicals. Most gins will include at least a few, especially cassia, citrus, and orris.

ANGELICA

Angelica archangelica, member of the Apiaceae (carrot family)

The third member of gin's "big three", angelica is often confused with juniper owing to its similar scent, though it's a little more musky and woody. The roots' primary aromatic constituents are alpha-pinene (like juniper) and beta-pinene. The seed oil is sweeter, with notes of mint and eucalyptus. Once distilled, angelica root has an earthy, woody, herbaceous flavour. Distillers sometimes say angelica "fixes" other flavours in a gin, particularly lighter and more volatile flavours, although there is little scientific evidence for this. A few gins, such as Beefeater, also use angelica seeds alongside the roots.

ALMOND

Prunus dulcis, member of the Rosaceae (rose family)

Almonds are closely related to apricots and peaches. They are cultivated mostly in California and, to a lesser extent, Spain and Italy. Their flavour is perhaps best described as a honeyed nuttiness – although almonds are not technically nuts at all, but rather drupes, a type of fruit that has a fleshy part surrounding a stone, which contains the seed. The almond seed is the part we eat. In gin, almonds give a certain dryness to the texture.

CARDAMOM

Elettaria cardamomum, member of the
Zingiberaceae (ginger family)

Cardamom is cultivated in tropical areas such as
Sri Lanka and Guatemala, but the best cardamom
comes from India. Its papery seed pods don't offer
much aroma, but the seeds within pack a big
floral-ginger-spicy punch. Cardamom can easily
overpower other botanicals, so distillers must use
it sparingly. Cardamom contains linalool and linalyl
acetate, flavour compounds that are also found in
lavender and citrus fruits. Black cardamom comes
from a different plant, *Amomum subulatum*, and is
typically dried over an open fire, which gives its
flavours a smoky tinge.

CASSIA BARK

Cinnamomum cassia, member of the Lauraceae
(laurel family)

In the UK, cassia is also called Chinese cinnamon to
differentiate it from "true" cinnamon (*Cinnamomum
verum*). No such distinction is made in the United
States, where cassia is sold as generic cinnamon.
Cultivated cassia comes mostly from Indonesia and
Sri Lanka and is used in gin to add complexity to the
base flavours. It is sweet, woody, and warmly spiced,
thanks to its essential oil, which contains the
compounds cinnamaldehyde and coumarin.

CASSIA IS SWEET, WOODY,
AND WARMLY SPICED, THANKS
TO ITS ESSENTIAL OIL.

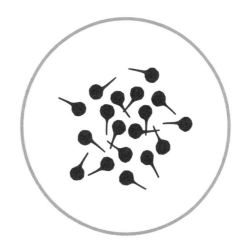

CITRUS

Various members of the Rutaceae (rue family)

What do distillers' favourite citrus peels and leaves all have in common? That would be limonene. This belongs to the strongly aromatic terpene group of compounds, which are responsible for the aromas, flavours, and colours of various types of plants. Many plants use them to deter animals from eating them. Bad luck, plants! Those terpenes are delicious: bright, zingy, zesty, and fresh on top with a background sweetness and, sometimes, a hint of bitterness too. As so many gin botanicals also contain limonene, citrus fruits are a natural match and easily slot into the overall flavour profile.

CUBEB

Piper cubeba, member of the Piperaceae (pepper family)

Cubeb is the fruit of a climbing vine from Indonesia, hence its other common name: Java pepper. Visually, it resembles its close relative black pepper (*P. nigrum*), although cubeb is usually sold with its stems still attached in order to make it easier to distinguish. Its essential oil contains piperine, which gives cubeb its pungent peppery bite, but also high amounts of limonene, which is common among many citrus and herbs. Cubeb can also contribute a minty flavour to gin, especially on the finish.

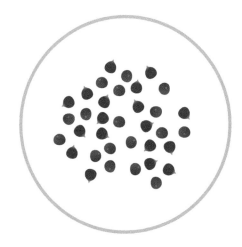

ELDER

Sambucus nigra, member of the Viburnaceae (viburnum family)

The elder is native to most of Europe (particularly the Nordic countries). The flavour derived from its flowers is common in the UK, appearing in all sorts of foods and drinks but most often in a non-alcoholic cordial. It's relatively unknown in the United States apart from the St Germain liqueur. Both the flowers and the berries of the elder tree are used in distilling. Elderflowers contain the compounds linalool, rose oxide, and a tiny hint of naphthalene. The frothy white flowers give a flavour of sweet, floral honey with a beguiling back note of pear or green-fleshed melon. The purple-black berries are jammier and quite tart.

GRAINS OF PARADISE

Aframomum melegueta, member of the Zingiberaceae (ginger family)

Grains of paradise are native to the coastal swamps of West Africa, and for this reason are sometimes called Guinea grains or peppers. The seed pods resemble peppercorns and can be used as a substitute for black pepper in all sorts of food and drink. They give a familiar pepper heat that is a little richer and spicier and somewhat reminiscent of its botanical relative, cardamom. Grains of paradise contain the compounds gingerol, paradol, and shogaol. Once distilled, grains of paradise give a minty, peppery flavour that adds depth to a gin's flavour profile and prolongs its finish.

BOTH THE FLOWERS AND THE
BERRIES OF THE ELDER TREE
ARE USED IN DISTILLING.

LIQUORICE ROOT

Glycyrrhiza glabra, member of the Fabaceae
(bean family)

Yes, liquorice is a bean. Who knew? But it's the root
we're interested in, with its rich store of anethole.
This is the compound that gives gin (and many other
spirits) a warm and sweetly aromatic note that pairs
so well with anise. It also contains plenty of
glycyrrhizin, a compound 30 to 50 times sweeter
than sugar. This is why liquorice is often used in
Old Tom gins (see pp74–75). Distillers mostly use
liquorice root in dried, powdered form not only for
its flavour but also to give their gin a smooth texture.

ORRIS ROOT

Iris florentina, member of the Iridaceae
(iris family)

Orris root is said to have fixative properties,
and its inclusion in gin probably stems from the
world of perfumery. It reduces the volatility of the
other botanicals found in gin – in other words, it
keeps gin tasting better for longer. The root itself
smells of violets (particularly Parma violet sweets),
though it's not often included for its flavour. The
orris root used in gin comes from irises grown in
southern France, northern Italy, and Morocco. It may
take up to five years for one to grow a root large
enough to harvest, and a further five to dry it.

MORE BOTANICALS

One of the reasons gin is so complex is the sheer number of ingredients that can wind up in the still. The leaves, seeds, and so on listed here have all appeared in at least one gin, although this is a long way off from being an exhaustive list of botanicals that have ever appeared in a gin. If you can smell it, you can distil it – and you probably won't be the first to try.

BOTANICAL	SWEET	NUTTY	EARTHY	WARMING	ANISE	SPICED	ACIDIC
BERRIES							
BILBERRIES	◉						◉
GOJI BERRIES							◉
LILLY PILLY BERRIES			◉			◉	◉
PEPPER BERRIES	◉					◉	
ROWAN BERRIES							
SEA BUCKTHORN	◉						◉
SLOES		◉	◉				◉
FLOWERS							
ACACIA	✳						
ARNICA							
DOG ROSE	✳						✳
HEATHER						✳	
HIBISCUS			✳				✳
HONEYSUCKLE	✳						
LINDEN	✳						
MEADOWSWEET	✳	✳					
SAKURA BLOSSOM	✳						✳
TANSY				✳		✳	

CITRUSSY	FRUITY	FLORAL	HERBAL	GRASSY	VEGETAL	PINEY	SALINE	BITTER	ASTRINGENT
	◉								
	◉								
	◉								
	◉								
	◉							◉	◉
◉	◉								
	◉							◉	
✽		✽			✽				
		✽				✽		✽	
		✽							
	✽	✽	✽						
	✽	✽							
		✽						✽	
✽		✽							
	✽	✽		✽					
	✽	✽							
								✽	

BOTANICAL	SWEET	NUTTY	EARTHY	WARMING	ANISE	SPICED	ACIDIC
FRUITS							
AMANATSU	●						●
FINGER LIME							●
KUMQUATS	●						●
POMELO	●						●
QUINCE	●						●
ROSE HIPS	●						●
LEAVES							
ANISEED MYRTLE	●		●	●			
BRAMBLE		●					
CAMOMILE	●						
CHERVIL					●		
CHINESE GREEN TEA	●	●	●				
CONIFER TIPS							●
LEMON MYRTLE	●					●	
LOVAGE					●		
MOUNTAIN PEPPERLEAF			●	●		●	
RASPBERRY			●				
RED SHISO					●	●	
SEA LETTUCE						●	
SORREL							●
SUGAR KELP	●	●					
SWEET GALE (bog myrtle)	●					●	
YARROW	●				●		

CITRUSSY	FRUITY	FLORAL	HERBAL	GRASSY	VEGETAL	PINEY	SALINE	BITTER	ASTRINGENT
								●	
●			●					●	
●									
●									
	●	●						●	
		●							
			●						
	●							●	●
	●	●							
			●						
		●	●		●				
●						●			
●			●						
			●						
			●						
	●		●					●	
●			●						
			●				●		
●				●					
					●		●		
			●			●		●	●
								●	

BOTANICAL	SWEET	NUTTY	EARTHY	WARMING	ANISE	SPICED	ACIDIC
OTHER							
FRANKINCENSE			◉	◉		◉	
HINOKI WOOD			◉				
MACADAMIA NUTS	◉	◉					
MARSH SAMPHIRE							
MYRRH	◉				◉	◉	
RHUBARB							◉
SANDALWOOD	◉	◉		◉			
PEELS							
BERGAMOT							◉
YUZU PEEL							◉
ROOTS							
BURDOCK	◐	◐	◐	◐			
CARLINE THISTLE			◐				
DANDELION		◐		◐			
HORSERADISH						◐	
SARSAPARILLA				◐			
TURMERIC			◐			◐	
SEEDS							
ALEXANDER						⬤	
ANISEED	⬤		⬤	⬤	⬤	⬤	
APRICOT KERNEL	⬤	⬤					
CARAWAY	⬤	⬤		⬤	⬤	⬤	
DILL	⬤	⬤			⬤		
FENNEL	⬤			⬤	⬤	⬤	
STAR ANISE	⬤		⬤	⬤	⬤		

CITRUSSY	FRUITY	FLORAL	HERBAL	GRASSY	VEGETAL	PINEY	SALINE	BITTER	ASTRINGENT
○						○			
○						○			
					○		○		
								○	○
	○								
		○							
◉		◉						◉	
◉	◉		◉					◉	
			⬮					⬮	
								⬮	
					⬮				
								⬮	
⬮								⬮	
		✸			✸				
								✸	
✸								✸	
			✸	✸				✸	

WHAT ABOUT BARRELS?

Some gins are barrel- or cask-aged. This gives them distinctive flavours on top of those imparted by the botanicals. These barrel-aged gins may taste familiar if you like whisky or bourbon, as those spirits get much of their flavour from barrels too.

CHARRING THE BARREL

Coopers (barrel makers) will often char a cask's inside surface before the distiller fills it with spirit. Charring forms a thin layer of charcoal inside the barrel that effectively filters the spirit and mellows it out over time by removing any sulphurous compounds. It also allows the spirit to get more easily into the subsurface of the wood, where more good things can happen.

SUGAR AND SPICE

The temperature of the spirit in the cask rises and falls with the natural rhythms of day and night, and the seasons. At the same time, the spirit moves in and out of the wood itself, almost as if the cask were breathing (see opposite). As the spirit moves into the wood's subsurface, it picks up some of the natural sugars there, which can give it sweet flavours of vanilla or coconut. The wood can also impart the flavours of baking spices, such as cloves, cinnamon, and nutmeg.

GHOSTS OF OTHER DRINKS

Most casks will be filled over and over again. Sometimes flavours from one drink can be carried over into the next one that is put into the cask. Many brewers make a virtue of this, and will age beers in casks that once held sherry, whisky, or bourbon to infuse those flavours into their beer. This is less common in gin but, done well, can lead to some very interesting drinks.

TIME AND FLAVOURS

The longer a drink spends in a cask, the more that cask will change its flavour character. The changes discussed above – the char, the sugar, the spice – will become more pronounced with prolonged aging. Duration in cask also brings other effects. Casks are not airtight, which means some oxygen will get in and some alcohol vapours will escape. As the liquid slowly evaporates, the portion left in the cask becomes more concentrated. Oxidized flavours will develop over time, which can lead to tastes reminiscent of sherry.

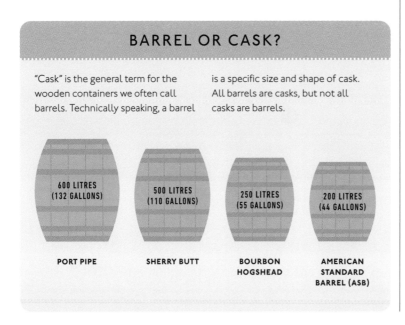

BARREL OR CASK?

"Cask" is the general term for the wooden containers we often call barrels. Technically speaking, a barrel is a specific size and shape of cask. All barrels are casks, but not all casks are barrels.

600 LITRES (132 GALLONS)

PORT PIPE

500 LITRES (110 GALLONS)

SHERRY BUTT

250 LITRES (55 GALLONS)

BOURBON HOGSHEAD

200 LITRES (44 GALLONS)

AMERICAN STANDARD BARREL (ASB)

WHAT HAPPENS IN THE BARREL?

A series of processes occurs once a spirit is put inside a barrel, which affects the final taste of the drink.

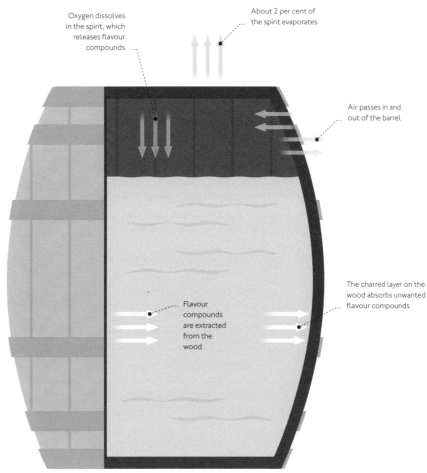

Oxygen dissolves in the spirit, which releases flavour compounds

About 2 per cent of the spirit evaporates

Air passes in and out of the barrel

Flavour compounds are extracted from the wood

The charred layer on the wood absorbs unwanted flavour compounds

THE LONGER A SPIRIT STAYS IN THE CASK, THE MORE THE CASK WILL CHANGE ITS FLAVOUR CHARACTER.

HOW FLAVOUR WORKS

It's worth taking a moment to understand how we experience flavour. By looking at the way our senses and the brain work together, we can deepen our understanding of what happens when we taste gin.

IT'S COMPLICATED

Flavour is what happens when our tongue, nose, and brain all cooperate to make sense of what we just put into our mouth. Our senses of sight, hearing, and touch all get in on the act too, along with our mood, expectations, memories, and our surroundings. These all combine to modify our experience of a flavour, so that everyone's perception ends up being truly unique to them.

TASTING IS MOSTLY SMELLING

Most of what we think of as flavour is actually aroma. The tongue can only pick up a few basic tastes: sweet, sour, salty, bitter, and umami. At least that's our current best understanding. Research suggests we can probably add fat as a sixth basic taste (or "oleogustus", if you're being fancy).

There may be another for "*kokumi*", or "richness", but scientists have yet to agree on that.

Everything else beyond these basic tastes is down to our sense of smell. Smell is hardwired into the limbic system of the brain, including the amygdala and the hippocampus, regions that relate to emotion and memory. This is why we can more easily recognize or recall smells that are linked to strong feelings or memories, and also why our experiences of flavour end up being so personal.

IT'S ALL IN YOUR HEAD

Most people think of smell as something that only happens outside our heads, usually somewhere just in front of our teeth and under our nostrils. This isn't true at all. Smell happens in our brain, and also inside our head somewhere just below and behind our eyes. That's where our olfactory receptors are, and the scents that we pick up there can just as easily come from inside our mouth as they can from outside. When the smell is inside, it's called retronasal tasting. Orthonasal tasting is when the smell comes from our surroundings.

VOLATILITY

Our senses of smell and taste are different from our other senses in that they work through "chemoreception". In other words, they rely on microscopic fragments of the thing we're smelling or tasting actually entering our body and interacting directly with our nervous system. When we smell a piece of fruit, for instance, what's actually happening is that the volatile compounds evaporating from the surface of the fruit enter our body through our nose. Remember that the next time you smell something really gross.

A UNIQUE TASTE SENSATION

Flavour is a complex, multi-sensory experience. It is the product of much more than just what's in the glass. Both physical and mental aspects combine to produce a sensation that is truly unique to each of us.

SMELL AND TASTE
Nerve signals from the olfactory receptors and the tongue are processed in the brain, making up most (but not all) of what we experience as flavour

EXPERIENCE
What we know about the gin, past flavour experiences, other memories, and even our mood can all affect how we experience a gin – even the same gin on different occasions

SIGHT
When we see a drink we quickly, often unconsciously, make judgments about its colour and clarity, the glass, the garnish, and so on. We form an expectation from these that can colour our enjoyment of the drink.

SOUND
Things we hear, like someone telling us to expect a certain quality or flavour, can affect our experience of the gin

SMELL
As we raise our glass, aroma compounds register in our olfactory receptors. Our nose gives its verdict on the gin. What will it do, warn or welcome?

AIR FLOW
As we drink our gin, some aroma compounds will reach our olfactory receptors from inside our mouth, enhancing our perception of its flavour

TOUCH
We feel the gin's temperature and viscosity in our mouth, and sometimes its alcohol sting too

TASTE
Our tongue will sense basic tastes (sweet, acid, salty, bitter, umami, fatty) as the gin passes across it

THINKING ABOUT FLAVOUR

Flavour is a great key for unlocking gin. If you understand it better, you will understand gin better. You will find it easier to know which mixers to choose, or why you enjoy a particular gin in any given cocktail.

BUILD A SCENT LIBRARY

One of the best things you can do to become a better gin taster is to become more familiar with flavours in general. By tasting widely, you have more experience to draw on when you're trying to work out and describe what your gin tastes like. Even more importantly, you must smell widely because flavour is mostly aroma (see pp94–95). Simply smelling an aroma is a good start, but if you want to really fix it in your mind, there are some tricks you can try – as long as you don't mind looking a bit odd. Most of these boil down to getting other senses involved as you smell, helping you form stronger memories of each odour.

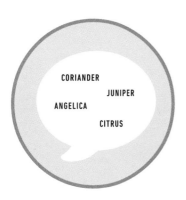

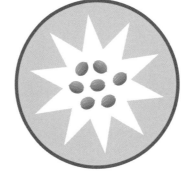

SAY MY NAME

As you smell something, repeat its name a few times. Close your eyes and really concentrate on the aroma, on the sound of its name, and on any memories that come to mind. By building linked multi-sensory pathways in your brain, you increase your chances of recognizing that scent the next time you encounter it.

CATCH SOME FEELS

You can also make use of the strong links between smell and emotion in your brain by trying to create a heightened emotional state as you smell something. A simpler method is to try linking scents to memories that have a strong emotional component. See if you can link a smell to a memory about a specific place or person.

TARGET YOUR TASTING

Many of gin's flavours come from ingredients we can actually find easily. If you want to recognize them better in gin, go and find some coriander seeds, liquorice, and angelica. Touch them and taste them for yourself, learn to recognize them in a context that makes sense to you. Build your own personal memory bank of gin's flavours.

BALANCING FLAVOURS

The basic tastes that we can pick up with our tongues don't exist in isolation – they swirl around together messing with our mouths. Different tastes can enhance one another. Sweet and salty are friends, each one increasing our perception of the other. Salted caramel ice cream, anyone? Sourness boosts umami and salty flavours. Picture that lemon with your fish and chips, or the lime with your tacos.

If one of the basic tastes is too dominant, you can use others to bring it back into balance:

• sweet balances sour or bitter (and also spicy heat)
• sour balances sweet or bitter (and also spicy heat)
• bitter balances sweet or salty
• salty balances bitter
• spicy heat balances sweet.

In drinks, the presence of alcohol can also be thought of as something akin to a basic taste. Just think back to drinks where you've taken that first sip and thought, "Wow, that's strong!" The good news is you can bring this back into balance by adding sweet or bitter flavours. (More dilution will also do the job.)

GIN'S FLAVOUR

There are many volatile flavour compounds that make it into a gin through distillation. These are all soluble in ethanol and water to a different degree. In other words, the stronger a gin is, the more it will hold on to some flavours and release others. If you add water (or any other mixer), it changes this balance, releasing a different combination of volatile compounds and altering the gin's flavour.

Sweetness isn't just about flavour – it also affects the gin's texture, making it thicker and stickier. See if you can detect the presence of sugar. If there's none, we call the spirit dry. If there's a little, we say off-dry or medium. If it's obvious, we call the spirit sweet.

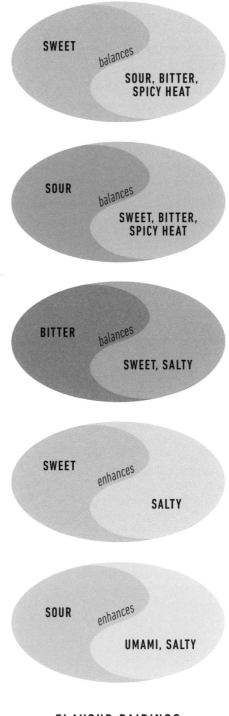

FLAVOUR PAIRINGS

Certain flavours counteract other flavours,
while some flavours enhance others.

GET READY TO TASTE YOUR GIN

Kicking back with a G&T with friends or in front of the TV is a wonderful experience, but that's not what we're talking about here. If your aim is to really taste your gin – maybe you want to evaluate its quality, become a better taster, or most likely a bit of both at once – you need to approach it differently.

NO DISTRACTIONS

The following pages set out how to taste your gin in a systematic way that's based on the methods the pros use. We'll also look at how to write memorable and insightful tasting notes (see pp102–03). But before you can tackle any of that, you need to make sure you've got everything you need.

There's no getting around it – you have to really concentrate on the gin and on your reactions to it. You can't do that if you're being interrupted every five minutes or distracted by noises. Worst of all are strong smells that will interfere directly with your tasting efforts. Pick a time and a place where you can turn your mind completely over to the gin, even if it's just for a short while.

THE PRACTICALITIES

Once you have everything ready, the practicalities, such as how much gin to use and whether to dilute it or not, are other things to consider.

HOW MUCH?
Stick to a single shot. You can always pour more if you need it, but usually a sip or two is plenty.

EVERYTHING TO HAND

You can't really focus if you have to keep on getting up to look for something. Get everything ready before you start. You will need your gin(s), clearly. If that was news to you, I'd give up now and pick another hobby. And on top of that, think about gathering the items shown here.

TASTING GLASS
A glass with a rim that tapers inwards will help to concentrate the aroma.

WATER OR TONIC FOR DILUTING
If you use tonic, avoid ones with strong flavours or artificial sweeteners that may mask the flavour of the gin (see p112).

WHAT TEMPERATURE?

Room temperature is fine. If your gin is too cold, you won't taste the flavours as much.

NEAT OR DILUTED?

Always start with neat gin. It helps to have some water or tonic to hand to see how the gin changes once you've diluted it, but that can always wait until after you try the spirit as it comes.

SHOULD I SPIT?

If you're only tasting a couple of gins, there's no need to spit. But if you have things to do afterwards, or if you have more than a handful of gins to taste, then spitting becomes a good idea. It minimizes alcohol absorption and prevents you from getting drunk. Definitely spit if you need to keep your concentration levels up over a long time.

WHAT GLASS?

Honestly, any clean glass will do. The pros use 200ml (7fl oz) International Organization for Standardization (ISO) glasses. If you have one with a rim that tapers inwards, like a wine glass, it will concentrate aromas at the top of the glass and make your job a little easier (see also pp104–05).

SPITTOON

If you want to minimize your alcohol intake, have something handy to use as a spittoon.

PALATE CLEANSER

If you're tasting a few gins, a palate cleanser is helpful – plain crackers are best.

NOTEPAD, PHONE, OR LAPTOP

Take notes with a notebook and pen, or use your phone or a laptop.

A SYSTEMATIC APPROACH TO TASTING GIN

Tasting consistently is your fastest route to a better appreciation of gin (or any other drink). This method is based on one the pros use. It's essentially a checklist to make sure you assess every aspect of the gin in front of you, every time you taste.

THE LOOK

The first step is always to check out the gin's clarity and colour. Most of the time, it will be clear and colourless and you can move on. Sometimes, you'll notice your gin has an almost silvery shine and looks brighter in the glass. This is a sign that it was chill filtered, which makes it more stable and less likely to louche (see pp62–63), but can also strip away some flavour and texture elements.

Some gins are coloured, which can hint at the flavours you might find; pink gins are often fruity, orange ones might have strong citrus flavours. Some have a colour that points to how the gin was made, perhaps cask aging (see pp92–93) or cold compounding (see pp70–71). Clues like this can guide you as you move on to assess the gin's aroma and flavour.

THE NOSE

To gauge the aroma's intensity, start by holding the glass at your chest. If you can smell the spirit from there, the aroma is intense. Then move the glass so it's at your chin. If you start to smell it there, the aroma's intensity is medium. Then hold it to your nose. If you only start to smell it here, it's light. If you still can't smell anything, then it's neutral.

Next, you work out what it is you can smell. Look for aromas from the raw materials, which in gin's case means the botanicals. There should always be juniper, and often a strong coriander note too, but that's just the beginning. Take your time here and try to tease out the separate smells (see pp80–91 for more on botanicals in gin).

YOUR PERSONAL REACTION TO THE GIN
IS NOT NECESSARILY THE SAME AS YOUR
TAKE ON ITS QUALITY – A GIN CAN BE
EXCELLENT BUT STILL NOT TO YOUR TASTE.

THE PALATE

Take a sip and hold it in your mouth for a few seconds. Allow the gin to move around a bit. This is important because you have tastebuds not just on your tongue but all over your mouth, in the sides of your cheeks, the roof of your mouth, and the back of your throat. See what you can taste and how that matches up with the aromas you picked out.

Concentrate also on how the gin feels in your mouth: does it sting and burn or is it smooth? Is its texture thin and light, or is it oily and mouth-coating?

Finally, take a moment to notice what happens after you've swallowed (or spat). Do the flavours linger for a while? Do they develop into something else? This aftertaste is also called the gin's finish, and a good one will have pleasant levels of complexity.

THE VERDICT

Put everything you've just noticed together and use that to reach an assessment of the gin's quality. How does it compare to others you've tasted? Was everything in balance or did one aspect stand out, and if so, was that good or bad?

This is also a good time to consider your personal reaction to the gin, which is not necessarily the same as your take on its quality – a gin can be excellent but still not to your taste. If you're making tasting notes (see pp102–03), now's the time to capture any emotional impressions too (see p96 for why this is a good idea). You might want to give each gin a score or a rating. Some pros, myself included, use a scale that runs through faulty, poor, acceptable, good, very good, and outstanding.

WRITING TASTING NOTES

We taste every day, yet many of us tell ourselves we're no good at it, especially when we compare ourselves to others. How is it that some people can rattle on about the flavours in their drink after just a couple of sips, whereas the best we can muster might be "I like it"?

TRUST YOUR NOSE

Everyone experiences flavour slightly differently. It's normal to look to others for guidance, but ultimately, you need to learn to trust your own experience.

WHAT'S THE SECRET?

The secret is that these chatterboxes are not necessarily better tasters than you. They've just had more practice at putting the flavours they experience into words. The more you do this, the better you get at figuring out what's going on inside your nose when you smell and in your mouth when you taste.

THE VALUE IN WRITING TASTING NOTES

Putting flavour into words is a skill, and one that will enrich your life if you let it. The good news is you don't need any special equipment. You can drop money on fancy-pants aroma-training kits if you like, but a simple notebook is going to have a much bigger effect.

Don't think of it as training your palate. What you're really doing is training your brain. It's true that some people's palates are more sensitive than others', but that doesn't matter. It just means the signal reaching their brains is louder than for others. What really counts is how good you are at interpreting that signal.

Writing notes as you taste helps you make sense of flavour. It fixes sensory impressions in your mind. This is especially true if you write your notes by hand, which research has shown will improve your memory. It also slows you down and helps you focus properly on what you're tasting.

WRITING MEMORABLE TASTING NOTES

To write memorable notes, all you need to do is pay attention to your drink, and write down what you find. It doesn't matter if this isn't much at first. If you want to get better, you just need to practise. Repetition is what counts.

Think about all the ways we can talk about flavour. It starts with basic reactions, "I love it" or "I hate it". After that come individual flavours, such as juniper, coriander, or citrus, and modifiers like muted, bold, or overpowering. You might use figurative language, such as "This gin is rich and creamy", or metaphor, "It's a rainy Sunday in my glass". You could use some technical language: "The alcohol is well integrated", meaning it doesn't burn or sting, or focus on basic tastes like sweet or bitter.

It's good to pick out any individual flavours that you can identify, but try to go beyond that. Take time to recognize how you feel about the drink. An emotional dimension adds richness to your experience. Because of the way our brains are wired, aroma is intimately connected with emotion. If you can bring that into your notes, it will help you to recall the aromas later on (see p96).

Writing notes, in conjunction with a systematic approach to tasting (see pp100–01), are your two most powerful tools to becoming a better taster.

WRITING NOTES AS YOU TASTE HELPS YOU MAKE SENSE OF FLAVOUR.

TASTING SHEET

Use this sheet as a guide to refine your tasting notes by focusing on the different facets of a gin's flavour. Then use your notes to give the gin a rating.

GIN NAME

☐ NEAT   ☐ TONIC

APPEARANCE	RATING
	☆ ☆ ☆ ☆ ☆

NOSE

PALATE

AROMA

NEUTRAL   LIGHT   MEDIUM   STRONG

FLAVOUR INTENSITY

NEUTRAL   LIGHT   MEDIUM   STRONG

JUNIPER

FRUIT

SAVOURY

SPICY

FLORAL

CITRUS

HERBAL

UMAMI

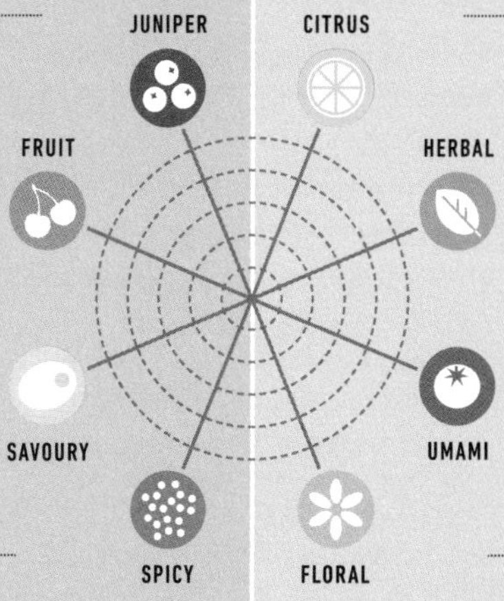

DOES THE GLASS MATTER?

What's the best glass for serving your gin?
Does its shape really affect the flavour or
is it just a question of which one looks best?

SHAPE AND FLAVOUR

There's a reason we have developed a variety of glass types for different drinks over time. The shape and style of your glass will affect how you taste the drink it contains. Sometimes it does this directly, and sometimes the mechanism is subtler and more indirect.

Direct effects include how the rim affects aromas, and the impact on temperature of a stemmed glass. Indirect effects include our judgment of whether the glassware is "appropriate" or not (whether that judgment is conscious or unconscious), and the influence of the weight of the glass.

Personal preference plays a part as well, but introduces a chicken-and-egg question: do I prefer a highball for my G&Ts because its shape suits the drink better, or does my preference for the drink served this way affect my perception as I drink?

DIRECT EFFECTS

The shape of a glass has direct effects on how we taste:

- A rim that tapers inwards concentrates aroma at the top of the glass.
- A rim that flares outwards opens the drink up to the air, letting all those volatile aromas escape.
- A tall, narrow glass holds onto carbonation better – G&T drinkers take note.
- A stem keeps your warm hands from the glass's bowl, so your drink stays cooler for longer; colder drinks release less aroma.

TAPERED RIM
Aroma is concentrated
at the top of a glass
with a tapered rim.

INDIRECT EFFECTS

Psychological research has revealed a number of factors that affect taste indirectly:

- We enjoy drinks more from glassware we consider "appropriate", and less from "inappropriate" glassware.
- We associate sweet-tasting food and drink with round forms, and sour or bitter ones with angular shapes. You can accentuate or tone down basic flavours in your drink depending on how you serve it. A Negroni may seem more mellow in a rounded glass, and have a sharper, bitter bite in an angular one.
- We associate weight with quality. Gin will taste better in a heavy-bottomed glass than it will in a plastic cup.

APPROPRIATE GLASSWARE
Champagne tastes better from
a flute than it does from a
chipped teacup.

THE SHAPE OF THE GLASS AFFECTS THE WAY YOU TASTE THE GIN IT CONTAINS IN DIRECT AND INDIRECT WAYS.

FLARED RIM
Volatile aromas
escape from a glass
with a flared rim.

TALL AND NARROW GLASS
Carbonation is retained
well in a tall, narrow glass –
perfect for a G&T.

STEMMED GLASS
Hold the stem, not the
glass, and your drink stays
cooler and crisper for longer.

ROUND SHAPE
We associate sweet-tasting food
and drink with rounder forms.
Bittersweet drinks can seem
more mellow in a round glass.

ANGULAR SHAPE
We associate sour or bitter food
and drink with angular shapes.
Bittersweet drinks can have a
sharper bite in an angular glass.

WEIGHT GAIN
Weight is associated with quality.
The same gin will taste better in a
heavy-bottomed glass than it will
in a lightweight plastic cup.

TYPES OF GLASSES

TUMBLERS

If your drink calls for ice, these are the glasses to choose. They have the space to accommodate the cubes. Low tumblers also have room for a good swirl, while, for mixers, a higher glass gives a narrow profile that will help your drink hold onto its carbonation. The heavy base means they're nice and stable too.

GLENCAIRN
These are made for whisky but they're great for small measures of other spirits. The bowl gives you room for a nice swirl, while the rim concentrates the aroma.

ROCKS, OLD FASHIONED, OR LOWBALL
These are the simplest way to serve a gin, particularly if you want to try it neat or on the rocks without any mixer. Very few people drink gin this way, but there's no reason not to give it a try sometime.

STEMMED GLASSES

If a cocktail recipe says to serve a drink "up", that means one of these stemmed glasses. The advantage here is that they help your drink stay cold, even though it is served without ice, by keeping your warm hand away from the chilled drink (as long as you hold them properly, that is, by the stem). They also look really glam.

NICK AND NORA
A Nick and Nora is great for cocktails when you want a little elegance, and when you want a drink to stay cold without putting ice in your glass. The drink is perched on a stem but remains balanced.

COUPE OR COUPETTE
This is the same idea as the Nick and Nora but a little more generous thanks to its wider bowl. It can look stunning used for cocktails that involve an egg white foam like the Clover Club (see p128).

STEMLESS TULIP

These glasses marry the heavy base of a tumbler with the roomy bowl and tapered rim of a wine or beer glass. They're good all-rounders offering stability, room for ice, and a rim that concentrates aroma.

HIGHBALL

Most G ends up mixed with a T, and this is the place to do it. A long glass for a long drink, room for lots of ice, and all balanced by a heavy base for no-nonsense enjoyment of a refreshing drink.

COLLINS

A collins is basically a highball that's taller and narrower. If you're wondering why bother, when you have a highball already, note that a collins often holds more liquid overall.

FASHIONABLE BUT AWFUL!

MARTINI

They look great but they're terrible in practice. They're a pain to clean and break easily. They hog shelf space. They're too easy to tip over. And worst of all, they're awful to drink from.

COPA OR BALON

Some people like them, but I can't get on with these terrible fishbowls. Like the martini glass, I find the balance is all wrong. Plus bartenders seem unable to resist over-garnishing in these.

THE IMPORTANCE OF ICE

Time for me to bang the ice drum. *Use! More! Ice!*
A room-temperature G&T is a travesty, a rainy Sunday
afternoon in a glass. What is this, a boring golf club
dinner? No! Sling some ice in that drink!

TEMPERATURE AND DILUTION

Here's the part we all know already: ice makes your
drink cold, which gives it a crisp texture and makes
it thirst-quenching and refreshing. The ice does much
more than just chill your drink though.

Eating and drinking are two of the most sensually
rich activities in our lives. Adding ice to your drink
brings the senses of sight, hearing, and touch into play,
alongside taste and smell.

Ice also softens your drink by diluting it – ideally,
just enough to calm any alcohol sting and no more.
If you overdilute, then your gin will become flabby
and lose its bite. It may seem counterintuitive, but you
avoid an overdiluted drink by adding more ice, not less.
This chills your drink faster and means the ice will melt
more slowly, giving you more time to sip and enjoy.

WHAT SORT OF ICE TO USE

For best results use fresh, "dry" ice cubes – that is, ice
that has not already started melting. "Wet" ice will
dilute your drink faster. You want them to be a decent
size, too – maybe 3cm (1in) cubes or large enough so
they just fit in your glass. Bigger cubes melt slower.
Clear ones look nicer, so I usually recommend buying
ice by the bag rather than making it yourself. You can
get a bag of "premium" ice cheaply. Three of these
chunky cubes fill a highball just right and they look
great. Totally worth it in my book.

CLEAR ICE

To make clear ice at home, you need it to freeze slowly and in a uniform direction. Fill an insulated cooler with water and leave it in the freezer with the lid open until it freezes. Any cloudiness will be confined to the side that was on the bottom. You can split your ice by scoring it with a serrated knife, then hitting the back of the knife with a mallet. (It may help to leave the ice out a while to temper first.) Divide the clear portion into manageable sizes and shapes for your drinks, then store them in a bag in the freezer until you need them. Or you could just buy it.

CRACKED AND CRUSHED ICE

Cracked ice is good for long drinks like a Red Snapper (see p144). If you have oversized cubes, you can crack them in your hand using a bar spoon. It takes a knack to pull it off, and you risk sending ice chips flying all over. A better way is to wrap your ice in a clean tea towel, pick up something blunt and hefty, such as a rolling pin, and crack away.

   Crushed ice is a pain. Unless you're dead set on making a Bramble (see p126), then honestly don't bother. If you must, though, you can crush ice in a plastic bag with a rolling pin, or use a blender or food processor.

CHILLING GLASSES

Chilling glasses in the freezer is best. They only need five or 10 minutes, then take them out just as you're ready to pour your drink. Alternatively, fill your glass with ice before you make your drink. Crushed ice works best as it makes more contact with the glass. If you're using cubes, add some water to speed up the cooling. Discard the ice when you're ready to pour your drink.

MAKING CRACKED ICE

Wrap the ice in a clean tea towel and smash it up with a rolling pin.

ROLLING PIN

ICE CUBES

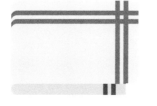

CLEAN TEA TOWEL

ADDING ICE TO YOUR DRINK BRINGS ALL YOUR SENSES INTO PLAY.

WAYS TO SERVE GIN

You absolutely can drink gin neat. There's no better way if you really want to get to know its flavours. Still, most of us will add mixers most of the time. Even so, there's more to life than tonic.

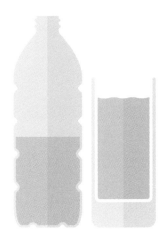

WATER

The English writer Kingsley Amis liked his gin this way. For Amis, adding tonic to a gin was like putting ketchup on caviar. He preferred to taste the gin, not the tonic, and even went as far as advising against adding a lemon slice (too aromatic) or ice (chill the bottle instead).

Adding water to a gin won't change its flavour much, but it will soften the texture and dampen any alcohol burn. It makes your gin more approachable, but many will probably still find this a pretty spartan way to drink it.

BITTER LEMON

Mixing lemon with gin is a no-brainer because so many of gin's botanicals already carry a citric edge, coriander especially (see p80). And that's not to mention the fact that lemon peel is often in the mix in its own right. The bitterness adds a touch of balance.

Try it with a sloe gin (see pp76–77). The gin is tart and fruity with earthy undertones, and all of this is brightened and balanced by the bitter lemon. You could also try adding it to gins that don't have much of a citrus note, which will round out the flavour profile of the drink as a whole.

GINGER BEER

Plenty of gins have an earthy, aromatic, spicy side (see pp198–205) that will lead smoothly into a warming and zingy ginger beer. Old Toms (see pp74–75), with their slightly thicker, sweeter texture, will stand up well to the flavour because sweetness generally balances out spicy heat. (See "How Flavour Works" on pp94–95.)

If you find lots of ginger beers a bit sugary, look for a really dry gin to pair it with. If the gin also has a touch of bitterness, it will work even better to balance out the sweetness.

BITTERS (PINK GIN)

No, I don't mean strawberry gin, raspberry gin, or any of that. Like the Gimlet (see p135), this is a classic drink with strong ties to the British Navy.

There's not much to it: roll three generous drops of Angostura bitters around the inside of an old-fashioned glass, pour out the excess, and then pour in your gin. About two shots should do it. Plymouth gin is the classic choice (navy strength, of course). You can add ice if you like.

This drink is a bit outdated so it can be hard to research online. Most search engine results are for modern, fruity gins instead. But it's so quick and simple to make that it's worth giving it a go at least once.

VERMOUTH (GIN & IT)

Mix equal parts gin and sweet vermouth (and perhaps a dash of orange bitters), stir with ice, and strain into an ice-filled old-fashioned glass. Garnish with an orange slice.

Choose a dry gin for this and a decent vermouth like Cocchi Vermouth di Torino. A good proportion of the botanicals in your gin will also be present in the vermouth, which is why this drink works so well.

At one time, it was called a Sweet Martini, but the shorter "Gin & It" eventually took hold during the prohibition era (1920–33) in the United States. The "It" in the name is short for "Italian" and refers to the sweet vermouth, which is sometimes also called Italian vermouth.

DUBONNET

Dubonnet is another old-school serve that's seen a spike of interest lately thanks to its association with the late Queen Elizabeth II. She liked it mixed with two parts Dubonnet to one part gin, stirred, and strained into a lowball glass over ice with a lemon garnish.

Dubonnet is a French sweet aperitif made with herbs, bitter barks, and spices. Technically, it's a wine-based quinquina, which means it contains quinine. It's also aged in oak vats. It comes across a bit like Campari but sweeter.

The Dubonnet you find in the United States is not the same stuff but is made from California wine fortified with grape brandy.

LET'S TALK TONIC

Just like gin, tonic has come a long way in the last couple of decades. Drinkers used to have two basic options: brand name (which meant Schweppes) or own-brand (normal or slimline). Now we have a huge choice of Ts to pour over our Gs. Tonic water falls into three broad groups: Indian (the classic tastes-of-quinine tonic waters), light, and flavoured.

INDIAN TONIC

For much of the 1900s, Schweppes was more or less synonymous with tonic water, but its supremacy was challenged with the launch of Fever-Tree Premium Indian Tonic Water in the early 2000s. This contains about 20 per cent less sugar than Schweppes and introduced the novel idea that tonic water need not be basic.

Most of these classic tonic waters have around 7–9g of sugar per 100ml (3½fl oz; see pp214–15), though some could easily be put among the light tonics, such as London Essence Original Indian Tonic Water, which has just 4.3g of sugar per 100ml (3½fl oz).

LIGHT TONIC

Less sugar means the gin's botanicals can come through more clearly, which is a great reason to choose one. Some light tonics replace sugar with sweeteners such as aspartame or stevia, which can mask the gin every bit as much as sugar. These are generally not as good as the tonics that simply use a touch less sugar.

SOPHISTICATED SCHWEPPES
An advertisement from the 1920s urges the young and elegant to add Schweppes tonic water to their drinks.

FLAVOURED TONICS

The most common ingredients in flavoured tonics are elderflower, grapefruit, orange, cucumber, and rosemary, although you'll also find flavours such as cranberry, pink rhubarb, ginger, yuzu, and black olive.

ELDERFLOWER

GRAPEFRUIT AND ORANGE

CUCUMBER

ROSEMARY

A WORD ON PACKAGING

Whichever tonic you choose, it must be fresh and fizzy. There's nothing sadder than a flat, lifeless tonic. Do yourself a favour and choose one that comes in a small can or bottle. Something between 150 and 200ml (5 and 7fl oz) is perfect. Depending on how much tonic you like in your G&T – which hopefully is not too much; see pp114–15 for advice on the perfect serve – you can get through the lot in just one or two drinks. If you opt for a bigger bottle, the tonic then sits around losing its fizz. It will never be quite the same after a day or two in the fridge compared to one you've just opened.

TONIC SYRUP

One option you don't see too often, but which is interesting nonetheless, is tonic syrup. This is basically a concentrate made with extracts of quinine and other botanicals that you mix with soda water to suit your taste. You can also add it directly to cocktails. Bermondsey Mixer Co. makes a version using natural cinchona extract that lends a sunset amber colour to the drink.

FLAVOURED TONIC

Flavoured tonics have become incredibly popular and offer all sorts of options for pairing your tonic with your gin. You can put like with like to increase the flavour profile of your drink, or choose combinations that will increase its complexity – for example, pairing a herbal tonic with a citrus-led gin. Some flavours that often feature are elderflower, grapefruit, orange, cucumber, and rosemary.

FEVER-TREE NATURALLY LIGHT TONIC WATER

This tonic has a good balance of quinine and citrus and lets the gin's character come across clearly without being too thin. It's a great all-rounder and is easy to find in 150ml (5fl oz) cans, which is also important.

I used this tonic when tasting the gins in this book (see pp154–213).

I tasted all of the gins neat first, but I also mixed them with tonic because that's how most people drink gin. I used equal parts tonic and gin, more or less – I'm not going to claim I was too precise. Anyway, this is the tonic to use if you want to recreate the tastings in this book.

MAKING AN ICON: THE GIN AND TONIC

Is there anything as lovely and inviting as a gin and tonic? The cheery rattle of the ice in the glass, the fresh lemon twist with its zesty citrus oils, the hiss of the bubbles fizzing on its surface, the sunlight catching the spray of tiny droplets dancing about its rim – what a delight.

THE DETAILS

And we haven't even had a sip yet. The only thing better than making a G&T yourself is being handed one by someone else – assuming they know what they're doing.

A G&T is such a simple drink that it pays to get the details right because it can bring so much pleasure when you do.

OTHER SPIRITS?

Tonic may be gin's best friend, but it can play nicely with other spirits too. Vodka's fine if you don't really want to taste anything; Cognac's better if you do. Tequila and mezcal provide a whole world to explore, but if you really want to dive down a rabbit hole, start exploring *amari* (singular, *amaro*), the bitter Italian liqueurs, with tonic.

AMARO AND TONIC

WHAT TEMPERATURE?

A G&T is meant be crisp and refreshing, which means it must be cold. The colder the better, so you have longer to enjoy it before it gets too warm and flabby. You don't need to chill the glass, and you could even get away without chilling your gin, though it's worth it if you can.

WHICH GLASS?

Highball. End of. It has room for all the ice you need, it has a heavy base for balance, it's narrow so it keeps the tonic from going flat too fast, it plays nicely with the dishwasher, and it doesn't unduly crowd your cupboard space.

HOW MUCH ICE?

Use ice and lots of it. Fill the glass all the way up. If the ice floats more than a centimetre or two above the bottom of your glass once you've poured the drink, then you're doing it wrong. There's nothing sadder than a G&T with two measly, cloudy ice cubes bobbing about on its surface like ducks in a pond. They'll melt before you know it. More ice means a slower melt and less dilution.

CHOOSE YOUR TONIC

The exact tonic to use depends on the gin you've chosen. Having said that, don't skimp. This is the largest element in your drink, so you want it to taste good. Look for something without too much sugar – you want to complement your chosen gin not hide it. A tonic that comes in a small bottle or can is best. Tonic in bigger bottles just hangs around losing flavour and carbonation before you finish it all.

FIND THE RATIO

I like a tonic to gin ratio of 1.5:1, though that can be a little strong for some. Lots of brands say 3:1. A good compromise is to use 2:1 as a starting point. If it's still too strong, you can always add more tonic, but if you start off too weak, then you can't take the tonic out.

FINALLY, THE GARNISH

A drink is always that little bit nicer with a garnish. With a drink as simple as a G&T, the right garnish can have a big impact. You can put a lot of thought into this (see pp150–53), but a simple lemon wedge or slice of cucumber will work with almost any gin.

THE PERFECT SERVE

There are a number of variables to tweak
if you want to elevate your G&T. Here's my
take on what goes into a perfect serve.

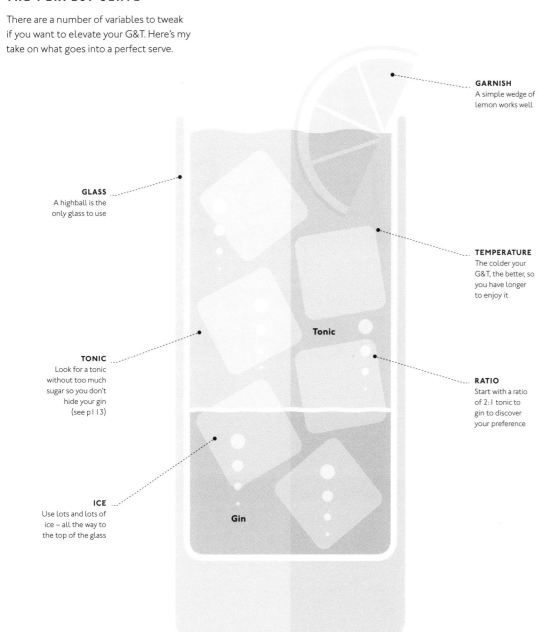

GARNISH
A simple wedge of
lemon works well

GLASS
A highball is the
only glass to use

TEMPERATURE
The colder your
G&T, the better, so
you have longer
to enjoy it

TONIC
Look for a tonic
without too much
sugar so you don't
hide your gin
(see p113)

Tonic

RATIO
Start with a ratio
of 2:1 tonic to
gin to discover
your preference

ICE
Use lots and lots of
ice – all the way to
the top of the glass

Gin

CLASSIC

···· GIN ····

COCKTAILS

THERE ARE COUNTLESS books on the subject, so rather than go into too much depth here, I've chosen a few classic recipes that will work with a wide variety of gins. All the recipes on the following pages are based on 30ml (1 fl oz) as a single measure (a shot), so you can adapt the amounts accordingly, if necessary. Whatever size measure you use, ensure the proportions stay the same. Be mindful of the few that call for teaspoons of some ingredients; these work out to one-eighth of a shot if your standard measure is 30ml (1 fl oz).

COCKTAIL-MAKING EQUIPMENT

You don't need any special equipment to make cocktails at home. You can use an eggcup as a measure, a measuring jug as your mixing glass, and any container with a tightly closing lid as a shaker. The reusable water bottles that so many of us have these days are great for this.

BARWARE TO BUY

If you want to make cocktails with a touch more consistency – or style – buying yourself a few bits of barware can make life a little easier. And nicer. You still don't have to break the bank though. Here are some useful tools in the order, more or less, you should consider buying them.

PEELER

Because garnishes. You probably own one already, but I've included it here just in case.

PARING KNIFE

Because garnishes, again. These are great for cutting wedges, tidying up twists, and so on. Keep it sharp.

JUICER

Fresh fruit juice is so much better than the bottled stuff, so invest in a decent juicer.

IT'S WORTH INVESTING IN SOME BARWARE TO MAKE COCKTAILS WITH A TOUCH MORE CONSISTENCY.

60ML
(2FL OZ)

Two shots

One shot

30ML
(1FL OZ)

Cap

Strainer

Shaker

JIGGER

A word on measures: use one! A good cocktail hinges on the balance of its ingredients in proportion to one another. Most jiggers come double-sided for measuring single or double shots. The better ones have marks etched inside for quarter-, half-, and three-quarter shots. Some are more like tiny measuring cups with gradations marking millilitres on one side and ounces on the other. You can get jiggers in 25ml/50ml (¾fl oz/1 ½fl oz) or 30ml/60ml (1 fl oz/2fl oz) sizes. I prefer the slightly larger ones where a single shot is 30ml (1 fl oz), as it makes for a more generous drink.

THREE-PART SHAKER

So now we're onto barware proper. This is also known as a cobbler shaker. This nifty bit of kit does three jobs in one: you can shake drinks in it, of course, but you can also use it as a mixing glass for stirred drinks, plus it has a strainer built right into its lid. Really, it's all you'll ever need. You might want more, but that's a different matter.

When you shake this, remember to keep a finger on the very top. The little cap that covers the strainer can fly off, and anyone standing behind you risks wearing your cocktail instead of drinking it. The problem with these is they often get stuck, and their components are not always easy to prize apart. For that reason, I tend to prefer a two-part shaker (see p121).

Counterbalance

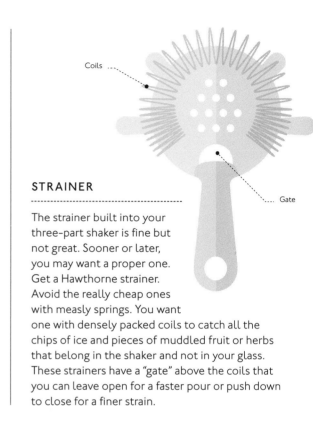

Coils

Gate

BAR SPOON

Yes, it's just a spoon. No, it doesn't perform any special function other than stirring. But it's cheap, and the long handle makes it a little easier to get a really good, fast stir going for when you want to chill that Martini right down to subzero crispy goodness. They're also good for reaching deep into the jar for that last cocktail cherry. Look for one with a nice weight on the end of the handle; it's a counterbalance and it's also good for muddling (mashing) ingredients.

STRAINER

The strainer built into your three-part shaker is fine but not great. Sooner or later, you may want a proper one. Get a Hawthorne strainer. Avoid the really cheap ones with measly springs. You want one with densely packed coils to catch all the chips of ice and pieces of muddled fruit or herbs that belong in the shaker and not in your glass. These strainers have a "gate" above the coils that you can leave open for a faster pour or push down to close for a finer strain.

SIMPLE SYRUP

Some cocktail recipes call for simple syrup in the mix. It will last in the refrigerator for about a month. "Rich" simple syrup uses two parts sugar to one part water.

SIMPLE SYRUP

1
Put equal parts sugar and water into a saucepan.

2
Stir over a medium heat until the sugar has fully dissolved.

3
Let it cool, pour it into a bottle, and seal, then refrigerate.

TWO-PART SHAKER

These are also called Boston shakers. If you shake more than you stir, this may be worth having even if you already have a three-part shaker. It's less finicky and you can shake with more gusto. It's also slightly more efficient, so will chill your drink faster without diluting it as much. The two parts can sometimes form a seal that's tough to break after a really good shake. The trick is to give the bottom part a gentle squeeze.

MIXING GLASS

If you stir more than you shake, this is definitely worth equipping your bar with. The heavy base keeps the glass stable, making it much easier to concentrate on building your drink without worrying that it's going to tip over and spill your hard work all over the table. Plus, it looks fancy, and cocktails are more fun when they're fancy.

USING A MIXING GLASS LOOKS FANCY, AND COCKTAILS ARE MORE FUN WHEN THEY'RE FANCY.

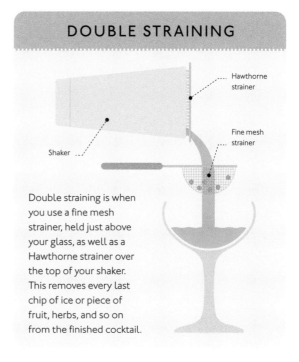

DOUBLE STRAINING

Hawthorne strainer

Fine mesh strainer

Shaker

Double straining is when you use a fine mesh strainer, held just above your glass, as well as a Hawthorne strainer over the top of your shaker. This removes every last chip of ice or piece of fruit, herbs, and so on from the finished cocktail.

ARMY AND NAVY

This is basically a gin sour that swaps out simple syrup for a sweet almond syrup called orgeat. The Army and Navy has a reputation for being tricky to balance, so be careful with your measures.

OTHER GARNISHES TO TRY

LUXARDO CHERRY

EDIBLE FLOWERS

Lemon twist to garnish

I shot fresh lemon juice

½ shot orgeat

2 dashes Angostura bitters (optional)

2 shots gin

WHICH GIN?

MELIFERA

NO. 3 LONDON DRY

HIGHCLERE CASTLE

METHOD

1. Add your liquids together in a shaker.

2. Throw in a couple of dashes of Angostura if you want to add a little more depth and edge to your drink.

3. Add ice and shake it all together until it is thoroughly chilled.

4. Double strain (see box on p121) into a chilled coupe glass and garnish with a lemon twist.

AVIATION

The Aviation is a pre-prohibition classic. There's some debate over whether this is better shaken or stirred. Shaken, it tastes a little lighter. Stirred, the flavours are more robust and the drink retains its violet colour better. I suggest you stir, but really it's your call.

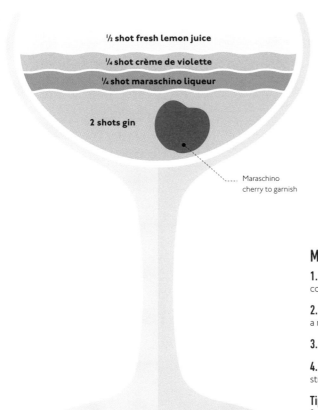

½ shot fresh lemon juice

¼ shot crème de violette

¼ shot maraschino liqueur

2 shots gin

Maraschino cherry to garnish

WHICH GIN?

AVIATION
BROCKMANS
THE BOTANIST
ISLAY DRY

METHOD

1. **Put a** maraschino cherry into a chilled coupe glass.

2. **Combine all** the liquid ingredients into a mixing glass or shaker.

3. **Add ice** then stir or shake.

4. **Strain the** drink into your glass. Double strain if you shook it.

Tip: **If you like**, you can express the oils from a lemon twist over the top and maybe wipe it around the rim before discarding.

BEE'S KNEES

This is a bright, light prohibition-era favourite that would, so the story goes, have hidden the flavour of all those terrible bathtub gins. You could replace the honey with honey syrup (three parts honey to one part water) if you want to be more refined.

| OTHER GARNISH TO TRY | THYME SPRIG |

Lemon twist to garnish

½ shot honey

1 shot fresh lemon juice

2 shots gin

WHICH GIN?

HEIGHT OF ARROWS

TANQUERAY LONDON DRY

MERMAID GIN

METHOD

1. Add your lemon juice and honey (or honey syrup) into a shaker and stir until the honey dissolves. (No need to stir if you choose to use syrup.)

2. Add your gin and some ice.

3. Shake until nicely chilled, then strain into a chilled Nick and Nora glass.

4. Garnish with a lemon twist.

BIJOU

Bijou means "jewel" in French, and this cocktail is so named, apparently, because its constituent spirits are the colours of diamond, emerald, and ruby. Some recipes suggest reducing the amount of green chartreuse by as much as half, but there's something appealing about the simplicity of an equal-parts cocktail.

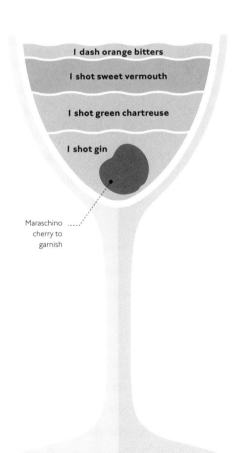

I dash orange bitters

I shot sweet vermouth

I shot green chartreuse

I shot gin

Maraschino cherry to garnish

WHICH GIN?

PLYMOUTH GIN
DEATH'S DOOR
PENRHOS
LONDON DRY

METHOD

1. Combine everything in a mixing glass and stir with ice.

2. Then strain into a chilled Nick and Nora or coupe glass.

3. Spear a maraschino cherry on a pick for a garnish or, alternatively, pop the cherry into the glass before you pour the drink.

BRAMBLE

English cocktail maker Dick Bradsell invented the Bramble in the 1980s. It calls for crème de mûre, a blackberry liqueur, but any berry liqueur will work well enough if you switch up your fresh berry garnish to match. You'll also need crushed ice, so have that ready in advance. Pick a gin with botanicals strong enough to make it through the cocktail's sweet and sour base.

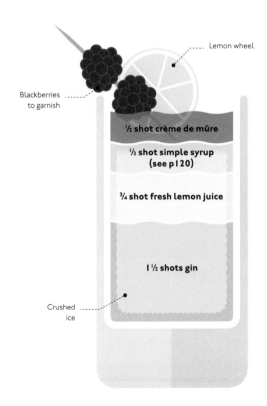

Lemon wheel

Blackberries to garnish

½ shot crème de mûre

½ shot simple syrup (see p120)

¾ shot fresh lemon juice

1 ½ shots gin

Crushed ice

WHICH GIN?

COTSWOLDS DRY

FORDS GIN LONDON DRY

CONKER SPIRIT NAVY STRENGTH

METHOD

1. Fill a lowball glass with crushed ice.

2. Shake the gin, lemon juice, and simple syrup with ice, and strain into your glass. Give it a quick stir to combine, then top up with a little more crushed ice.

3. Float your berry liqueur over the top and garnish with some fresh blackberries on a pick. If you want to be extra fancy, add a lemon wheel too.

BRONX

Bronx recipes vary a lot in their proportions. Here's a basic one to get you started. You can make this as a perfect cocktail (using equal measures of sweet and dry vermouth), or you can dial the dry vermouth back, up the gin, use more or less orange juice, and so on.

Orange twist to garnish

1 dash orange bitters

½ shot fresh orange juice

⅓ shot dry vermouth

½ shot sweet vermouth

1 shot gin

WHICH GIN?

BROOKLYN GIN

CONNIPTION AMERICAN DRY

HAYMAN'S EXOTIC CITRUS

METHOD

1. Shake everything with ice and strain into a chilled coupe.

2. Garnish with an orange twist.

3. Wonder whether you got the proportions right. Make another. Have someone else taste both.

CLOVER CLUB

This is another pre-prohibition classic that is at once light, fruity, and smooth. The egg white gives this drink a wonderful silky smooth texture and a dense white head of foam that looks superb.

OTHER GARNISH TO TRY

MINT SPRIG

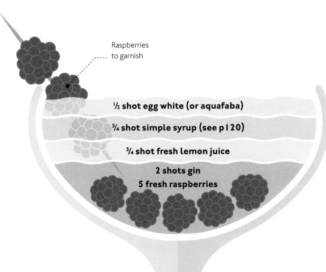

Raspberries to garnish

½ shot egg white (or aquafaba)

¾ shot simple syrup (see p120)

¾ shot fresh lemon juice

2 shots gin
5 fresh raspberries

WHICH GIN?

BEEFEATER LONDON DRY

LIND & LIME

PERRY'S TOT NAVY STRENGTH

METHOD

1. **Put everything** into a shaker, remembering to keep a few raspberries back for your garnish, and whip (shake without ice) for a count of 10.

2. **Then add** ice to the shaker and shake again until properly chilled.

3. **Strain into** a chilled coupe glass. If you can double strain (see box on p121), even better.

4. **Garnish with** your reserved raspberries on a cocktail pick and, if you like, a sprig of mint.

CORPSE REVIVER NO. 2

This was originally designed as a quick pick–me–up for the morning after. The original recipe called for Kina Lillet, which is no longer made. You can substitute Lillet Blanc, Cocchi Americano, or even a dry vermouth.

2 drops absinthe

¾ shot fresh lemon juice

¾ shot Cointreau

¾ shot Cocchi Americano or Lillet Blanc

¾ shot gin

Maraschino cherry to garnish

WHICH GIN?

HENDRICK'S
MARTIN MILLER'S
BOBBY'S
SCHIEDAM DRY

METHOD

1. Add everything apart from the absinthe into a shaker with ice and shake.

2. Roll two drops of absinthe around a chilled Nick and Nora glass to coat it. You can tip away any excess.

3. Put a maraschino cherry into the glass for garnish, then strain your drink over the top. Adding the cherry first avoids wasteful splashing.

DIRTY MARTINI

Like a Martini but better – or worse, depending on how you feel about drinking the salty-umami brine from an olive jar. This drink is dry, boozy, and, all in all, a rather grown-up affair. Serve up alongside some smooth jazz.

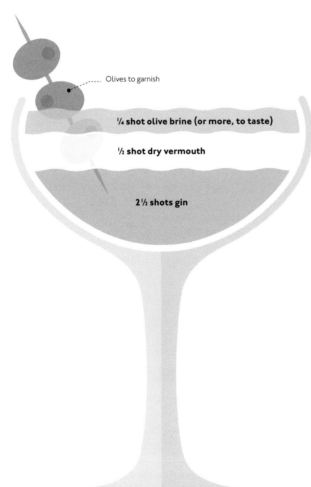

Olives to garnish

¼ shot olive brine (or more, to taste)

½ shot dry vermouth

2½ shots gin

WHICH GIN?

ISLE OF HARRIS

AN DÚLAMÁN IRISH MARITIME GIN

THE BOTANIST ISLAY DRY

METHOD

1. Combine your ingredients in a mixing glass. You can vary the measure of olive brine to taste; this recipe calls for a rather small amount.

2. Add ice and stir until very well chilled.

3. Strain into a chilled coupe glass and garnish with one or three olives on a cocktail pick.

DRY MARTINI

This is about as naked as a cocktail can get. The gin has nowhere to hide. The drink highlights the gin's quality and its interaction with your chosen vermouth. Ideally, one should glide elegantly into the other so each is elevated and the drink really shines.

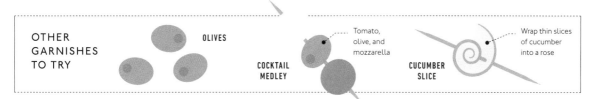

OTHER GARNISHES TO TRY

OLIVES

COCKTAIL MEDLEY

Tomato, olive, and mozzarella

CUCUMBER SLICE

Wrap thin slices of cucumber into a rose

Lemon twist to garnish

1 dash orange bitters

½ shot dry vermouth

2½ shots gin

The stem helps to keep your drink chilled

WHICH GIN?

TANQUERAY NO. TEN

MANGUIN OLI'GIN

HEPPLE

METHOD

There are endless variations on how to mix a Martini. Take this recipe as a starting point rather than the definitive version.

1. Combine the ingredients in a mixing glass with ice and stir until the outside is frosted with condensation. You want the glass to become just slightly too cold to hold comfortably in your hand.

2. Strain into a chilled glass and garnish as you see fit.

ENGLISH GARDEN

This is a refreshing drink that's reminiscent of a summer afternoon in an English orchard. Some recipes feature an elderflower liqueur like St Germain rather than the cordial, or lime juice in place of lemon. The proportions vary wildly also. Here's a version to get you started.

Lemon and cucumber slices to garnish

½ shot elderflower cordial

¾ shot fresh lemon juice

2 shots apple juice

2 shots gin

WHICH GIN?

KI NO TEA

LE GIN DE CHRISTIAN DROUIN

BOMBAY SAPPHIRE

METHOD

1. Fill a highball glass with ice.

2. Shake everything but the garnish with ice and strain into your glass.

3. Garnish with lemon and cucumber slices. This also makes a good fizz if you lengthen it with soda water.

FRENCH 75

A early 1900s classic from Harry's New York Bar in Paris, it is very similar to a Tom Collins but fancier, thanks to the champagne. Of course, it doesn't have to be champagne. There are all sorts of things you could try swapping it out with: Prosecco, crémant, perry, dry cider, or kombucha.

Lemon twist
to garnish

chilled
champagne
(or alternative)
to top

½ shot simple
syrup (see p120)

½ shot fresh
lemon juice

1 shot gin

WHICH GIN?

SILENT POOL

BARRA ATLANTIC GIN

SANTA ANA

METHOD

1. Combine the gin, lemon juice, and syrup in a shaker with some ice and shake well.

2. Once the shaker is so cold your fingers start to complain, strain into a chilled champagne flute.

3. Top with your chosen fizz and garnish with a lemon twist.

GIBSON

The Gibson is a variation of the Dry Martini that relies on a picked cocktail onion as its visual marker. This adds a pleasing umami note along with its acidity. At a time when most Martinis were made with bitters, the Gibson went without. The proportions aren't set in stone, so start with this recipe and then experiment.

Cocktail onion on a pick to garnish

½ shot dry vermouth

2 ½ shots gin (some recipes use vodka, but we'll have none of that here)

WHICH GIN?

LUSSA
FOUR PILLARS
OLIVE LEAF
HEIGHT OF ARROWS

METHOD

1. Stir your gin and vermouth over ice in a mixing glass.

2. Strain into a chilled coupe.

3. Skewer a cocktail onion on a pick to garnish.

GIMLET

This is an old naval cocktail made from what the sailors had to hand: navy strength gin and lime cordial. It *must* involve lime cordial. Don't listen to the siren song of those who say you can get by with fresh lime juice and a little simple syrup. It won't be the same.

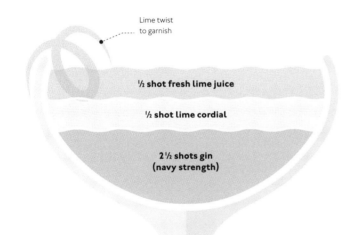

Lime twist
to garnish

½ shot fresh lime juice

½ shot lime cordial

2 ½ shots gin
(navy strength)

WHICH GIN?

PLYMOUTH NAVY
STRENGTH

OXLEY

PROCERA

GREEN DOT

METHOD

1. Drop the lot in your shaker over ice and shake.

2. Strain into a chilled coupe glass and garnish with a lime twist.

GIN BASIL SMASH

This is a fruity and herbal drink that screams of summer. Drink it in a sunny garden to kick off a late, lazy lunch with friends. This is a great cocktail because it only needs one bottle of booze, and its ingredients are easy to find.

Basil leaves to garnish

½ shot simple syrup (see p120)

I shot fresh lemon juice

2 shots gin

basil leaves

WHICH GIN?

GIN MARE

HENDRICK'S

KNUT HANSEN DRY

METHOD

1. Muddle a couple of basil leaves in your shaker, then add the other ingredients with ice and shake hard.

2. Double strain (see box on p121) into a rocks glass over ice and garnish with some more basil leaves.

GIN FIZZ

This cocktail is often overlooked because it's so simple, but it's definitely worth your time. With a nice balance of sweet and sour and a light and fluffy texture, this is a delightful showcase for any number of gins. Sloe gins are great in a Fizz too.

soda water to top

½ shot egg white
(or aquafaba)

¾ shot simple syrup
(see p120)

1 shot fresh
lemon juice

2 shots gin

WHICH GIN?

ROKU

SACRED PINK
GRAPEFRUIT

MEDITERRANEAN GIN
BY LÉOUBE

METHOD

1. Combine everything except the soda water in a shaker and whip (dry shake without ice) for a few seconds.

2. Then add ice and shake again vigorously.

3. Strain into a chilled highball glass and top with the soda water. Don't add ice to the glass for this one and don't garnish it either. It's enough to enjoy just as it is.

HANKY PANKY

Created at the Savoy Hotel in London in the early 1900s, this is basically an adapted Martinez (see p141). A small amount of the intensely bitter Italian herbal liqueur Fernet-Branca cuts through the sweet vermouth.

OTHER GARNISH TO TRY   MINT SPRIG

Orange twist to garnish

I dash fresh orange juice (optional)

I tsp Fernet-Branca

I shot sweet vermouth

2 shots gin

WHICH GIN?

TARQUIN'S CORNISH DRY

GREATER THAN LONDON DRY

EAST LONDON KEW GIN

METHOD

1. Stir your ingredients over ice in a mixing glass.

2. Strain into a chilled Nick and Nora glass.

3. You can freshen it up with a tiny dash of fresh orange juice.

Tip: Some recipes have two measures of gin to one of vermouth, while others call for equal measures. Try both and see what you like.

JULIET AND ROMEO

This was created in 2007 to mark the opening of The Violet Hour bar in Chicago. Its creator, Toby Maloney, described it as a gin cocktail for people who think they don't like gin cocktails.

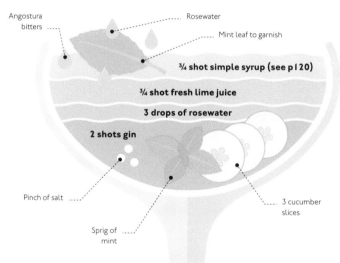

Angostura bitters

Rosewater

Mint leaf to garnish

¾ shot simple syrup (see p120)

¾ shot fresh lime juice

3 drops of rosewater

2 shots gin

Pinch of salt

Sprig of mint

3 cucumber slices

WHICH GIN?

WA BI

ARC ARCHIPELAGO BOTANICAL

FOUR PILLARS RARE DRY

METHOD

1. Pop three cucumber slices into your shaker with a small pinch of salt and muddle together.

2. Then add your gin, simple syrup, lime juice, three drops of rosewater, and a sprig of mint. Add ice, shake, then double strain (see box on p121) into a chilled coupe.

3. Now we get fancy: float a single mint leaf on the surface of your drink and place a single drop of rosewater on top of that.

4. Dot three drops of Angostura bitters on the surface around your leaf. Take a picture. Post it online. Get likes.

LAST WORD

I came close to leaving this one out given the slightly outré ingredients it requires, but in the end, it was too good to ignore. It's tart but balanced. You can substitute the green chartreuse with St Germain in a pinch.

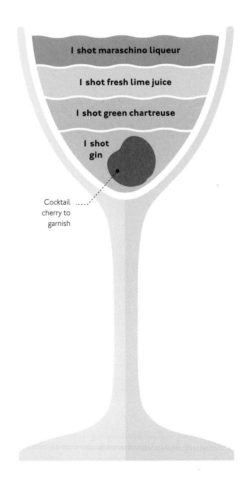

I shot maraschino liqueur

I shot fresh lime juice

I shot green chartreuse

I shot gin

Cocktail cherry to garnish

WHICH GIN?

NO. 3 LONDON DRY

SILENT POOL

XORIGUER MAHÓN

METHOD

1. Shake everything with ice and strain into a chilled glass – a Nick and Nora is good for this.

2. Pop a cocktail cherry in to garnish. Choose a decent one though, like a Luxardo, rather than one of those bright red monstrosities.

MARTINEZ

A forerunner to the Martini, this drink is more complex and a little sweeter but every bit as delicious. Use an Old Tom gin if you can for a little extra oomph.

Orange twist
to garnish

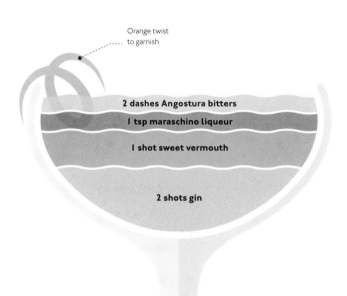

2 dashes Angostura bitters

I tsp maraschino liqueur

I shot sweet vermouth

2 shots gin

WHICH GIN?

YORK GIN OLD TOM
HERNÖ NAVY STRENGTH
ROCK ROSE PINK
GRAPEFRUIT
OLD TOM

METHOD

1. Stir in a shaker or mixing glass over ice until wickedly cold and strain into a chilled coupe glass.

2. Garnish with an orange twist.

NEGRONI

This cocktail sees the interaction of gin and vermouth amped up and given a bitter kick from the Campari. It packs a delicious punch, but the gin can get rather lost if you're not careful. You won't go wrong if your gin has robust juniper and orange notes, but it's worth experimenting with other flavour profiles to see what works well in the mix.

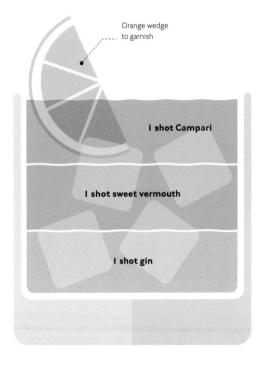

Orange wedge to garnish

I shot Campari

I shot sweet vermouth

I shot gin

WHICH GIN?

SIPSMITH VJOP

O'NDINA

DOROTHY PARKER

METHOD

You can make this cocktail in two steps, as below, or build it directly into the glass.

1. Combine the ingredients and stir over ice to chill and dilute.

2. Strain into a chilled glass over more ice and garnish with an orange wedge or peel.

OLD FRIEND

Just when the gin and the elderflower liqueur threaten to fly away, along comes Campari to ground the cocktail in some bitterness, while the pink grapefruit adds a tart complexity that makes this a real pleasure to drink.

OTHER
GARNISH
TO TRY

ORANGE TWIST

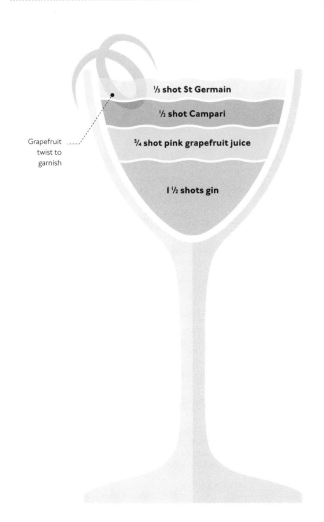

Grapefruit twist to garnish

⅓ shot St Germain

½ shot Campari

¾ shot pink grapefruit juice

1 ½ shots gin

WHICH GIN?

ROCK ROSE PINK
GRAPEFRUIT OLD TOM

HAPUSĀ HIMALAYAN DRY

JENSEN'S
BERMONDSEY DRY

METHOD

1. Put it all in a shaker, add ice, and shake it.

2. Double strain (see box on p121) into a chilled Nick and Nora glass.

3. Garnish with a grapefruit twist.

RED SNAPPER

Is it the weekend? Are you hungover again? Is it time for brunch? Do you want to taste some botanicals in your pick-me-up? Step aside, Bloody Mary. This calls for a Red Snapper! Fair warning, this one's a little involved. Maybe have someone else make it up for you.

OTHER GARNISHES TO TRY

OLIVES

COCKTAIL ONION

ROSEMARY

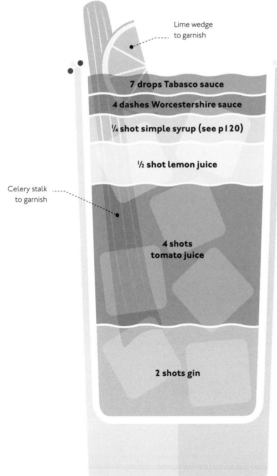

Lime wedge to garnish

Two grinds of black pepper and two pinches of celery salt around rim

7 drops Tabasco sauce

4 dashes Worcestershire sauce

¼ shot simple syrup (see p120)

½ shot lemon juice

Celery stalk to garnish

4 shots tomato juice

2 shots gin

WHICH GIN?

AUDEMUS UMAMI

BARRA ATLANTIC GIN

SEVEN HILLS VII ITALIAN DRY

METHOD

1. Prepare your glass first. Put the black pepper and celery salt onto a small plate, and wipe the lip of a pint glass with the cut side of your lime wedge.

2. Dip the glass into the salt and pepper so they stick to the rim, then fill it with ice.

3. Now the drink: add your gin, tomato juice, lemon juice, simple syrup, plus Worcestershire and Tabasco sauces into a shaker. Shake until well chilled and strain into your glass. (Some say a gentler shake is best here.)

4. Garnish with a stick of celery and your lime wedge.

SATAN'S WHISKERS

This is an old classic from Harry Craddock's *The Savoy Cocktail Book*. There are two versions. The straight version uses Grand Marnier and packs an orange punch. The curled version calls for curaçao and emphasizes the vermouth a little more.

Orange twist to garnish

I dash orange bitters

½ shot Grand Marnier or curaçao

¾ shot sweet vermouth

¾ shot dry vermouth

¾ shot gin

WHICH GIN?

CITADELLE

AUDEMUS PINK PEPPER

BROOKIE'S
BYRON DRY

METHOD

1. Put everything into a shaker with ice and do what comes naturally in this situation.

2. Once you've had enough of shaking, strain into a chilled coupe glass and garnish with an orange twist.

SOUTHSIDE RICKEY

This one's going to feel quite familiar to any Mojito lovers out there. It's light and refreshing and great for long, hot summer evenings. If you leave out the cracked ice, this Rickey turns into a Fizz. Cocktails are magic like that.

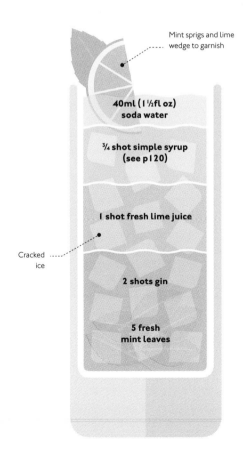

Mint sprigs and lime wedge to garnish

40ml (1½fl oz) soda water

¾ shot simple syrup (see p120)

1 shot fresh lime juice

Cracked ice

2 shots gin

5 fresh mint leaves

WHICH GIN?

G'VINE FLORAISON

INVERROCHE CLASSIC

MANLY SPIRITS COASTAL CITRUS

METHOD

1. Fill a highball with cracked ice.

2. Add gin, lime juice, simple syrup, and the mint leaves together with ice in your shaker, and shake.

3. Strain into your glass. Top with soda water and garnish with a lime wedge and mint sprigs.

20TH CENTURY

This is similar to the Corpse Reviver No. 2 but builds on pairing lemon and chocolate. It uses white crème de cacao, but if you also have some of the dark stuff, you can elevate the whole thing by freezing a teaspoonful in the bottom of your glass.

Lemon twist to garnish

¾ shot fresh lemon juice

¾ shot white crème de cacao

¾ shot Cocchi Americano (or Lillet Blanc)

¾ shot gin

WHICH GIN?

HEPPLE

PALMA

NIKKA COFFEY

METHOD

1. Combine all your ingredients with ice in your shaker. Give it a shake. You want the contents to rebound off both ends of the shaker, not just swill around the bottom.

2. Strain into a chilled glass and garnish with your lemon twist.

WHITE LADY

This recipe went through some pretty major changes before settling down to the cocktail we recognize today. When it was first invented, it didn't contain gin at all but instead was built around crème de menthe.

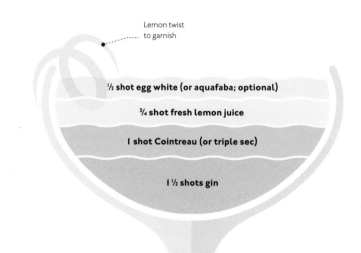

Lemon twist to garnish

½ shot egg white (or aquafaba; optional)

¾ shot fresh lemon juice

1 shot Cointreau (or triple sec)

1 ½ shots gin

WHICH GIN?

MARTIN MILLER'S

DRUMSHANBO GUNPOWDER IRISH GIN

LONDON TO LIMA

METHOD

1. Combine everything in a shaker. If you're using egg white, give it a dry shake first before adding ice. If not, skip straight to the next step.

2. Add ice, shake, double strain (see box on p121) into a chilled coupe glass, and garnish with a lemon twist.

Tip: If you find this too sharp, drop the Cointreau down to a three-quarter shot and add a quarter shot of simple syrup (see p120).

WHITE NEGRONI

An all-French take on a classic Italian drink, the White Negroni replaces Campari with Suze, which has a stronger bitter flavour thanks to gentian. It has a pleasantly drying finish, so it's great as an appetizer before a meal. Like the Negroni, this is made with equal parts, but if you up the gin to one and a half shots and drop the Suze and Lillet Blanc to a three-quarter shot each, you may find it more balanced.

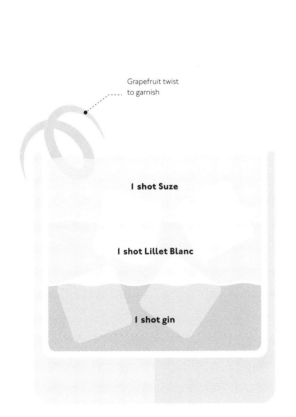

Grapefruit twist to garnish

I shot Suze

I shot Lillet Blanc

I shot gin

WHICH GIN?

**HAPUSĀ
HIMALAYAN DRY**

ACHROOUS

GEOMETRIC

METHOD

1. Combine the ingredients in a mixing glass, add ice, and stir.

2. Strain into a double rocks glass over ice.

3. Wipe the rim with your grapefruit twist for a little extra flavour kick, then drop it into the drink as a garnish.

Tip: It's also fine to make this straight in the glass.

THE GARNISHES

A drink without a garnish is like a joke without the punchline. It may seem like faff and frippery when all you want is to move onto the drinking part of the evening, but it's worth taking that extra step.

HEIGHTENED FLAVOUR

A good drink is an occasion, not just something you tip down your neck. We taste with our eyes first. Anticipation, excitement, and delight do more than you realize to heighten a drink's flavour once it reaches your lips.

WHICH GARNISH?

There are three main approaches to choosing which garnish to pair with your gin: complement, contrast, and harmonize. Generally speaking, upping the complexity of your drink makes it more interesting. So if your gin is heavy on the juniper and citrus, with more subtle herbal back notes, you might choose a herbal garnish such as rosemary or a cucumber slice to bring these back notes forward in the finished drink.

If your drink leans heavily on one particular flavour, you might choose a garnish to contrast with that. For instance, a fruit garnish will add some depth to a floral gin, while citrus can brighten up an earthy and aromatic gin. Think

also about the ways in which basic tastes interact (see "How Flavour Works" on pp94–95).

Your third option is to pick up what your gin throws down and run with it. A harmonizing garnish accentuates the gin's predominant flavour, but in a way that also adds complexity. For example, a lemon twist brings a slightly different hit of acidity to a sloe gin's tartness.

CITRUS GARNISHES

Lemons, limes, oranges, and other citrus fruits do a lot of work in cocktail-land. Their peels contain compounds such as limonene (also found in many of gin's ingredients), which impact the taste of the finished drink.

For a twist, cut a swathe of zest from your fruit. Don't go too deep,

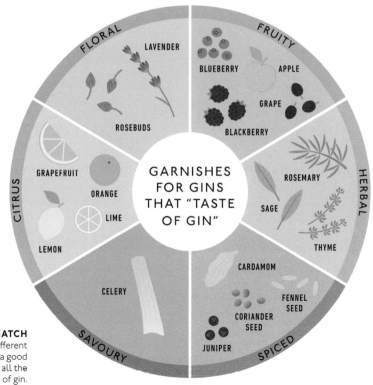

MIX AND MATCH
A variety of different garnishes are a good match for all the categories of gin.

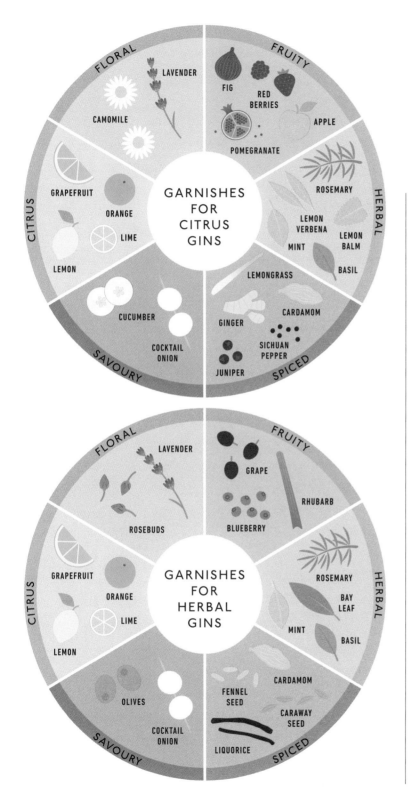

as you don't want the bitter white pith in your glass. You can fold this zest-side out to send a mist of oils over your drink. Or you can rub it around the rim of your glass to add a subtle flavour kick. And you can drop the whole thing into the drink, trimming it first if you want it to look fancy.

You can also cut wheels, slices, or wedges of the whole fruit to drop into your drink. If you're doing this, squeezing a few drops of juice from the fruit into your drink can heighten the whole flavour experience even more.

HERBAL GARNISHES

Mint is the classic herbal garnish. A fresh sprig of bright green leaves looks lovely and adds an extra dimension to your drink. It's great with a Clover Club cocktail (see p128), for instance.

A sprig of rosemary is another good option that marries well with gin's juniper notes. Thyme and lemon thyme work well also, but rosemary's a little less likely to leave tiny leaves floating in your drink.

I'm a big fan of a cucumber slice in a G&T. Although it's a herbal taste, it's a little more laid back than rosemary or mint, less in your face. The popularity of cucumber tonics shows I'm not alone on this.

WOODY AND SPICY GARNISHES

An obvious option, if you want to accentuate the G in your G&T, is to float a few juniper berries on the surface. It looks fine, and obviously the flavour works just great, but still, not everyone is a fan. The berries float, so they're drawn inexorably to your lips when you sip and end up getting in the way. They only work if you're going to use a straw, and many people would rather not.

Another floater, but a little less annoying, is star anise. This can add a lovely hint of deep, earthy aromatics to your drink. Cinnamon can work well too. Black pepper and coffee beans are also good garnishes.

ACID, SALT, AND UMAMI GARNISHES

These flavours cover some of the classic gin cocktail garnishes. Take the humble olive. There it sits, in the noble Dry Martini (see p131), and you think to yourself, "That has no earthly business being in my glass". Or you do until you taste

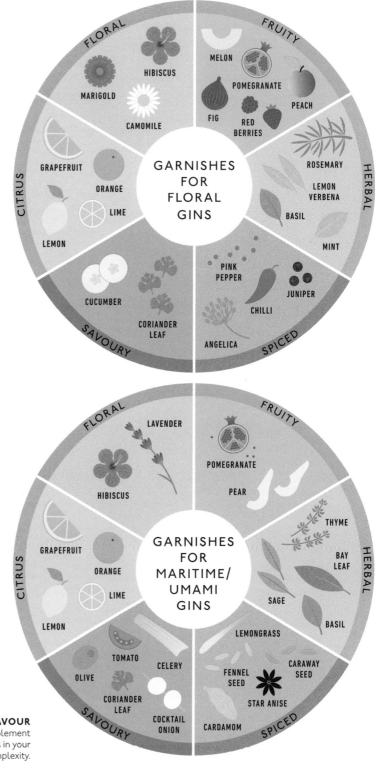

ENHANCE THE FLAVOUR
Use garnishes to complement or contrast the flavours in your gin, or to add complexity.

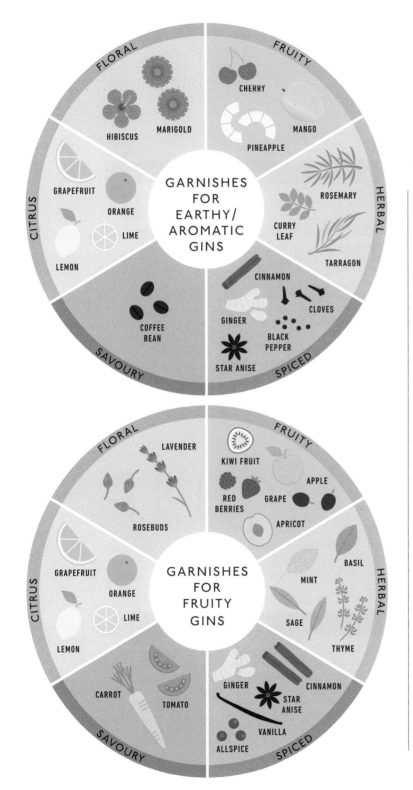

it for the first time, after which you'll never question it again.

Swap your olive for a tiny silverskin cocktail onion, and you exchange salty and umami for piquant and sharp, with perhaps just a little hint of umami still. Your Martini becomes a Gibson (see p134), but the same rules apply: looks weird, tastes glorious. A salted rim, pickle slice, celery, or tomato slice can also work.

FRUITY GARNISHES

All hail the mighty maraschino cherry, a little drop of heaven here on earth. These are the proper ones, you understand: your Luxardo, your Hotel Starlino – dark, glossy jewels floating in a syrup more addictive than any drug. Forget the cocktail, let's just swig it straight from the jar!

Other berries, such as raspberries, strawberries, and so on, are also delicious paired with the right gin or cocktail. A blackberry in your G&T would be delightful if you're using Hepple Gin (see p160), which is distilled with blackcurrants. They're different fruits, of course, but their flavours work together well, and blackberries are easier to find. A slice of apple or pear, or grapes also work well.

NAVIGATING
GIN
----- BY -----
FLAVOUR

THIS SECTION USES flavour as a key to explore the many different kinds of gin on offer today. With tasting notes for more than 100 gins, you'll discover gins that "taste of gin" – which use bold juniper flavours backed up with choirs of classic botanicals – as well as citrus-forward gins, herbal gins, floral gins, fruity gins, earthy and aromatic gins, and maritime and umami gins. For each of these flavour groups, you'll learn about the typical botanicals that go into them, the source of the flavours that bind the gins in each group together, plus suggestions for garnishes, mixers, and cocktails that will enhance your enjoyment every time. Grab a glass, a splash of tonic or another mixer, and get ready to taste the delicious world of gin.

GINS THAT "TASTE OF GIN"

These are the classics and those more modern gins that follow in their path. They have a definite tilt towards juniper, but beneath that they're often quite rounded and balanced.

THE BOTANICALS

No surprises here. We're looking at juniper, coriander, angelica, orris, lemon, and liquorice. It's not unusual to see cubeb or grains of paradise joining in to add a peppery kick. As well as common juniper, some distillers are starting to experiment with other species (see p21).

CORIANDER

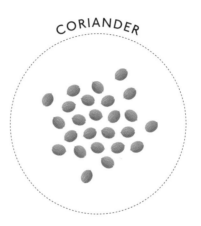

ANGELICA

ORRIS

LEMON

LIQUORICE

MIXERS	GARNISHES	COCKTAILS	OTHER GINS TO TRY
FEVER-TREE Premium Indian Tonic Water	LEMON	**GIN AND IT** see p111	HAYMAN'S OLD TOM
Q SPECTACULAR Tonic Water	LAVENDER	**DRY MARTINI** see p131	JAWBOX CLASSIC DRY
STRANGELOVE No. 8 Indian Tonic Water	ROSEMARY	**NEGRONI** see p142	WILDJUNE WESTERN STYLE

BEEFEATER LONDON DRY

40% (47% EXPORT STRENGTH) ABV

LONDON, ENGLAND

FLAVOUR

Perhaps the archetypal London Dry gin, with strong links to the city that endure to this day, Beefeater has used the same recipe since 1876. It's a mix of nine classic botanicals including angelica as both seed and root. It's clean on the nose, first all juniper and oily orange peel, then developing a subtle floral undertone. On the palate, juniper dominates, as you'd expect, but beneath that there's a warming balance of citrus and spice.

There are other expressions to try, including Beefeater 24 (made with tea) and Beefeater Crown Jewel (strong, lots of grapefruit), but the classic London Dry remains a dependable cocktail workhorse.

BLUECOAT AMERICAN DRY

47% ABV

PHILADELPHIA, PA, USA

FLAVOUR

When this launched in 2006, using "citrus peels not found in most gins", it was notably different. These days, its flavour seems rather classic. It goes to show how tastes can change. Don't go getting the wrong idea though: it remains a very good gin and one well worth seeking out if you haven't tried it.

There's soft juniper on the nose with bitter orange, and on the palate these are joined by some gentle, earthy spice. There's cardamom (or something like it) in the mid-palate and zesty, fruity red grapefruit. It ends with a fair bit of angelica, all musky, woody, and drying. It's very good indeed with tonic.

BOMBAY SAPPHIRE LONDON DRY

40% ABV

LAVERSTOKE, ENGLAND

FLAVOUR

JUNIPER · CITRUS · HERBAL · FLORAL · SPICE · FRUIT

Gin might never have had its renaissance without Bombay Sapphire. But if it once redefined its category, it tastes quite classic now. If gin were a town, Bombay Sapphire's aroma would put your feet firmly in its central market square rather than any of its weirder backstreets.

Lemon takes the lead, but juniper and gentle spice are there too. It retains that light palate that lured drinkers back from Vodkaville, but seek and you shall find subtle juniper and orris. There's an elusive vegetal note, perhaps angelica's musky side coming through, then pepper and spice build to a woody finish overlaid with citrus.

FORDS GIN LONDON DRY

45% ABV

LONDON, ENGLAND

FLAVOUR

JUNIPER · CITRUS · HERBAL · FLORAL · SPICE · FRUIT

This is a real gin-lover's gin, created by two legends: Simon Ford, one-time US brand ambassador for Beefeater and Plymouth Gin, and master distiller Charles Maxwell (whose family has been making gin since the 1680s).

Juniper leads with its camphoric, floral side rather than the usual piney-terpsy profile. Perhaps this is down to the long, 15-hour maceration, or maybe it's that it is distilled so slowly over five more hours. Balanced and complex, there's juniper and citrus building through woody cassia to a finish that's long and warming with rich, deep grapefruit notes. With tonic, the juniper softens to a damp woodland walk in April showers brightened by citrus sunshine.

GREATER THAN LONDON DRY

40% ABV

NEW DELHI, INDIA

FLAVOUR

JUNIPER CITRUS

FRUIT HERBAL

SPICE FLORAL

While bartending in New Delhi, India, NÄO Spirits co-founders Anand Virmani and Viabhav Singh were frustrated by a lack of homegrown gins. They wanted a solid London Dry gin, but one made locally. Greater Than is just that.

There's enough of a twist from the ginger, fennel, lemongrass, and camomile to keep it interesting, but it's classic enough that the gin's story can focus on its Indian roots for the home market. And while that market is potentially huge, this gin deserves to spread much further. It's delicious, balanced, and classic without feeling staid – a great option for a G&T or Dry Martini (see p131).

HEIGHT OF ARROWS

43% ABV

EDINBURGH, SCOTLAND

FLAVOUR

JUNIPER CITRUS

FRUIT HERBAL

SPICE FLORAL

Height of Arrows is one of those gins that is notable for how little goes into it rather than how much. There's just juniper in here, modified by sea salt and beeswax to coax out all sort of other flavours. It's resinous on the nose with a soft lemon note, and just the slightest hint of something else deeply warm and sweet. On the palate, there's the juniper again, but it morphs through rosemary and lavender and anise towards a soft and herbal finish.

Honestly, I'm not sure how they've done all this, but if anyone can claim to be carrying on with distilling's alchemical roots, then perhaps it's this distillery. Try it in a Gibson (see p134).

HEPPLE

45% ABV

HEPPLE, ENGLAND

FLAVOUR

One of the best. Earthy juniper leads the aroma with grassy, mossy scents of the Northumberland moors. Savoury-sweet bog myrtle gives way to blackcurrants. On the palate, fennel, fir, coriander, and lovage build to a finish bursting with cedar and sandalwood from the fresh, unripe juniper berries harvested on the Hepple estate.

Distiller Chris Garden (ex-Sipsmith) employs pot distillation, vacuum distillation, and supercritical extraction (see pp64–65) to bring out the best from his 12 botanicals. The effect is to beam the moors right into your soul. Stupendous. At once classic and modern, quietly complex, and thoroughly delicious however you drink it – though in Martinis (see pp130–31), it is to die for.

HERNÖ NAVY STRENGTH

57% ABV

DALA, SWEDEN

FLAVOUR

This navy strength gin from Sweden's first gin distillery is a lovely mix of bold and crisp juniper, earthy pepper, and fresh meadowsweet. There's vanilla in there too, lending a soft sweetness, as well as lingonberries. Lemons stomp around in the top notes, lifting everything with a nice citric twang, and making this a rather contemporary navy strength gin compared to some of its fellow seadog spirits.

It packs a punch, as you'd expect for its strength, but that soon settles down to a nice, warming glow. Tame with some tonic to enjoy at its best.

HIGHCLERE CASTLE LONDON DRY

43.5% ABV

HIGHCLERE, ENGLAND

FLAVOUR

JUNIPER · CITRUS · HERBAL · FLORAL · SPICE · FRUIT

Far from the old Mother's Ruin, this gin is less drinking to forget poverty and more English upper classes at play (with the addition of one American spirits entrepreneur, Adam von Gootkin). It hails from the "real Downton Abbey", home to the Earl and Countess of Carnarvon, and celebrates its reputation for entertaining to the highest standards.

It's a bit hot tasted neat, but once mixed with tonic, it really sings: earthy, aromatic base tones, angelica and soft cardamom joined by lavender in the alto register, and citrus and juniper on the descant.

JENSEN'S BERMONDSEY DRY

43% ABV

LONDON, ENGLAND

FLAVOUR

JUNIPER · CITRUS · HERBAL · FLORAL · SPICE · FRUIT

Bermondsey lies southeast of London Bridge and Borough Market. Christian Jensen created his gin as a reaction to the crummy paint-by-numbers gins of the 1980s and 90s. It uses a 1920s recipe based on ingredients that would have been available in Bermondsey at the time, which he developed with Charles Maxwell of Thames Distillers.

It opens with a classic, earthy balance on the nose driven by softly insistent piney juniper. On the palate, there's a floral, earthy note that turns rooty and sweet, then juniper and citrus lift it all back up. A true gin that "tastes of gin" if ever there was.

JUNIPERO

49.3% ABV

SAN FRANCISCO, CA, USA

FLAVOUR

JUNIPER · CITRUS · HERBAL · FLORAL · SPICE · FRUIT

One of the American craft-distilling pioneers, this gin is fast closing in on its third decade. Plenty has changed in the gin world since this was released back in 1996, and these days, it tastes pretty classic compared to what else is around – yet it's no standard London Dry. The woody juniper has more oomph and the herbal notes are stronger too.

Coriander and cardamom dance right through this, conjuring lemongrass even though there's none in the mix. It's complex on the palate and surprisingly smooth given its strength, even when tasted neat. It's punchy in all the right ways.

MARTIN MILLER'S

40% ABV

LONDON, ENGLAND

FLAVOUR

JUNIPER · CITRUS · HERBAL · FLORAL · SPICE · FRUIT

I score each gin I taste. If it's getting up there in the marks, I ask myself: how could it be any better? If I can't think of anything, the gin maxes out. Top marks. Perfect score. This gin is one such.

It's light and balanced but wonderfully complex also, with liquorice and lemon dancing around nutmeg and iris, plus cucumber over all, like the sun from above. It's smooth on the palate, sweet and herbal at first, then warming rooty spice builds into floral orris-iris, before sending us on our way with a long, complex aftertaste of woody, drying spice, pine, angelica, liquorice, and lemon again. A modern classic.

PLYMOUTH GIN

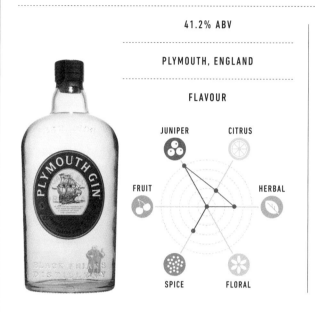

41.2% ABV

PLYMOUTH, ENGLAND

FLAVOUR

JUNIPER · CITRUS · HERBAL · FLORAL · SPICE · FRUIT

This is softer than a London Dry, and driven by a pleasing balance of stiff juniper pine and earthy, aromatic cardamom and coriander on the nose. The palate is smooth and creamy. There's a quick flash of orange before the soft, rooty-herbal flavours wash through and begin their build-up to juniper again. It's a little sweet. Or off-dry, rather: not actually sweet but departed from dry and headed in that direction.

The finish is long and drying, woody and piney from angelica and juniper, but mixed with tonic, coriander, lemon, and orange come out more here. It's a hugely versatile classic and a must for any cocktail lover.

PROCERA GREEN DOT

47% ABV

NAIROBI, KENYA

FLAVOUR

JUNIPER · CITRUS · HERBAL · FLORAL · SPICE · FRUIT

This is a love letter to juniper and an exploration of every facet of its flavours. It contains some common juniper, but the star is the local *Juniperus procera* (African pencil cedar), the only juniper native to the southern hemisphere. Fans of nose-to-tail eating will approve of how the distillery uses it, treating us to its flavours from leaf (young tips only) and berry (fresh and dried) to toasted heartwood.

On the nose, its 2022 vintage showed soft, earthy juniper, nutty notes, a tea-like, deep herbal note, and some woody base notes. On the palate, it was piney and grassy, building through wood to a resinous and oily finish.

SIPSMITH VJOP

57.7% ABV

LONDON, ENGLAND

FLAVOUR

JUNIPER · CITRUS · FRUIT · HERBAL · SPICE · FLORAL

The "VJOP" stands for "Very Junipery Over Proof", and it certainly delivers on that. Sipsmith uses twice as much juniper in this gin as it does in its London Dry Gin. The result is a big, bold, juniper party in your mouth, but also with some pleasing complexity underneath if you care to look.

Juniper and woody notes dominate the nose above orange zest and coriander. Angelica and rich spice come along on the palate, and mixed with tonic, there's a lemon-meringue-pie character as well. The finish is long and dry and woody again, with juniper sailing off into the sunset. It makes a really killer Negroni (see p142).

TANQUERAY LONDON DRY

43.1% ABV EUROPE; 47.3% ABV USA

CAMERON BRIDGE, SCOTLAND

FLAVOUR

JUNIPER · CITRUS · FRUIT · HERBAL · SPICE · FLORAL

The rock that, as gin's tides swirl around it, remains classic, rounded, balanced, and delicious. It's proof you need not spend lots of money to get a gin that deserves a spot in any kitchen and in every bar.

The most junipery juniper greets your nose alongside citric coriander. On the palate, angelica blends almost seamlessly with the juniper, then adds its own woody and perfumed element. Liquorice brings depth with a touch of sweetness. The finish is long and dry with coriander and pine and a pleasing tingle of alcoholic warmth. Superb in a G&T, but for cocktails, maybe reach for the Tanqueray No. Ten (see p173) instead.

TARQUIN'S CORNISH DRY

42% ABV

ST ERVAN, ENGLAND

FLAVOUR

JUNIPER · CITRUS · HERBAL · FLORAL · SPICE · FRUIT

This has a pretty classic London Dry flavour profile given a little lift and twist from grapefruit and violet, which come out even more when the T hits the G. It's made from wheat-based neutral spirit with 12 botanicals, none of them too unusual other than the grapefruit and violet.

What is slightly unusual, these days at least, is that the distillers heat their three 250-litre (55-gallon) copper pot stills over an open flame and seal the joints with bread dough. What this does to the flavour, I couldn't say, but it can't be anything bad because this is a tasty gin.

YORK GIN OLD TOM

42.5% ABV

YORK, ENGLAND

FLAVOUR

JUNIPER · CITRUS · HERBAL · FLORAL · SPICE · FRUIT

What a revelation. This Old Tom is only very slightly sweetened with a sugar syrup infused with white alba rose, bronze fennel, star anise, angelica, and pink peppercorns, giving the gin a silky and elegant texture.

Its aroma greets you with anise and cinnamon that give way to an earthy floral note. On the palate, there's juniper and the cinnamon again. Herbaceous notes spiral up with floral flavours, then cardamom comes through in a wave that is, in turn, replaced by a building peppery spice. The finish is long and earthily spiced. It's great with tonic but even better if you have the wherewithal to make a Martinez (see p141).

CITRUS-FORWARD GINS

Almost all gins have a citric edge to lift the other botanicals. What these ones share is a more intense citrus character that drives the gin's flavour profile onwards. Some are tart and zesty while others go down a richer, fruitier route.

BOTANICALS

There are plenty of oranges, lemons, limes, and grapefruits here. You will also find more exotic citrus fruits, such as Buddha's hand, *dalandan*, *calamansi*, and kumquat. From Japan, we find yuzu, which is starting to become familiar in the West, and also *hirado buntan*, *kabosu*, *komikan*, and *natsudaidai*.

BUDDHA'S HAND

DALANDAN

CALAMANSI

KUMQUAT

YUZU

MIXERS	GARNISHES	COCKTAILS	OTHER GINS TO TRY
FRANKLIN & SONS Rosemary Tonic Water with Black Olive	THYME	**BRONX** see p127	**BEEFEATER CROWN JEWEL**
LONG RAYS Premium Australian Pacific Tonic	MINT	**JULIET AND ROMEO** see p139	**BOMBAY SAPPHIRE PREMIER CRU**
LONDON ESSENCE Grapefruit and Rosemary Tonic Water	CUCUMBER	**20TH CENTURY** see p147	**KOMASA GIN SAKURAJIMA KOMIKAN**

ARC ARCHIPELAGO BOTANICAL

45% ABV

CALAMBA, PHILIPPINES

FLAVOUR

JUNIPER · CITRUS · HERBAL · FLORAL · SPICE · FRUIT

It's citrus, but not as we know it – for those of us who grew up in the West, at least. But, remember, this gin is from the Philippines, so for Filipinos, the flavours of *dalandan* and *calamansi* are probably more familiar.

Citrus drives this gin, along with floral notes from ylang-ylang, Arabian jasmine (*sampaguita*), and camia flowers. Woody base notes on the palate keep it all from becoming too cloying and make for a very pleasant gin. There are 28 botanicals in all, 22 of which are foraged from across the Philippines. Some go into the pot and some are vapour infused.

BRIGHTON GIN PAVILION STRENGTH

40% ABV

BRIGHTON, ENGLAND

FLAVOUR

JUNIPER · CITRUS · HERBAL · FLORAL · SPICE · FRUIT

This gentle, balanced gin is led by citrus notes and touch of sweet, floral milk thistle. There's a little pinch of spice in there, for balance, and just enough juniper. I found lime peel first on the nose, but mixed with tonic, this migrated over to orange – both are actually in there.

Kathy Caton, the founder of Brighton Gin, says this makes a great G&T garnished with an orange slice. I have to agree with one caveat: choose your tonic wisely. It would be a shame to wash this gentle gin away with anything too sweet or too strongly flavoured (see pp112–13 and 214–15).

BROOKLYN GIN

40% ABV

NEW YORK, NY, USA

FLAVOUR

JUNIPER   CITRUS

FRUIT   HERBAL

SPICE   FLORAL

This gin's distillers crush fresh juniper berries by hand instead of using dried ones, cut up four kinds of fresh citrus instead of using dried peels or concentrates, and so on. The result is a zesty, vibrant, complex gin, with layers of fruit over woody and camphoric floral notes from the juniper and lavender. There are cocoa nibs to counter the acidity from all that citrus.

The corn (maize) in its base spirit made itself felt on the nose when I tried the gin neat, but melted away as soon as I diluted it with some tonic. Try this in a Bee's Knees (see p124) or an equal-parts Martini (see pp130–31).

DRUMSHANBO GUNPOWDER IRISH GIN

43% ABV

DRUMSHANBO, IRELAND

FLAVOUR

JUNIPER   CITRUS

FRUIT   HERBAL

SPICE   FLORAL

This is a popular gin, and with good reason. A lovely balance of botanicals adds up to a rounded and flavourful spirit, which will do a great job in a tonic or in a cocktail.

The aroma is clean and light but also complex. Citrus and pine come first, then earthy-herbal green tea notes from the gunpowder tea – so named because the leaves, rolled into small balls, resemble it. After that come caraway and grapefruit with a peppery kick. The palate adds to this with aromatic spice and a warming touch of cardamom and angelica.

HAYMAN'S EXOTIC CITRUS

41.1% ABV

LONDON, ENGLAND

FLAVOUR

JUNIPER   CITRUS

FRUIT   HERBAL

SPICE   FLORAL

There must be some sleight of hand going on here. How else does Hayman's manage to have such depth at the same time as such zesty vibrancy? It starts off juicy and fruity and lush, then the kumquat, mandarin, pomelo, and Persian lime go in two ways at once. One side goes off into the air, all peels and zests and oils. The other burrows down into a cooked-down, syrupy, sticky-puddingy loveliness.

The finish is smooth and fresh, with long, zesty notes calling you back for more. The citrus is the star, but the reassuring ginny-gin base is there all along. It's a real winner.

LIND & LIME

40% ABV

EDINBURGH, SCOTLAND

FLAVOUR

JUNIPER   CITRUS

FRUIT   HERBAL

SPICE   FLORAL

There's a lovely, straightforward nature to this bright, fresh, modern gin. It has seven botanicals – not many by modern standards – but they all work together and the flavours are right there in your mouth, clean and defined. Juniper, pink pepper, and lime deliver the main notes, with coriander, angelica, liquorice, and orris on backing vocals. The pink pepper and lime in particular run through this from start to finish, and their flavours make a really good pair.

Whereas some gins can become a bit lost when you add tonic, this gin seems to stand out even more. I don't know how the distillers have done that, but it's great.

NIKKA COFFEY

47% ABV

MIYAGIKYO, JAPAN

FLAVOUR

JUNIPER
CITRUS
FRUIT
HERBAL
SPICE
FLORAL

This may look fairly robust from its flavour diagram. You should think of it instead as well defined – high scores here denote clarity, not strength. This gin is unique, delicate, and delicious. It has a mix of traditional botanicals and Japanese ingredients like *amanatsu*, *kabosu*, and *yuzu* (all kinds of citrus), plus *shikuwasa* (hirami lemon) and sansho pepper.

It starts off with citrus and herbal notes, then develops a light pepper edge and an almost floral fruit note from the inclusion of apple. It's all delivered with a silky texture that comes from its distillation on the original Coffey still (see p52), which was imported to Japan in the 1960s.

OXLEY LONDON DRY

47% ABV

LONDON, ENGLAND

FLAVOUR

JUNIPER
CITRUS
FRUIT
HERBAL
SPICE
FLORAL

The first gin (that I know of) to be distilled without any heat at all. Distillers run it through a vacuum still at subzero temperatures, which sounds like a right hassle, but obviates any risk of "cooking" the botanicals. These include cocoa, nutmeg, vanilla, and meadowsweet. The real stars are the "fresh-frozen" orange, lemon, and grapefruit peels, which drive the aroma from the outset.

There's complexity if you take the time to look for it, with a creamy vanilla-and-hay tone mingling with the coriander and juniper. It's more earthy and rooty on the palate, with warming peppery notes building before those zesty citrus oils sweep through again.

PALMA

46.6% ABV

PALMA, MALLORCA, SPAIN

FLAVOUR

This could sit in any number of flavour groups, but its deep, zesty citrus-oil note edged into the lead for me. Mallorcan oranges, lemons, and limes play their part, so perhaps it's no surprise. You'll also find rhubarb root, almond flowers, lavender, and – a touch of genius – tomato branches.

Its fresh, vibrant aroma takes me to sun-drenched courtyards bright with lime, juniper, and earthy-woody lavender. Feel your shoulders loosen in the Mediterranean heat, take a sip, and find sweet, gentle spice, honeyed floral notes, and a prolonged finish with juniper and earthy spice. And all the time, like the sun on your face, those citrus oils work their magic. Bliss.

ROCK ROSE PINK GRAPEFRUIT OLD TOM

41.5% ABV

DUNNET, SCOTLAND

FLAVOUR

Distilled in two John Dore stills named Elizabeth and Margaret, this is an exercise in balance: an Old Tom but not too sweet, packed with citrus but not too sour, full of berries and roots but the juniper still shines through. Each batch is just 500 litres (110 gallons), and the bottles are all filled, sealed, and signed by hand. You'll spot a vintage and a batch number on there too. I tasted batch 9.

Its zesty aroma keeps pink grapefruit and juniper delicately balanced. The palate adds extra depth and sweetness, before moving on to a warming finish with juniper and pithy citrus. Tonic deepens and softens the grapefruit notes.

SACRED PINK GRAPEFRUIT

43.8% ABV

LONDON, ENGLAND

FLAVOUR

JUNIPER   CITRUS

FRUIT   HERBAL

SPICE   FLORAL

My recommendation here is to skip trying this gin neat and put it straight into a cocktail – a Gin Fizz (see p137) or a Tom Collins would be a good choice – or give it a splash of tonic to wake it up. This is a gin made for tonic.

Once it's diluted (which will make it louche; see pp62–63), it bursts with zesty, oily, vibrant pink grapefruit on the nose and on the palate. The flavours take you from the skin through the pith and deep down into the glistening pink flesh of the fruit, with just a bit of cardamom and piney juniper to back it all up. There are other botanicals in there, frankincense among them, but they're the stage hands to grapefruit's strutting star.

SILENT POOL RARE CITRUS

43% ABV

ALBURY, ENGLAND

FLAVOUR

JUNIPER   CITRUS

FRUIT   HERBAL

SPICE   FLORAL

Now, when I say there's a lot going on in this gin, I mean a *lot*. There are 21 botanicals, some in the pot and some in the basket for vapour infusion. Four more get distilled separately and blended back in: *natsudaidai*, *hirado buntan*, and Buddha's hand are the rare citruses after which the gin is named, with number four being Seville orange.

The citrus is balanced against a peppery spice profile from sansho pepper, wild forest pepper, and voatsiperifery pepper. It all adds up to something delicious: sweet and zesty citrus, pepper that's bright and warm, a hint of juniper, and a breath of lavender to tie it together.

TANQUERAY NO. TEN

47.3% ABV

CAMERON BRIDGE, SCOTLAND

FLAVOUR

JUNIPER · CITRUS · HERBAL · FLORAL · SPICE · FRUIT

If Tanqueray's London Dry Gin (see p164) proves you need not shell out extra for a great gin, its No. Ten Gin shows what you can get when you do: something truly glorious.

Its citrus heart is distilled from fresh oranges, limes, and grapefruits. This is redistilled with camomile, quartered fresh limes, and the classic Tanqueray mix of juniper, angelica, liquorice, and coriander. The distillers cut the tails early to emphasize the more citric part of the spirit. You'll spot that immediately on the nose: lime and grapefruit leap over earthy-floral camomile and woody juniper. This gin is complex, rounded, zesty, and vibrant. Hard to beat in almost any cocktail.

WA BI

47% ABV

MINAMISATSUMA, JAPAN

FLAVOUR

JUNIPER · CITRUS · HERBAL · FLORAL · SPICE · FRUIT

This gin comes from Minamisatsuma, near Kagoshima, on the southwestern tip of Japan's Kyushu island. With the exception of its juniper (imported from Albania and North Macedonia), this is where all of its botanicals are found. There's *hetsuka daidai* (a type of bitter orange), yuzu, and kumquat, cinnamon leaf, shell ginger, green tea, and shiso (also called curly perilla, part of the mint family).

The resulting gin has floral and perfumed citrus on the nose undercut by soft juniper and a light, herbal, grassy-minty note from the shiso. There's more spice on the palate, with a hit of bitter orange and kumquat, before the juniper and shiso reassert themselves.

HERBAL GINS

These gins take me places. It might be the Mediterranean scrub, droning with insects, a Japanese teahouse filled with the soothing, slightly smoky scent of green tea, or a windswept beach in the Hebrides. The herbal notes in these gins always float to the top.

BOTANICALS

There are tonnes of herbs that find their way into a gin maker's still: basil, bay leaf, lemon myrtle, marjoram, rosemary, shiso (a Japanese member of the mint family), and thyme. You'll find different sorts of green tea. And while cucumber and fennel aren't actually herbs, they taste like they ought to be.

BASIL

BAY LEAF

SHISO

LEMON MYRTLE

ROSEMARY

MIXERS	GARNISHES	COCKTAILS	OTHER GINS TO TRY
FEVER-TREE Aromatic Tonic Water	**APPLE**	**BIJOU** see p125	**KYRÖ**
FRANKLIN & SONS Rosemary and Black Olive	**BAY LEAF**	**ENGLISH GARDEN** see p132	**VARA HIGH DESERT**
STRANGELOVE Dirty Tonic Water	**ROSEMARY**	**GIN FIZZ** see p137	**WYE VALLEY**

135° EAST HYOGO DRY

42% ABV

AKASHI, JAPAN

FLAVOUR

JUNIPER
CITRUS
FRUIT
HERBAL
SPICE
FLORAL

This blends traditional botanicals with some uniquely Japanese ingredients, including *ume*, *yuzu*, *shiso*, *sansho* pepper, and *sencha*, plus a splash of saké distillate. Some or all of these (it's not entirely clear) are vacuum distilled, which results in a gin that is bright, light, leafy, and fresh.

It opens with a mix of citrus and spice, then develops to a herbal green-tea note that builds to a climax, then lingers on the delicate finish. Dilution brings out soft, aromatic spice notes and a peppery bite that livens up the finish. There are exotic flavours here, but they're deftly woven in rather than painted on. It's smooth for its strength, too.

CONNIPTION AMERICAN DRY

44% ABV

DURHAM, NC, USA

FLAVOUR

JUNIPER
CITRUS
FRUIT
HERBAL
SPICE
FLORAL

Here's something different. For a start, it's made with corn (maize) spirit rather than wheat, rye, or barley. Then there's the method, which again is somewhat unusual. The distillers vapour infuse juniper, coriander, angelica, caraway, and cardamom. Then they individually vacuum distil citrus peels, cucumber, fig, and honeysuckle. Neither the botanicals nor the methods are extraordinary in isolation, but this gin piles these slight departures from the norm atop one another.

The end result is mighty tasty: a herbal nose with juniper and coriander over cucumber, cardamom, and caraway. The palate runs along the same lines, with cucumber and orange over woody angelica. Try it in a Bee's Knees (see p124).

COTSWOLDS DRY

46% ABV

STOURTON, ENGLAND

FLAVOUR

JUNIPER CITRUS

FRUIT HERBAL

SPICE FLORAL

This gin is packed with botanicals to the point that it may louche (see pp62–63) when you dilute it. That's not a bad thing, it just means there are lots of flavour-bearing essential oils knocking about in it. Give it a sip, and you'll see what I mean.

Juniper leads on the nose over black pepper, cardamom, and grapefruit. It's smooth on the palate with grapefruit and lavender, then there's rooty warmth under bay leaf and cardamom. It finishes with lingering juniper, lavender, and lime. Overall, there's a nice balance and complexity that sits on the cusp of herbal and earthy aromatic. It's superb with tonic. Try a bay leaf and slice of grapefruit for your garnish.

DEATH'S DOOR

47% ABV

CAMBRIDGE, WI, USA

FLAVOUR

JUNIPER CITRUS

FRUIT HERBAL

SPICE FLORAL

Death's Door has a blend of just three botanicals: juniper, coriander, and fennel. Some of each goes into the pot and into the vapour infusion basket. The aroma is herbal overall but there's a real breadth – citrus from the coriander, anise from the fennel, woody juniper beneath all that.

The alcohol heat is there but, at this strength, it's to be expected. It's racy on the palate, like each flavour can't wait to be your best buddy. Here they come, juniper's pine thwack, fennel's perfumed herbal spice, coriander's citrus and earthy spice. This gin is a whole lot of fun on its own, but it was born to be mixed into cocktails. Don't deny it that birthright.

FOUR PILLARS OLIVE LEAF

43.8% ABV

HEALESVILLE, AUSTRALIA

FLAVOUR

When a label mentions olive leaf and Australia, I want a gin that's bright, fresh, modern, and savoury. This delivers everything and more. There's a lot of olive action. The leaves themselves are infused as a tea, which gives herbaceous green notes and light tannins to the gin. On top of that there's extra-virgin olive oil from three different varieties: Picual, Hojiblanca, and Coratina.

It makes for a gin that's olive first on the nose, swiftly followed up by herbal and citrus notes from the lemon verbena, and undertones of nutty sweetness and bay leaf. Grapefruit and lavender lift the palate and keep it from getting too heavy.

GIN MARE

42.7% ABV

VILANOVA I LA GELTRÚ, SPAIN

FLAVOUR

Apparently, the distillers macerate both bitter and sweet orange peel with regionally grown lemons for a year in neutral wheat spirit before distilling this gin. Given that, you might think this gin would turn out to be citrus led, but instead, the herbs are the star.

Basil, rosemary, and thyme lead each other on a dance from start to finish, with first one then the other taking the lead. Tonic sorts them out and lets basil shine first, while the woodier herbs are kept to the finish. The Arbequina olives feature prominently on the nose and come out again towards the finish. Juniper takes a bit of a back seat.

KI NO TEA KYOTO DRY

45.1% ABV

KYOTO, JAPAN

FLAVOUR

JUNIPER · CITRUS · HERBAL · FLORAL · SPICE · FRUIT

The Kyoto Distillery makes this alongside the tea grower Horii Shichimeien, featuring two teas harvested from the Okunoyama tea garden, which dates from the 1300s: *tencha* gives bright green matcha flavours, and *gyokuro* gives deeper fuller notes with a savoury edge. They combine with yuzu and *akamatsu* (Japanese red pine) to make a superb gin.

The aroma is immediately herbal, but over time, reveals a deeper complexity with notes from the *shōchū* base spirit (see p67) and yuzu. The palate proceeds from gentle, almost sweet matcha, through perfumed, zesty yuzu, piney *akamatsu*, and into juniper. The finish is long and lingering with notes of roasted green tea. A total delight.

KOMASA GIN HOJICHA

45% ABV

HIOKI, JAPAN

FLAVOUR

JUNIPER · CITRUS · HERBAL · FLORAL · SPICE · FRUIT

Well now, this is quite something. Complex, even a little challenging, but I just love it. *Hojicha* – green tea roasted to drive off its bitterness – dominates the aroma, all vegetal, smoky, and almost iodized. It's part green tea and part nori (the seaweed used to wrap sushi rolls). After that comes woody pine and juniper.

The green tea's smoky richness comes over clearly on the palate, along with coriander and herbal notes. The finish lingers and builds in some hints of liquorice. The distillers use locally made *shōchū* (see p67) for their base spirit, and infuse the botanicals separately to extract the best flavour.

MEDITERRANEAN GIN BY LÉOUBE

41.5% ABV

BORMES-LES-MIMOSAS, FRANCE

FLAVOUR

JUNIPER
CITRUS
FRUIT
HERBAL
SPICE
FLORAL

If this is what distilling botanicals separately can do, then I'm all for it. The deep flavours on show somehow speak to the core of you. They're distinct also, no mishmash muddiness here. The aroma sings with rosemary, olive, and orange, instantly transporting me to the scrubby, sun-warmed garrigue of southern France. On the palate, it is simply delicious. The rosemary and orange are present, but there are floral notes plus a breadth of soft, herbal warmth that resolves towards juniper.

The finish is long, with fennel and a rosemary-menthol kick. Tonic softens everything and allows lighter citrus and floral notes to play a greater role. It's stunningly good.

O'NDINA

45% ABV

ITALY

FLAVOUR

JUNIPER
CITRUS
FRUIT
HERBAL
SPICE
FLORAL

This is a premium Italian gin from the Campari Group, which has kept tight lipped about where and how it's made. What we do know is that it uses 19 botanicals, including juniper, basil, fennel seeds, marjoram, nutmeg, orange, and lemon.

It's light and refreshing, with a herbal hit of basil, fennel, and possibly thyme. A strong, bright spark of orange acidity runs through it to keep things interesting. The base hums with earthy, aromatic warmth. Tonic opens it up nicely, bringing the herbs further forward. There's a good balance overall. The herbs don't shout, just quietly insist. Given the makers, it's a no-brainer to try this in a Negroni (see p142).

ROKU

47% ABV

OSAKA, JAPAN

FLAVOUR

JUNIPER CITRUS

FRUIT HERBAL

SPICE FLORAL

"*Roku*" means "six" in Japanese, so this gin's name reflects the six Japanese botanicals used to make it: sansho pepper, yuzu peel, cherry blossom, cherry leaf, plus two sorts of green tea (sencha and *gyokuro*).

Herbal tea and citrus come on the nose. Beneath them, you'll find smoky pepper and a light floral character. All is held in a beautiful balance. The palate is a wave of yuzu, juniper, and green tea that culminates with a light, herbal bitterness plus an almost grapefruit peel note. (There's none in there. My guess is it's the bitter orange and yuzu together.) Piney juniper and the perfumed cherry blossom finish it off nicely.

SEVEN HILLS (VII) ITALIAN DRY

43% ABV

MONCALIERI, ITALY

FLAVOUR

JUNIPER CITRUS

FRUIT HERBAL

SPICE FLORAL

Ah, I thought to myself, seven hills, that must mean Rome. But no, turns out this is distilled near Turin in Piedmont. The camomile in it is Roman at least. There are seven botanicals (I'm sensing a theme here), with the other six being juniper, celery, rosehip, pomegranate, blood orange, and artichoke – all vacuum distilled at 65°C (149°F).

It's a unique flavour profile, rather rich and sophisticated. On the nose, it's lightly herbal with citrus and soft juniper, and some intriguing depth from the camomile and rosehip. Early batches used sugar cane spirit, but this has been swapped out for neutral grain spirit.

THE BOTANIST ISLAY DRY

46% ABV

BRUICHLADDICH, ISLAY, SCOTLAND

FLAVOUR

This gin is "achingly slow" to make, maybe thanks to its thumping 31 botanicals. Nine of the usual lot go into the pot. Others are vapour infused: three kinds of mint, gorse, lady's bedstraw, tansy, sweet cicely... Anyway, my point is this: take your time tasting. It's oddly delicate for a gin with so many ingredients, but rewards prolonged attention.

It starts honeyed and herbal on the nose with soft citrus and juniper. Meadowsweet and lady's bedstraw fluff up on the palate, working up to a herbal symphony with bog myrtle singing a solo. The finish is camomile and soft juniper, then more gentle citrus and herbal notes. Lovely.

XORIGUER MAHÓN

38% ABV

MAHÓN, MENORCA, SPAIN

FLAVOUR

This gin's a belter. Piney juniper runs the show, but with all sorts of delicious herbal and softly citric business underneath. We know, from details filed to support this gin's EU protected geographical indication (PGI) status, that it's made in wood-fired copper stills. We also know it uses common juniper berries in the pot.

The legal stuff forbids further flavourings or extracts, but the distillery website says "other aromatics" go into a vapour basket, "but these are a closely guarded secret", so unless those other botanicals are, in fact, just more juniper, then I'm afraid I don't know what's going on – other than a whole lot of great flavour.

FLORAL GINS

Floral may suggest to you an English country garden in June. There are some gins here that do capture exactly that, but floral can be other things as well, from the sun-drenched south of France to the South African fynbos.

BOTANICALS

Perhaps the most common source of floral aromas in gin is orris root. Many gins include this as a fixer, but it also gives violet aromas of its own. Other floral botanicals include camomile, elderflower, hibiscus, immortelle, jasmine, lavender, mimosa, rose, and yarrow.

ORRIS ROOT

MIMOSA

ELDERFLOWER

HIBISCUS

LAVENDER

MIXERS	GARNISHES	COCKTAILS	OTHER GINS TO TRY
LONG RAYS Premium Australian Pacific Tonic	GRAPEFRUIT	**AVIATION** see p123	ADNAM'S COPPER HOUSE
LUSCOMBE Light Tonic Water	CAMOMILE	**BEE'S KNEES** see p124	BLUECOAT ELDERFLOWER
TOP NOTE Bitter Lemon Tonic Water	STAR ANISE	**FRENCH 75** see p133	RIVER TEST LONDON DRY

44°N

44% ABV

ROURE, FRANCE

FLAVOUR

JUNIPER · CITRUS · HERBAL · FLORAL · SPICE · FRUIT

I'm reasonably certain you can't distil sunshine. Yet, somehow, Comte de Grasse, the makers of 44°N, have done just that. Its aroma is a perfumed blast from the Côte d'Azur, a whoomph of flowers and dried grasses and citrus. It's complex and intense. The floral notes dominate on the palate too, supported by a herbal, piney backbone. The juniper is light, fresh, and somehow sun-drenched.

The gin is made in a perfume distillery, which dates back to 1820, using all sorts of perfumers' tricks: ultrasonic maceration, vacuum distillation, and supercritical extraction. Alongside the usual botanicals, you'll find littoral goodies such as cade, mimosa, immortelle (curry plant), rose centifolia, and samphire.

AVIATION

42% ABV

PORTLAND, OR, USA

FLAVOUR

JUNIPER · CITRUS · HERBAL · FLORAL · SPICE · FRUIT

One of the pioneering New Western gins (see p74) that soften their juniper so the other botanicals can shine, this gin offers a subtle but interesting complexity. It's quite rounded on the nose with citrus and earthy spice first out, followed by a woody-floral note that builds into a slightly mentholic aroma similar to wintergreen – that's probably the sarsaparilla. As you'd expect, there's not much juniper here, just a hint, and it stays that way on the palate.

Tonic livens it up nicely, bringing out bitter orange and lavender, but you need a light touch. It's worth trying in its namesake cocktail (see p123).

COTSWOLDS NO. 1 WILDFLOWER

41.7% ABV

STOURTON, ENGLAND

FLAVOUR

JUNIPER • CITRUS • FRUIT • HERBAL • SPICE • FLORAL

This is a bold and original gin that shows a different side of florality. No twee English gardens here – more like a mashup of a wildflower meadow with a sun-baked citrus grove. It's made from a base of Cotswold Dry Gin (see p176) with extra cornflowers, lavender, orange, and rhubarb. These are all processed separately before being compounded together.

There's a slightly dusky floral aroma with orange and juniper floating around. It's smooth and oily on the palate, a little bit potent, with fruity orange notes building to a bittersweet orange and earthy rhubarb finish with floral overtones. It's good with tonic but worth trying with lemonade also.

DOROTHY PARKER

44% ABV

NEW YORK, NY, USA

FLAVOUR

JUNIPER • CITRUS • FRUIT • HERBAL • SPICE • FLORAL

There's a lot going on in this. It teeters between earthy aromatics, spiced fruits, and lush floral notes. Juniper leads front and centre on the nose, with cardamom playing backup. Then hibiscus sashays over, all soft, downy, and luscious. Beneath that, cinnamon and elderberry combine for a spiced fruit edge. It's similar on the palate except the juniper is a touch more piney and assertive.

The finish is long and complex, with spiced orange and floral warmth. This gin feels generous to me. I'm not sure how else to put it. Also, it has Negroni (see p142) written all over it.

EAST LONDON KEW GIN

42% ABV

LONDON, ENGLAND

FLAVOUR

JUNIPER

CITRUS

FRUIT

HERBAL

SPICE

FLORAL

Conceived by the East London Liquor Co. to reach a hand of friendship across the city to West London, this gin is made using Douglas fir and lavender hand picked by the head botanist at the Royal Botanic Gardens, Kew. It has eight botanicals in all, the other six being juniper, coriander, sweet orange, angelica, fennel seed, and liquorice.

The aroma starts off herbaceous with coriander spice, then sweet orange citrus and floral lavender develop over time. The citrus is more forward on the palate, which is smooth despite the slightly raised ABV. Overall, it's a pleasant balance of herbal and floral notes cut through with bright citrus.

G'VINE FLORAISON

40% ABV

MERPINS, FRANCE

FLAVOUR

JUNIPER

CITRUS

FRUIT

HERBAL

SPICE

FLORAL

This gin is named for the short time in the spring when flowers blossom on the vine – an ugni blanc vine to be precise. Both the grapes and the flowers make their way into this gin, along with ginger, cubeb, nutmeg, liquorice, and a few of the usual suspects. Its base spirit is made from grapes too.

The gin is light, herbaceous, and floral on the nose, with grassy citrus notes and a vinous white-wine character. It gets a little heavier on the palate, which is oily, then creamy, with the grape coming through again. It's quite delicate on the finish.

HENDRICK'S

41.4% ABV

GIRVAN, SCOTLAND

FLAVOUR

JUNIPER · CITRUS · FRUIT · HERBAL · SPICE · FLORAL

Many reviews lean on how floral this is, how herbal. And yes, it is both those things. But for me, the juniper still comes through first, cubeb on its coat-tails. Only after that did I find roses and camomile asserting themselves. On the palate, the flavours play in reverse order: a big wash of rose, then a sweet haze of yarrow and elderflower, then spice and juniper building.

It settles into a long finish, where cucumber wafts over a gentle alcohol warmth and lingering complexity. Groundbreaking when it launched in 1999, it remains very good to this day, even if its flavour profile no longer seems quite so unusual.

INVERROCHE CLASSIC

43% ABV

STILL BAY, SOUTH AFRICA

FLAVOUR

JUNIPER · CITRUS · FRUIT · HERBAL · SPICE · FLORAL

This gin was born from the South African fynbos that grows on the limestone hills of the Western Cape. Fynbos isn't one plant, but a unique biome of more than 9,500 species, 70 per cent of which grow nowhere else in the world.

Inverroche's founder, Lorna Scott, chose citrus buchu for the gin's main flavour, which blends juniper and soft flowers on the nose. There's rose alongside the buchu, plus a soft anise note. The palate is earthy and floral, with woody flavours lightening towards a spicy, floral finish. There are 15 botanicals in total, eight of which remain a secret, all vapour infused into a sugar cane base spirit.

LBD

43% ABV

EDINBURGH, SCOTLAND

FLAVOUR

JUNIPER — CITRUS — HERBAL — FLORAL — SPICE — FRUIT

Edinburgh's Little Brown Dog Spirits tells drinkers not just what botanicals go into its gin, but also where each one grew and what it contributes to the spirit. I wish more did the same.

The gin bursts with myriad flavours. Citrus notes come from vapour-infused lemon and grapefruit peel, but also wood sorrel and beech leaves that go into the basket with them. Bee pollen lends a sweet and honeyed-floral note to the palate. Parsnips contribute to the creamy texture and add a little peppery kick. Birch sap adds mineral notes and a soft, woody sweetness. The flavour from the rhubarb is jammier but also tart. It's a lovely little sipper.

MELIFERA

43% ABV

SAINT-GEORGES-D'OLÉRON, FRANCE

FLAVOUR

JUNIPER — CITRUS — HERBAL — FLORAL — SPICE — FRUIT

Melifera is made on Oléron, off France's southwest coast, to evoke "the sweet scents of a walk back from the beach". It makes me want to roll through the island's dunes all summer long. It's floral, warm, mineral, and slightly citric, with velvety juniper and a breath of the seaside.

Immortelle (curry plant) flowers combine with gentian and alexanders for a floral punch on the palate, under which woodier aromatics resolve towards earthy cardamom and camphoric floral notes. The finish has floral and citrus notes, but also that fresh and coastal character (perhaps from one of the two secret botanicals). It's so good that even the empty glass still smells delicious.

MONKEY 47 SCHWARZWALD DRY

47% ABV

LOSSBURG, GERMANY

FLAVOUR

How can you make sense of a gin like this? With so much thrown in, pinning down the aroma is like stepping into the same river twice: it can't be done. But in the broadest possible terms, it is a great big, lovely dollop of fruity-spicy-floral exuberance.

For me, aromas of citrus and fruity-floral pepper come early on, then it's berries and menthol-camphor herbs. For you, who knows? There are 47 different botanicals, so you're almost guaranteed to find a different combination. It's a bit too much of a bully for most cocktails, I reckon, but great softened with tonic, in a Dry Martini (see p131), or just neat with ice.

PENRHOS DRY

40.5% ABV

KINGTON, ENGLAND

FLAVOUR

Penrhos sounds Welsh but isn't: the distillery is in Herefordshire. Apple country. They hit me first even though there aren't any in here. I was transported to a stand of soft, young junipers and firs in the corner of a springtime orchard and saw the sunlight on the dew-damp grass.

This gin bursts with blossom and soft fruit, gentle juniper, and light citrus. The palate adds depth with pink peppercorn, warming spice, and earthy cardamom, but they're the soil at the roots of the trees whose blossom fills the air around us. The lingering finish is rose petals and camomile, juniper, and gentle orange, then hibiscus. Just lovely.

SANTA ANA

42.3% ABV

CHARENTE, FRANCE

FLAVOUR

Santa Ana contains some unusual botanicals. Alongside the usual juniper, bitter orange, angelica, orris root, and fennel, you will find ylang-ylang (also used to make Chanel No. 5 perfume), alpinia (lesser galangal), and two types of tropical citrus, *calamansi* and *dalandan*. They add up to a gin that's atypical in the best way.

It opens with beguiling tropical floral notes, which make me picture bougainvillea on a warm summer night, the darkness filled with the promise of hidden delights. The citrus is light and fresh. There's soft, earthy spice for depth and juniper to wave you goodbye.

SILENT POOL

43% ABV

ALBURY, ENGLAND

FLAVOUR

Potent and complex, this is one of those gins that could fit into any number of flavour profiles, but for me, the floral notes just edge it. Juniper drives without dominating. There's a deep base of earthy cassia and cubeb spice overlaid with fruit, and floral notes bursting with camomile, lavender, and rose.

To make this, the distillers undertake two separate macerations, then add yet more botanicals to a gin basket for vapour infusion. There are 24 in all, including two types of juniper (Bosnian in the pot, North Macedonian in the basket), dried pears, honey, makrut lime leaves, linden, and elderflower. The result is well rounded and utterly delicious.

FRUITY GINS

What we're looking for here are fruit from beyond the citrus grove. First, we stop at bushes where the berries grow. Next, we head into the orchard for apples and quinces. There are gins here with sloes and rosehips, and even tropical tastes of the Amazon.

BOTANICALS

Berries feature a lot, which is no surprise: blueberry, blackberry, blackcurrant, raspberry, rowanberry, strawberry. Look out for apple, quince, grape, even melon. From South America, you can find açaí, *seje* (a palm-tree fruit), and *túpiro*.

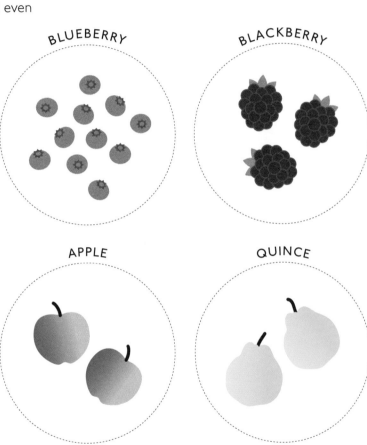

BLUEBERRY

BLACKBERRY

RASPBERRY

APPLE

QUINCE

MIXERS	GARNISHES	COCKTAILS	OTHER GINS TO TRY
FRANKLIN & SONS Elderflower and Cucumber	GINGER	**CLOVER CLUB** see p128	CAORUNN
SANPELLEGRINO Tonica Oakwood	LAVENDER	**GIN BASIL SMASH** see p136	ELEPHANT SLOE
DOUBLE DUTCH Pomegranate and Basil	LIME	**SOUTHSIDE RICKEY** see p146	YORK GIN ROMAN FRUIT

BROCKMANS

40% ABV

WARRINGTON, ENGLAND

FLAVOUR

This gin bills itself as classic with a twist, and I'm inclined to agree. The usual line-up of gin botanicals is augmented by blueberry and blackberry, both of which are front and centre on the nose. Underneath, piney juniper is lifted by citrus. If the initial flavour is a little unclear, it's soon swept away by a wave of juicy dark berry, which builds to orange and angelica over liquorice sweetness.

You might hear berries and think sweet. Think again. The finish is dry, with soft juniper, a grassy note, and lingering berries. The dryness keeps it from becoming cloying. It's a gin with berries rather than a berry-flavoured gin.

BROOKIE'S BYRON DRY

46% ABV

MCLEODS SHOOT, AUSTRALIA

FLAVOUR

This gin could easily sit in the earthy aromatic section, but it's here because of a raspberry note that adds an extra kick of complexity and lifts this gin from good to great. There are 25 botanicals in all, 17 of which are native to the subtropical rainforest of Australia's Byron Bay.

Notable ingredients include macadamia, finger lime, anise and cinnamon myrtles, and river mint. There's juniper on the nose followed by earthy and herbal spice. The palate starts off with citrus and raspberry, then moves through bold, spicy notes of ginger and anise myrtle to a warming, peppery finish.

CANAÏMA

47% ABV

LA MIEL, VENEZUELA

FLAVOUR

From the home of Diplomático Rum, this gin has a pleasing blend of tropical notes and a slight vegetal hint that suggests the lush, damp greenery of the Amazonian rainforest. There's some fairly firey juniper and pepper going on also that I really liked.

There are 19 botanicals in total, 10 of which the distillers deem exotic, including *merey* (cashew), açaí, *uva de palma*, *túpiro*, *seje*, and *copoazú*. All of these are macerated and distilled individually before blending to create the final gin. A portion of the profits from this gin support reforestation of the Amazon as well as preserving the culture and heritage of the Indigenous people.

CITADELLE JARDIN D'ÉTÉ

41.5% ABV

ARS, FRANCE

FLAVOUR

I counted 22 botanicals in this gin, including melon flesh (unusual) and yuzu (a little less so), plus all manner of spices: cubeb, cumin, cinnamon, Sichuan pepper, nutmeg, green cardamom, fennel, star anise… So I was surprised when I tasted it neat to find this gin holding back much of its flavour. Once you dilute it though, all that exuberant complexity bursts forth – and it's lovely.

There are fruity, herbal, and citrus notes underpinned by an earthy aromatic complexity. It's like remembering a summer garden versus visiting one on a sunny afternoon and basking in its lush foliage. It makes a great G&T.

FOUR PILLARS BLOODY SHIRAZ

37.8% ABV

HEALESVILLE, AUSTRALIA

FLAVOUR

This is a beaut! It's Four Pillars' Rare Dry Gin macerated for eight weeks on Shiraz grapes, hence the colour. These impart a deep, rich fruit note that is almost raspberry but retains that vinous grape character.

Fresh pine and soft pepper sit alongside this on the nose, and a big whack of pepperberry drifts somewhere between the two camps. Its palate is thick, off-dry, almost sweet, with fruity notes to the fore again. There's a perfumed lemon myrtle and cardamom interlude, then pepperberry rushes in again over star anise and lavender. It goes in a similar direction to sloe gin but is very much its own thing.

HAYMAN'S SLOE GIN

26% ABV

LONDON, ENGLAND

FLAVOUR

This is *technically* a liqueur rather than a straight gin. It's made from Hayman's London Dry, which is macerated with sloes for up to four months post-distillation. The resulting flavour is dominated by the fruit, but keeps a good balance with the base gin and doesn't get too sweet.

The nose has sloe's characteristic plummy-tart note with a nutty depth to it and a hint of citrus. It's a subtle but rich aroma. The texture is thick, smooth, and sweet. The sloes dominate again, but there's also a suggestion of subtle spice.

HEPPLE SLOE & HAWTHORN GIN

29.9% ABV

HEPPLE, ENGLAND

FLAVOUR

JUNIPER · CITRUS · HERBAL · FLORAL · SPICE · FRUIT

Sloe gins can end up sticky and syrupy. No such worries here. Chris Garden, head distiller at Hepple Spirits, has slipped in some hawthorn berries. These contribute a sloe-like taste but with an additional drying character that lifts this liqueur and keeps it from seeming too sweet.

Quiet complexity lurks on the horizon of its flavour profile from botanicals such as fennel seeds, Douglas fir, bog myrtle, blackcurrant (both berry and leaf), clove, black pepper, and bay leaf. This works really well with bitter lemon as a mixer. I'm also told adding a slug of it to your Guinness makes for a deliciously festive pint.

KNUT HANSEN DRY

42% ABV

HAMBURG, GERMANY

FLAVOUR

JUNIPER · CITRUS · HERBAL · FLORAL · SPICE · FRUIT

This gin has been around since 2017, when it was launched by Kaspar Hagedorn and Martin Spieker. They began on a tiny tabletop still in Spieker's home, but by 2019, had opened their own distillery.

It has a deliciously light and fresh character underpinned by apples and herbal notes from basil and cucumber. The full list of botanicals has not been declared, but from the softly hay-like floral and vanilla notes, I'd guess it also contains meadowsweet. The finish is complex and warming, with juniper, apple, and some floral woody notes. This will work wonders in a Gin Basil Smash (see p136).

LE GIN DE CHRISTIAN DROUIN

42% ABV

PONT-L'ÉVÊQUE, FRANCE

FLAVOUR

JUNIPER · CITRUS · HERBAL · FLORAL · SPICE · FRUIT

When most people hear "fruity gin", their thoughts often turn first to berries, but it doesn't have to be that way. This gin explodes with orchard fruit and takes us in another direction entirely. Its neutral spirit is aromatized with distilled apple cider made from more than 30 apple varieties.

On the nose, expect juniper mingled with spiced apple, ginger, and brioche-like vanilla. It's like a French bakery had a baby with a barrel store in an orchard. The palate is dry and spicy, with sherbert lemon, apple pie, and that vanilla sweetness again. Finally, we end on a lingering note of apple skin, juniper, and spice. A real treat.

MERMAID PINK GIN

38% ABV

RYDE, ENGLAND

FLAVOUR

JUNIPER · CITRUS · HERBAL · FLORAL · SPICE · FRUIT

If you fear pink gin will be sickly sweet, think again. This gin from the Isle of Wight manages to flaunt its fruity side without getting too saccharine. The strawberry is the star but it doesn't hog the limelight. There's still room for complexity from the base of Mermaid Dry Gin, in which the distillers steep locally grown fruit for four days before redistilling it.

The flavour starts with strawberries and peppery grains of paradise, then mellows into a rootier liquorice note. The all-important juniper is soft on the finish but it's there, and there's a lingering fragrant strawberry sweetness. It only gets better with tonic.

PUERTO DE INDIAS STRAWBERRY

37.5% ABV

CARMONA, SPAIN

FLAVOUR

JUNIPER CITRUS

FRUIT HERBAL

SPICE FLORAL

If you like pink gins, then this is the business, bursting with bright, fresh strawberry. Strawberry is pretty much all there is on the nose. There's perhaps just the slightest hint that there could be juniper and maybe lime.

On the palate, that is confirmed, and, in fact, the juniper comes through quite strongly and mixes surprisingly well with the strawberry flavour. The citrus (maybe lime, maybe grapefruit) just lifts the finish a little. It's quite thick and off-dry when you have it neat, but most people will be enjoying this with a good glug of tonic, which it deals with very well.

RAMSBURY SINGLE ESTATE

40% ABV

RAMSBURY, ENGLAND

FLAVOUR

JUNIPER CITRUS

FRUIT HERBAL

SPICE FLORAL

An elegant, balanced, and complex gin, it could sit in any number of flavour groups, but it's here because the perfumed quince just edges into first place on the aroma for me. (It's also the only botanical that's not one of the gin classics.)

It's clean and light on the nose with soft juniper, grassy and fruity quince, citrus notes, and a gentle, musky woody base from the angelica. On the palate, there's a floral note that develops through rooty sweetness to pithy citrus and piney juniper over gentle spice. Ramsbury makes its own base spirit and is also heavily invested in making its production as sustainable as possible.

TANQUERAY BLACKCURRANT ROYALE DISTILLED

41.3% ABV

CAMERON BRIDGE, SCOTLAND

FLAVOUR

JUNIPER · CITRUS · HERBAL · FLORAL · SPICE · FRUIT

The purpley-black sweets are always the best, aren't they? This brings all the blackcurrant to the yard, but without seeming too confected. It drifts ever closer to the line of being too sweet, but pulls up just short.

What it leaves you with is lip-smacking dark fruits, backed up by vanilla in its lighter, more vibrant mode rather than its gooey sweet ice-cream persona. Juniper lurks around unwilling to get involved until the main event is over, at which point it creeps over to see what all the fuss was about. Definitely made for mixing.

THE SOURCE

47% ABV

WĀNAKA, NEW ZEALAND

FLAVOUR

JUNIPER · CITRUS · HERBAL · FLORAL · SPICE · FRUIT

This is a gin in which a combo kick of rosehip and angelica stars. Floral, musky, tart, woody, and perfumed, it's first out of the glass and into your nose, and it's last to fade from your tongue a few moments later. In between, juniper dances with coriander and orange-and-lemon citrus. All in all it's a pleasing balance with some real moments of complexity.

This gin is not chill filtered, so it may develop a slight haze when you dilute it. It's also slightly unusual in that nothing goes into the pot. All the botanicals are vapour infused, though it's certainly not the only gin to use this approach: Bombay Sapphire (see p158) does the same.

EARTHY AND AROMATIC GINS

These are some seriously delicious gins, but this is not all about heat. Think more spiced than spicy.

BOTANICALS

From the peppery side are cubeb, grains of paradise, pink peppercorns, and Sichuan pepper. Pepperberry matches heat with fruity and pungent sweetness. Others commonly used are cardamom, cinnamon, cumin, ginger, nutmeg, star anise, tonka beans, turmeric, and vanilla.

CUBEB
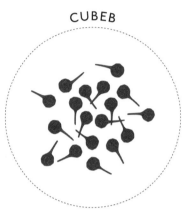

GRAINS OF PARADISE

PEPPERBERRY

CARDAMOM

STAR ANISE

MIXERS	GARNISHES	COCKTAILS	OTHER GINS TO TRY
FRANKLIN & SONS Grapefruit and Bergamot	**BAY LEAF**	**MARTINEZ** see p141	**AVAL DOR CORNISH DRY**
FENTIMANS Oriental Yuzu Tonic Water	**MARIGOLD**	**SATAN'S WHISKERS** see p145	**LUMBER'S BARTHOLOMEW NAVY STRENGTH**
DOUBLE DUTCH Cucumber & Watermelon	**ORANGE**	**WHITE NEGRONI** see p149	**SCILLY SPIRIT ISLAND**

ACHROOUS

41% ABV

LEITH, SCOTLAND

FLAVOUR

JUNIPER CITRUS
FRUIT HERBAL
SPICE FLORAL

This is a bright, modern gin that mixes juniper with some pleasantly complex woody and spiced notes. It is earthy and peppery on the nose, with grassy fennel midtones and hints of citrus over the top. The palate comes in woody then builds through sweetness from the liquorice to bright citrus notes from the Sichuan pepper, which brings the zing but not the fire. The finish is long with anise warmth.

It's definitely one to try in a Negroni (see p142), where it will lead the vermouth and Campari a merry dance. Tonic brings out the mellow side of the aromatic, rooty, warming flavours to give you a hug from the inside.

AUDEMUS PINK PEPPER

44% ABV

COGNAC, FRANCE

FLAVOUR

JUNIPER CITRUS
FRUIT HERBAL
SPICE FLORAL

First of all: this is delicious. Second, but also important: it's very light on the juniper, most likely too light for some. Third, though: it's still delicious. Two of its nine botanicals remain secret, but the rest are pink pepper, juniper, cardamom, cinnamon, honey, vanilla, and tonka beans. Audemus distils them separately at low temperatures on a rotovap still, then blends them back together.

The result is earthy and alluring on the nose with lots of pink pepper and tonka. If you don't know it, tonka's flavour is a cola-adjacent mix of vanilla, cinnamon, marzipan, caramel, and darkly perfumed honey. Yum.

BERTHA'S REVENGE IRISH MILK

42% ABV

CASTLELYONS, IRELAND

FLAVOUR

Your first question is probably: "Does the whey make a difference?" Well, gentle reader, yes, it does. It makes for a silky gin without the edge that grain-based spirits can have. This releases its botanicals' flavours over time. There are plenty in here – 18 in all – including juniper and its usual mates, plus cloves, cumin, alexander seeds, and elderflower.

The overall impression is one of gentle spice lifted by citrus. It's rooty and warming, liquorice and lime, cardamom and pepper. Give it a go in a Gibson (see p134) or mix it into a Martini (see pp130–31), but whatever you do, don't gulp it down. This gin rewards the slower drinker.

BOBBY'S SCHIEDAM DRY

42% ABV

SCHIEDAM, NETHERLANDS

FLAVOUR

The "Bobby" here is distiller Sebastiaan van Bokkel's grandfather, who came to Schiedam in 1950 from Indonesia and made gin using the spices he grew up with.

This gin could be the poster child for earthy, aromatic gins. Cloves and cubeb pair up from the start to drive its flavour profile, with the other botanicals dancing around the leading duo. The supporting cast are juniper, coriander, fennel, lemongrass, and rosehips. The finish, in particular, is lovely. Juniper finally muscles its way forwards, along with lingering peppery spice notes that work wonders in a Negroni (see p142) or Corpse Reviver No. 2 (see p129).

CITADELLE

44% ABV

ARS, FRANCE

FLAVOUR

JUNIPER • CITRUS • HERBAL • FLORAL • SPICE • FRUIT

Maison Ferrand is better known for its Cognac, but we should be glad it makes this gin too. It's quite delicate on the nose, with fresh floral notes mixed with earthy pepper spice. On the palate, juniper takes charge before yielding to complex flavours that run through herbal to rooty to peppery, and then we're back to juniper and woody notes for the finish.

There are 19 botanicals in all, among them fennel, star anise, violet, cumin, Sichuan pepper, and sunflower seeds. Back in 1995, when it first appeared, its flavour profile would have been very unusual. Today, it sits somewhere between contemporary and classic.

CONKER SPIRIT NAVY STRENGTH

57% ABV

BOURNEMOUTH, ENGLAND

FLAVOUR

JUNIPER • CITRUS • HERBAL • FLORAL • SPICE • FRUIT

OK, real talk, friends: this gin is stunning. It's delicious and deftly done. The head distiller runs nine botanicals through his copper stills: marsh samphire, elderberry, juniper, coriander, angelica, cassia bark, orris root, lime peel, and Seville orange peel. It's big, oily, and potent on the palate but smooth with it – that navy strength alcohol doesn't burn or sting.

Juniper and elderberries lead on to orange and warming spice. There's a beautiful depth of flavour and a long, complex finish. It stands up really well to tonic. Five pounds from every bottle sold goes to support the RNLI – a charity that operates lifeboats and rescue services around the UK coastline.

FOUR PILLARS RARE DRY

41.8% ABV

HEALESVILLE, AUSTRALIA

FLAVOUR

This gin is smooth and approachable, and although it's definitely modern, it also manages to feel somewhat classic. Maybe it's the balance of the botanicals, which reminds me of a classic London Dry from an alternative dimension.

The juniper is soft and subtle, and instead, lemon myrtle and pepperberry leaf take the lead. There's a fair amount of citrus, with coriander and cardamom brightening up the mid-palate, before star anise and lavender come along to join the pepperberry on the finish. For me, it needs waking up a little by mixing with a tonic or into a cocktail. A Red Snapper (see p144) should do the job nicely. Bonza.

GEOMETRIC

57% ABV

CAPE TOWN, SOUTH AFRICA

FLAVOUR

One to seek out. Flavours of the South African fynbos meld with traditional gin botanicals to make an elegant gin that works wonders in a Dry Martini (see p131). Its cardamom-and-cloves aroma is gently spiced with a herbal edge. The palate deepens with flavours of buchu leaf (think blackcurrant meets rosemary meets peppermint) and Cape snowbush (wild rosemary and pepper). Piney juniper plus more buchu linger on the finish.

It is the result of a complicated distillation process involving a blend of one main batch and three smaller sub-batches, some of which are vapour infused. It sounds like a lot of work, but for a gin like this, it's definitely worth it.

HAPUSĀ HIMALAYAN DRY

43% ABV

NEW DELHI, INDIA

FLAVOUR

Quite simply a triumph. Earthy and spicy, perfumed and nutty, and lifted by citrus. Himalayan juniper is earthy on the nose, leading into earthy-sweet mango, cardamom, and rangpur lime. There's a pleasant touch of oiliness on the palate, which leads with juniper, lime again, and some turmeric warmth.

All well and good, but it's the finish where this gin really shines. It's a flavour-nerd's dream that will keep you exploring the inside of your cheeks to find flavours reappearing in different combinations – ginger and coriander, mango and ginger, coriander and turmeric, lime and coriander. What could the distillers possibly do to improve on this? Nothing, that's what.

LONDON TO LIMA

42.8%

LIMA, PERU

FLAVOUR

The stars of the show here are pink peppercorns, Cape gooseberry, and key lime. They swirl around one another, giving tart, fruity spiced notes cut through with citrus. The finish is long and warming with a satisfyingly robust hit of piney juniper.

This Anglo-Peruvian gin is made from a grape-based spirit called pisco, which is unique to Peru. The pisco used here is made from Quebranta grapes, and its flavours are the final piece of the puzzle that make a fabulous drink well worth savouring neat. It's great in a G&T too, if you're light on the T. The aroma responds really well and leaps out of the glass.

NO. 3 LONDON DRY

46% ABV

LONDON, ENGLAND

FLAVOUR

JUNIPER   CITRUS

FRUIT   HERBAL

SPICE   FLORAL

Classic but far from austere, this gin shows what can be done with just a few good ingredients and a sure touch on the still. There are six botanicals – juniper, coriander, orris root, grapefruit, orange, cardamom – delivering bags of flavour.

It starts off familiar enough on the nose, showing just an edge of earthy spice on the otherwise classic London Dry gin aroma profile to hint at what's to come. On the palate, though, it bursts with juniper, orris, and cardamom before citrus and coriander sweep through. It's crisp and fresh, building to an earthy dry angelica-and-juniper finish that never seems to show any signs of falling off.

PERRY'S TOT NAVY STRENGTH

57% ABV

NEW YORK, NY, USA

FLAVOUR

JUNIPER   CITRUS

FRUIT   HERBAL

SPICE   FLORAL

This is a bit much on its own. Once you've tamed it with tonic, it's another matter altogether: complex and aromatic on the nose, with juniper and some of the honey and citrus appearing plus some of the cardamom. The finish is excellent, showing a real depth of flavour with a nice mix of juniper and aromatic aniseed.

Even so, tonic doesn't feel like its natural home. This gin is one to use judiciously in a cocktail. It'll turn your Negroni (see p142) up to 11, but it might work in something more delicate like a Clover Club (see p128) too, if you're open to dialling the measure back a little.

PROCERA BLUE DOT

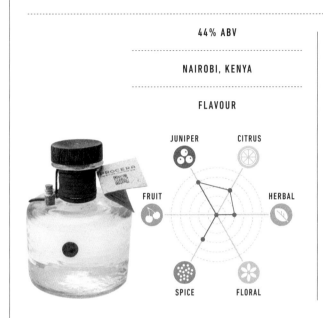

44% ABV

NAIROBI, KENYA

FLAVOUR

JUNIPER
CITRUS
FRUIT
HERBAL
SPICE
FLORAL

This mixes common juniper and a local species, *Juniperus procera* (African pencil cedar), from which it takes its name. This is the only juniper native to the southern hemisphere. The distillers use its berries fresh and "never dried", giving a bright and nutty flavour, which they bottle in vintages.

My sample (2022 vintage) was gentle and balanced on the nose with earthy notes, juniper, honey, cardamom, and a smoky hint of green tea. There was a soft yet persistent finish with orange and lime and some pink pepper spice. It's marketed as a "Martini and sipping gin", and sold with a special botanical salt garnish that really ups its G&T game.

SANDY GRAY

46% ABV

SPREYTON, AUSTRALIA

FLAVOUR

JUNIPER
CITRUS
FRUIT
HERBAL
SPICE
FLORAL

Deftly made, this. Distiller Bob Connor wanted a higher ABV to carry his botanicals' flavour, and by using grape neutral spirit rather than grain, plus distilling carefully, he managed to do that without the boozy sting that other spirits might show at this strength.

It's non-chill filtered so may louche (see pp62–63) when you dilute it. Mine didn't. It opens rich and warm on the nose with scents of juniper and lime followed by pepperberry spice. It's smooth on the palate, rooty and warm, rich with cardamom and cassia undercut by citrus. The finish is long and complex and ends up perfumed and peppery with juniper over the top. Delicious.

MARITIME AND UMAMI GINS

This is fast becoming my favourite category of gins.
These savoury gins carry a saline smack of the sea;
or, in another direction, a juicy hit of lush, green olives.
Either way, it's a delicious and refreshing new
side to gin that's well worth exploring.

BOTANICALS

Seaweeds first: carrageen, channelled wrack, dulse, sea lettuce, sugar kelp. You'll also see rock samphire, olives, and capers, even Parmesan. Supporting roles are played by fennel, bog myrtle, water mint, and the like.

CARRAGEEN

SEA LETTUCE

ROCK SAMPHIRE

OLIVES

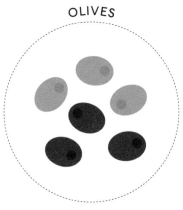

CAPERS

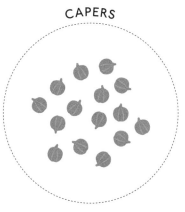

MIXERS	GARNISHES	COCKTAILS	OTHER GINS TO TRY
FEVER-TREE Refreshingly Light Cucumber Tonic Water	ORANGE	**DIRTY MARTINI** (see p130)	GRAY WHALE
STRANGELOVE Coastal Tonic Water	LEMONGRASS	**GIBSON** (see p134)	GREENWICH MARINE LONDON DRY
LONDON ESSENCE Pomelo and Pink Pepper Tonic Water	SAGE	**RED SNAPPER** (see p144)	NEWFOUNDLAND SEAWEED

AN DÚLAMÁN IRISH MARITIME

43.2% ABV

DONEGAL, IRELAND

FLAVOUR

Distiller Sliabh Liag's copper pot still is called Meabh, which means "bringer of great joy" or "she who intoxicates". Was a name ever more apt? An Dúlamán is an intoxicating joy right from the get-go, an umami gin with a coastal kiss and a spicy kick.

It opens smoky, earthy, maritime, saline, and vegetal. The palate is dry but also silky. There's sweetness and salinity, tobacco and liquorice, and herbal juniper swaying in the breeze on the distant hills, while we splash in rock pools below. The warming finish whispers to you about how this gin might work with oysters or dark chocolate. I think a Martini (see pp130–31) might be in order.

AUDEMUS UMAMI

42% ABV

COGNAC, FRANCE

FLAVOUR

Designed for the Experimental Cocktail Club in London, which wanted a savoury gin to use in its cocktails, this gin contains vacuum distillates of juniper, Sicilian capers, lemon, bergamot, and Parmesan cheese. The latter is flash-infused so that the gin gets the depth of umami from its salty, crunchy crystals without any of the cheesy notes. Capers provide a constant top note, while juniper and citrus dance underneath.

The gin rests for three to five months in Cognac barrels, which also lend it a woody snap that plays nicely into the juniper on the finish, while the capers linger on. Try it in a Red Snapper (see p144).

BARRA ATLANTIC GIN

46% ABV

CASTLEBAY, SCOTLAND

FLAVOUR

Oh my goodness. If this gin were playing pool, you'd be well and truly hustled. It comes on all delicate on the nose and then whammo! What a gin! Robust, bursting with flavour, and strangely exciting in a way I can't quite place.

It features 17 botanicals, among which are mint, elderflower, camomile, heather, cubeb, and pink pepper. The star, though, is the carrageen seaweed that brings its wild, maritime edge. The distillery (Scotland's most westerly) uses vapour infusion to capture all that flavour and cram it into a gin that you really should seek out. Go light on the tonic if you're mixing this into a G&T.

DÀ MHÌLE ORGANIC SEAWEED

45% ABV

LLANDYSUL, WALES

FLAVOUR

To smell this is to hold seaweed in your hand still glistening wet. Iodized salinity is cut through with citrus and black pepper, and underneath lies juniper's piney rasp. Just lovely. The distillers rest their gin on seaweed for three weeks after distillation, which explains the delicate green colour and its glorious savoury smack. Some rose-fennel-cardamom business in the mid-palate lifts the whole experience into a realm of seaside gardens and flower beds beaded with sea spray.

Dà Mhìle's copper pot still is named Ceridwen after the Welsh goddess of the cauldron, to whom we should all lift a glass in thanks for this luxuriously silky and off-dry spirit.

DEWI SANT COASTAL

40% ABV

CARDIFF, WALES

FLAVOUR

JUNIPER   CITRUS

SAVOURY   HERBAL

SPICE   FLORAL

An interesting one. The distillers kept the botanicals quiet, but we do know it contains fennel, citrus, and "aromatic herbs". I'd lay money on there being grains of paradise in it and some kind of seaweed, possibly laver.

Its aroma is a pleasing mix of savoury, citrus, and peppery notes. In time, fennel and liquorice sweets join to round it out. On the palate, these are supported by a woody anise base note and a growing perfumed peppery heat. The coastal element is gentle but persistent, not in your face but evocative none the less. "Dewi Sant", in case you're wondering, is Welsh for "Saint David", the nation's patron saint.

GIN EVA LA MALLORQUINA OLIVE

45% ABV

LLUCMAJOR, MALLORCA, SPAIN

FLAVOUR

JUNIPER   CITRUS

SAVOURY   HERBAL

SPICE   FLORAL

The climate in Mallorca's Valldemossa Valley is perfect for growing olives. This gin, made in that same valley, bursts with their juicy flavours. The distillers macerate their wheat spirit on olive pomace for weeks before distillation, at which point they add just juniper and coriander. No messing around here!

On the palate, the olives pick up a saline note, then a herbal wash of juniper sweeps them away. It finishes with pine, citric coriander, and a hint of the olives returning to the background. It's a really lovely gin that proves you don't always need a lot of botanicals, as long as you treat the ones you do have well.

ISLE OF HARRIS

45% ABV

TARBERT, SCOTLAND

FLAVOUR

JUNIPER · CITRUS · SAVOURY · HERBAL · SPICE · FLORAL

This is a gin that demands space in the special cupboard where you keep the really good stuff. The distillers macerate juniper, cassia, coriander, angelica, bitter orange, cubeb, liquorice, orris, and sugar kelp together ahead of distillation, but remove the kelp just before they fire the still. This keeps its coastal note light and fresh – you won't be attracting seagulls the moment you pull the stopper.

What you get is a glorious procession of citrus, gentle spice, warming, rooty sweetness, savoury herbal coastal notes, and juniper, then bitter citrus again to round it off. It's fantastic with tonic but revelatory neat or in Martinis (see pp130–31).

LUSSA

42% ABV

ARDLUSSA, SCOTLAND

FLAVOUR

JUNIPER · CITRUS · SAVOURY · HERBAL · SPICE · FLORAL

About 250 people live on Jura, Scotland's eighth-largest island but one of its least populated. Three of them (all women) distil this gin from 15 botanicals grown or gathered on the island, including lemon thyme, lemon balm, bog myrtle, and Scots pine needles.

Its aroma melds these with juniper and base notes of sea lettuce and ground elder. The palate adds elderflower and honeysuckle alongside lime, and then goes on for a long finish where the lemon thyme and juniper reappear. The distillers say theirs is probably one of the most "ungetatable" distilleries. If you can't visit, do the next best thing and seek out a bottle.

MAINBRACE CORNISH DRY

40% ABV

HELFORD PASSAGE, ENGLAND

FLAVOUR

JUNIPER CITRUS

SAVOURY HERBAL

SPICE FLORAL

The Mainbrace name goes back to when sailors enjoyed an extra tot of rum after successfully "splicing the mainbrace" – repairing a crucial bit of rigging during battle. This developed over time to involve less rope and more drinking, legitimized with a toast: "The King, God Bless Him" or "The Queen, God Bless Her".

Mainbrace released this gin to mark Queen Elizabeth II's Platinum Jubilee in 2022, so in a way, you're still raising a glass to the monarch when you taste it. The flavour has bold juniper, citrus, and coriander to the fore, after which come saline and umami notes from kelp, dulse, and sea spaghetti.

MANGUIN OLI'GIN

41% ABV

AVIGNON, FRANCE

FLAVOUR

JUNIPER CITRUS

SAVOURY HERBAL

SPICE FLORAL

The second you open this bottle, it's olives everywhere. The meaty, fruity ones you devour on holiday, in some little corner bar perhaps, and before you know it, the dish is gone and you're agitating for more, your drink forgotten for the moment…

Now then, don't fret: there's juniper here too and our old pal fennel. The gin is wondrous neat. You should try it that way, then in a Martini (see pp130–31). But if you do mix it with tonic, you're also in for a treat. It softens and deepens the umami note and lets the fennel and orange shine through more. Garnish with three cherry tomatoes on a pick.

MANLY COASTAL CITRUS

43% ABV

SYDNEY, AUSTRALIA

FLAVOUR

That's Manly as in the place – in Sydney, Australia. Now, let me tell you about this gin. It is fantastic. It begins with an earthy, herbal citrus note that I took to be the lemon aspen, although lemon myrtle is also contributing, as well as Meyer lemon (smaller, sweeter, less tangy).

Next comes delicate sea parsley – herbal, savoury, and saline – then juniper stiffening everything up. There's coriander leaf rather than the usual seeds, which also leans into the herbal and citrus vibe. The whole thing takes off if you add a little tonic, becoming deeper, richer, softer. Glorious.

MERMAID

43% ABV

RYDE, ENGLAND

FLAVOUR

Some well-chosen botanicals give this gin layers of interest. Elderflower adds subtle, lighter notes to the aroma. Hops from the nearby botanical gardens in Ventnor add earthy spice to the finish. But, above all, it's the rock samphire that elevates this gin above the run of the mill. It lends a refreshing saline and citrus note that floats through like a breath of sea air.

Grains of paradise and liquorice keep things grounded in the mid-palate, providing a rooty warmth to balance all the other elements. This will work well in a Bee's Knees (see p124) garnished with a lemon twist and a sprig of lavender.

NO. 6 LAVER ATLANTIC SPIRIT

42% ABV

BIDEFORD, ENGLAND

FLAVOUR

JUNIPER · CITRUS · HERBAL · FLORAL · SPICE · SAVOURY

Funny thing – there's a delicious citrus edge to this gin without there being any citrus in it. Instead, the flavour comes from the coriander and the laver, a seaweed that also gives this gin its gently iodized sea-breeze character. It's foraged from Abbotsham cliffs on the rugged North Devon coast and tastes of a pleasant sunny morning splashing about in rock pools.

Beneath that, though, you'll find a very balanced and rather classic gin base. There's a nice balance of juniper, angelica, and orris, plus grains of paradise and cubeb giving it a rooty and peppery back note. It's a lovely balance that you'll likely find quite moreish.

ROCK ROSE CITRUS COASTAL EDITION

41.5% ABV

DUNNET, SCOTLAND

FLAVOUR

JUNIPER · CITRUS · HERBAL · FLORAL · SPICE · SAVOURY

A delicate gin, this one. When you look at the list of botanicals (19 in all), you might expect otherwise, but this is no brash pot pourri. The more interesting ones are bilberry, hawthorn, rowanberry, lemon verbena, and rose root – but these are all shared with the distillery's Original Edition. The extra seaside pop comes from kelp and liquorice salt, which give this gin its delicate but definite oceanic edge.

A little drop of tonic wakes this gin up very nicely. Try it in a G&T with a slice of pink grapefruit and, if you can find them, a few goji berries.

SUGAR IN TONICS

Tonic waters vary greatly in their sugar content.
Choose one that doesn't contain too much sugar
so that you don't mask the flavour of your gin.

BRAND	PRODUCT	TYPE	SUGAR (g/100ml)
LUSCOMBE	Elderflower	Flavoured	7.9
LUSCOMBE	Grapefruit	Flavoured	7.9
SANPELLEGRINO	Tonica Citrus	Flavoured	7.9
SANPELLEGRINO	Tonica Oakwood	Flavoured	7.9
FENTIMANS	Pink Rhubarb	Flavoured	7.8
FEVER-TREE	Aromatic	Flavoured	7.8
FEVER-TREE	Elderflower	Flavoured	7.8
LUSCOMBE	Cucumber	Flavoured	7.8
FENTIMANS	Valencian Orange	Flavoured	7.7
FEVER-TREE	Lemon	Flavoured	7.6
FEVER-TREE	Mediterranean	Flavoured	7.4
STRANGELOVE	Coastal	Flavoured	6
DOUBLE DUTCH	Cranberry and Ginger	Flavoured	4.9
FENTIMANS	Oriental Yuzu	Flavoured	4.9
FRANKLIN & SONS	Elderflower and Cucumber	Flavoured	4.9
FRANKLIN & SONS	Rosemary and Black Olive	Flavoured	4.9
FRANKLIN & SONS	Pink Grapefruit and Bergamot	Flavoured	4.9
FRANKLIN & SONS	Rhubarb and Hibiscus	Flavoured	4.9
STRANGELOVE	Dirty	Flavoured	4.9
TOP NOTE	Bitter Lemon	Flavoured	4.8
DOUBLE DUTCH	Cucumber and Watermelon	Flavoured	4.7
DOUBLE DUTCH	Pomegranate and Basil	Flavoured	4.6
LONDON ESSENCE	Pomelo and Pink Pepper	Flavoured	4.5
DOUBLE DUTCH	Pink Grapefruit	Flavoured	4.3
LONDON ESSENCE	Bitter Orange and Elderflower	Flavoured	4.3

BRAND	PRODUCT	TYPE	SUGAR (g/100ml)
LONDON ESSENCE	Grapefruit and Rosemary	Flavoured	4.2
LONG RAYS	Premium Australian Citrus	Flavoured	4
LONG RAYS	Premium Australian Pacific	Flavoured	3.8
Q MIXERS	Spectacular	Indian	11
CAPI	Tonic	Indian	8.7
SCHWEPPES	Indian	Indian	8.6
LUSCOMBE	Devon	Indian	7.9
FENTIMANS	Connoisseurs	Indian	7.7
BERMONDSEY MIXER CO.	Bermondsey	Indian	7.6
DOUBLE DUTCH	Indian	Indian	7.5
FEVER-TREE	Premium Indian	Indian	7.1
STRANGELOVE	Distiller's	Indian	7
STRANGELOVE	Tonic No. 8 Indian	Indian	7
TOP NOTE	Classic Indian	Indian	6.6
FENTIMANS	Premium Indian	Indian	4.9
LIXIR	Classic Indian	Indian	4.9
TOP NOTE	Indian	Indian	4.8
LONDON ESSENCE	Original Indian	Indian	4.3
LONG RAYS	Premium Australian	Indian	3
CAPI	Dry	Light	6.2
FRANKLIN & SONS	Natural Light	Light	4.9
FEVER-TREE	Refreshingly Light Cucumber	Light	4.8
DOUBLE DUTCH	Skinny	Light	4.7
SCHWEPPES	Signature Light	Light	4.6
FEVER-TREE	Refreshingly Light Mediterranean	Light	4.2
FEVER-TREE	Refreshingly Light	Light	3.8
LUSCOMBE	Light	Light	3.6
SANPELLEGRINO	Tastefully Light	Light	3.5
FENTIMANS	Naturally Light	Light	3.4
STRANGELOVE	Light	Light	2.9

GLOSSARY

Aldehyde
An organic compound formed when oxygen reacts with an alcohol such as ethanol or methanol.

Alpha-pinene
See **Pinene**.

Anethole
An organic compound responsible for the aroma and flavour of anise. It is also present in fennel, star anise, and liquorice. Anethole is 13 times sweeter than sucrose. It is highly soluble in ethanol but only slightly so in water, and so causes **louching** when present in some spirits.

Azeotropic point
The point at which a mixture of liquids being distilled, such as water and ethanol, reach a constant boiling point – meaning no further separation is possible. The vapour and liquid mixture have the same composition, no matter how much more **reflux** takes place.

Beta-pinene
See **Pinene**.

Charge
The mixture of alcohol, water, and any flavourings loaded into a still before distillation.

Flash infusion
Also known as rapid infusion, this technique involves combining a flavouring ingredient with alcohol under pressure for a short time, using nitrous oxide as a solvent.

Foreshots
The very first fractions to come through the still during distillation. These are high in poisonous methanol, as it has a lower boiling point than ethanol.

Glycyrrhizin
A substance present in liquorice root that is 30 to 50 times sweeter than sucrose.

Heads
The fractions that come through the still after the **foreshots** and before the **hearts**. These are filled with undesirable solvent aromas so won't be used in the finished spirit. Nevertheless, they contain useful ethanol so may be mixed into the **charge** for the next distillation (especially in Scotch whisky) or sold on to be made into lighter fluid, hand sanitizer, and so on.

Hearts
The good stuff. Technically, the distillation fractions that contain the highest concentration of ethanol and the best flavours. This is what distillers want and what is bottled and sold to customers.

Isomers
Compounds with the same numbers and types of atoms but different molecular structures.

Limonene
A **monoterpene** that is the major component in the oils of citrus peels. One of its **isomers** is responsible for the aroma of oranges.

Linalyl acetate
An organic compound found in many flowers and spices. It is one of the main components of bergamot and lavender.

Louching
When a clear alcoholic liquid becomes cloudy upon dilution. Also commonly called the ouzo effect.

Malted grains
Grains such as barley, wheat, or maize that have been dried partway through germination. Malting makes the grains' starch available for fermentation.

Monoterpene/monoterpenoids
A **terpene** that has 10 carbon atoms.

New-make spirit
Spirit that has been distilled but not diluted, flavoured, matured, or otherwise altered.

Piperine
An alkaloid responsible for the pungency of black pepper. It activates tongue receptors that are sensitive to heat and acidity.

Pinene
A **monoterpene** present in juniper oil, turpentine, and other natural extracts. One of its **isomers**, alpha-pinene, is the most common natural **terpenoid** and is produced by pine trees, sage, cannabis, and many other plants. The other isomer, beta-pinene, occurs in hops and many other plants.

Rectification
The separation of the volatile fractions and the production of a high-strength spirit.

Reflux
The interaction between vapours in liquids inside the still, whereby the less volatile fractions within the vapours condense back into a liquid and return to the lower portions of the still, while the more volatile fractions remain vaporized and pass further up the still.

Rotovap
Short for "rotary evaporator", a device first invented for chemical laboratories that has since found uses in distillation and molecular gastronomy. It allows distillers to process botanicals at low pressure, and therefore low temperatures, preserving more of the botanicals' delicate aromas and flavours.

Sabinene
A **monoterpene** found in many plants. It contributes to the spicy flavours of black pepper.

Stillage
The liquid left in a pot still once a distillation has been completed, plus any botanicals that were present in the pot.

Stripping
The process of separating all the volatile fractions from some of the water and non-volatile fractions.

Tails
The final fractions to pass through the still. These have a lower concentration of ethanol than the **hearts** and may have vegetal, plastic, bitter, or rubber flavours, depending on what is being distilled. As with the hearts, they may be redistilled or sold on for repurposing.

Terpene/terpenoid
A natural hydrocarbon produced by plants, particularly conifers.

Wash
A fermented, alcoholic liquid that is ready is to be distilled for the first time.

INDEX

Page numbers in **bold** indicate main entries.

A

absinthe: Corpse Reviver No. 2 **129**
Achroous **199**
acid garnishes **152–53**
aged gin 14, 72
agricultural distillers **68**
alcohol 13, 41, 49, 68
  low(er)-alcohol gins **75**
alembic stills 22
almonds 81
American bars **38**
An Dúlamán Irish Maritime **207**
angelica 81, 156
apple juice: English Garden 132
apples 190
ARC Archipelago Botanical **167**
Army and Navy **122**
aromatic compounds **78–79**
aromatic and earthy gins 153, **198–205**
Audemus Pink Pepper **199**
Audemus Umami **207**
Australia 14, 17, 43
Aviation (cocktail) **123**
Aviation (gin) **183**

B

Balfour, William 36
bar spoons 120
Barra Atlantic Gin **208**
barrels 72, **92–93**
barware **118–21**
base spirits 44, **68–69**
basil **174**
bathtub gins 39, 70, 72, 73
bay leaves **174**
Beefeater London Dry **157**
beer 31
Bee's Knees **124**

berries **86–87**
Bertha's Revenge Irish Milk **200**
Bijou **125**
bitter lemon 110
bitters 32, 111
blackberries 190
blueberries 190
Bluecoat American Dry **157**
Bobby's Schiedam Dry **200**
Bombay Sapphire London Dry **158**
Bond, Erasmus 36, 37
Boston shakers 121
botanicals 45, **80–91**
  citrus-forward gins **166**
  earthy and aromatic gins **198**
  floral gins **182**
  fruity gins **190**
  gins that "taste of gin" **156**
  herbal gins **174**
  maritime and umami gins **206**
  for vapour infusion 56
  see also individual botanicals
The Botanist Islay Dry **181**
bottles and bottling 33, **46–47**, 49
Bramble **126**
Bright Young Things 39
Brighton Gin Pavilion Strength **167**
Britain see UK
Brockmans **191**
Bronx **127**
Brookie's Byron Dry **191**
Brooklyn Gin **168**
Buddha's hand **166**

C

calamansi **166**
Campari: Negroni 142
  Old Friend 143
Canaïma **192**
capers 206
cardamom 82, 198
carrageen 206

casks 92
cassia bark 82
champagne: French 75 133
charring barrels 92
chartreuse: Last Word 140
chill filtering 63
Citadelle **201**
Citadelle Jardin d'Été **192**
citrus fruit 16, 83
  citrus-forward gins **166–73**
  garnishes **150–51**
Clive, Robert 35
Clover Club **128**
coastal gins **72–73**
cobbler shakers 119
Cocchi Americano: Corpse Reviver No. 2 129
  20th Century 147
cocktails 38, 39, 41, 42, **116–53**
  Army and Navy **122**
  Aviation **123**
  Bee's Knees **124**
  Bijou **125**
  Bramble **126**
  Bronx **127**
  Clover Club **128**
  Corpse Reviver No. 2 **129**
  Dirty Martini **130**
  Dry Martini **131**
  English Garden **132**
  equipment **118–21**
  French 75 **133**
  garnishes **150–53**
  Gibson **134**
  Gimlet **135**
  Gin Basil Smash **136**
  Gin Fizz **137**
  Hanky Panky **138**
  Juliet and Romeo **139**
  Last Word **140**
  Martinez 33, **141**
  Martini 33
  Negroni **142**

Old Friend 143
Red Snapper 144
Satan's Whiskers 145
Southside Rickey 146
20th Century 147
White Lady 148
White Negroni 149
Coffey, Aeneas 32, 52
Coffey still 52
Cointreau: Corpse Reviver No. 2 129
White Lady 148
cold-compounded gins 70–71, 72, 73
colonization 34–37, 40
column stills 49, 52–53
compounded gins 14, 70–71
condensers 54–55
Conker Spirit Navy Strength 201
Conniption American Dry 175
continental method 65
copper stills 60–61
coriander 16, 80, 156
Corpse Reviver No. 2 39, 129
Cotswolds Dry 176
Cotswolds No. 1 Wildflower 184
Craddock, Harry 39, 145
craft distilleries 42
crème de cacao: 20th Century 147
crème de mûre: Bramble 126
crème de violette: Aviation 123
cubeb 83, 198
Culpeper, Nicholas 18

D

Dà Mhìle Organic Seaweed 208
dalandan 166
Death's Door 176
Defoe, Daniel 25
Dewi Sant Coastal 209
dimethyl sulphide 61
dimethyl trisulphide 61
Dioscorides 18
Dirty Martini 130

distillation 13, 14, 48–65
the condenser 54–55
copper stills 60–61
distilling vs rectifying 69
environmentally friendly 44–45
fractions and flavours 58–59
history of 22–23
louching 62–63, 70
multi-shot 44, 45, 65
other methods of 64–65
pot stills 50–51
vapour infusion 56–57
Dorothy Parker 184
double straining 121
Drumshanbo Gunpowder Irish Gin 168
Dry Martini 131
Dubonnet 111
Dutch East India Company 34

E

earthy and aromatic gins 153, 198–205
East India Company (EIC) 35–36
East London Kew Gin 185
East London Liquor Co. 47
Egypt 18, 22
elder 84, 182
elderflower cordial: English Garden 132
England see UK
Empire 34–37, 40
English Garden 132
environment, gin and 44–47
essences 75
esters 61
EU 13, 21
extracts, gins made from 71

F

fermentation 48–49
Fernet-Branca: Hanky Panky 138
Fever-Tree tonic water 113
Fielding, Henry 28

flavour: balancing flavours 97
casks and 92
flavour compounds 78–79
flavour pairings 97
fractional flavours 59
glassware and 104–105
heightening 150
how flavour works 94–95
juniper 16
navigating gin by flavour 154–213
scent libraries 96
flavoured gins 14, 72, 73
Fleischmann Brothers 33
floral gins 152, 182–89
flowers 86–87
Fords Gin London Dry 158
foreshots 58, 59, 216
Fortnum & Mason 39
44°N 183
Four Pillars Bloody Shiraz 193
Four Pillars Olive Leaf 177
Four Pillars Rare Dry 202
fractional stages 58
French gin 43
French 75 133
fruit 88–89
cold compounding with 71
fruity garnishes 153
fruity gins 153, 190–97
fungal root rot 20–21

G

garnishes 118, 150–53
genever 15, 24
Geometric 202
Gibson 134
Gimlet 135
gin: alcohol strength 13, 41, 68
and the environment 44–47
Gin Craze 24–29
gin tasting 98–103
history of 22–43

ingredients **66–67**
legal definitions of **12–15**
styles of **72–75**
Gin & It 39, 111
Gin & Tonic 37, **114–15**
Gin Acts (1729, 1733, 1736) 26, 27, 28
Gin Basil Smash **136**
gin cordial 14
gin de Mahón 13
Gin Eva La Mallorquina Olive **209**
Gin Fizz **137**
Gin Flip 38
gin liqueur 14
Gin Mare **177**
gin palaces **30–31**
Gin Twist 38
ginger beer 110
gins that "taste of gin" 150, **156–65**
glass bottles **46–47**
glassware: chilling glasses 109
    Gin & Tonic 114
    history of 33
    mixing glass 121
    shape and flavour 104
    tasting glasses 98
    types of **106–107**
global trade 32, **34–35**
graangenever 15
grains 48, 66, 68, 216
grains of paradise 84, 198
Grand Marnier: Satan's Whiskers 145
grapefruit juice: Old Friend 143
grapes 67
Greater Than London Dry 159
Greece 18, 22
green chartreuse: Bijou 125
G'Vine Floraison **185**

H

Hanky Panky **138**
Hapusā Himalayan Dry **203**
Hayman's Exotic Citrus **169**

Hayman's Sloe Gin 77, **193**
heads 58, 59, 63, 216
hearts 58, 59, 216
Height of Arrows **159**
Hendrick's **186**
Hepple Gin **160**
Hepple Sloe & Hawthorn Gin 77, **194**
herbal gins 151, **174–81**
Hernö Navy Strength **160**
hibiscus 182
Highclere Castle London Dry **161**
history of gin **22–43**
Hogarth, William, *Gin Lane* 27
honey: Bee's Knees 124
hybrid stills 64
hydraulic distillation 22
hydrogen sulphide 61

I

ice 38, **108–109**
    Gin & Tonic 114–15
Indian tonic 37, 112
Inverroche Classic **186**
Islamic scholars 22–23
Isle of Harris 47, **210**

J

Jensen's Bermondsey Dry **161**
jiggers 118, 119
jonge genever 15
juicer 118
Juliet and Romeo **139**
juniper **16–21**, 80
    amount in gin 17
    common juniper 17
    flavours of 16
    fungal root rot **20–21**
    harvesting 17
    historical uses of **18–19**
    medicinal uses 18
    role of 16

species 13, 21
taste 19
uses in magic **18–19**
vapour infusion 56
Junipero **162**

K

Ki No Tea Kyoto Dry **178**
Knut Hansen Dry **194**
Komasa Gin Hojicha **178**
korenwijn genever 15
kumquat 166

L

Lark, Bill 43
Last Word **140**
lavender 182
LBD **187**
Le Gin de Christian Drouin **195**
leaves **88–89**
lemon juice: Army and Navy 122
    Aviation 123
    Bee's Knees 124
    Bramble 126
    Clover Club 128
    Corpse Reviver No. 2 129
    English Garden 132
    French 75 133
    Gin Basil Smash 136
    Gin Fizz 137
    Red Snapper 144
    20th Century 147
    White Lady 148
lemon myrtle 174
lemons 156
Lillet Blanc: Corpse Reviver No. 2 129
    White Negroni 149
lime juice: Gimlet 135
    Juliet and Romeo 139
    Last Word 140
    Southside Rickey 146

limes 32
Lind, James 36
Lind & Lime **169**
liquorice 85, 156
London **24–29**, 35, 39, 40
London Dry gins 13, 32, 73, 74, 75
London to Lima **203**
louching **62–63**, 70, 216
low(er)-alcohol gins **75**
Lussa **210**

M

Magarian, Ryan 43, 74
Mainbrace Cornish Dry **211**
malaria, quinine and 36
Maloney, Toby 139
Mandeville, Bernard 15
Manguin Oli'Gin **211**
Manly Coastal Citrus **212**
maraschino liqueur: Aviation 123
  Last Word 140
  Martinez 141
maritime and umami gins 152, **206–13**
Martin Miller's **162**
Martinez 33, **141**
Martinis 33
  Dirty Martini **130**
  Dry Martini **131**
mashing 48
Mediterranean Gin by Léoube **179**
Melifera **187**
Mermaid **212**
Mermaid Pink Gin **195**
milling 48
mimosa 182
mixers 32, **110–11**
mixing glass 121
Monkey 47 Schwarzwald Dry **188**
monoterpene/monoterpenoids 16, 216
Moorish alcohol 22
Mother's Ruin 25, 39
multi-shot distillation 44, 45, 65

N

Navy strength gins 74
Negroni **142**
New Western Dry gins 43, **74**
New Zealand 14, 17
Nikka Coffey **170**
No. 3 London Dry **204**
No. 6 Laver Atlantic Spirit **213**

O

Old Friend **143**
Old Tom gins 33, **74–75**
olives 206
O'ndina **179**
135° East Hyogo Dry **175**
orange juice: Bronx 127
  Hanky Panky 138
orgeat: Army and Navy 122
orris root 85, 156, 182
oude genever 15
oude graangenever 15
Oxley London Dry **170**

P

packaging **46–47**, 113
Palma **171**
paring knife 118
peelers 118
peels **90–91**
Pegu Club 39
Penrhos Dry **188**
pepperberry 198
Perry's Tot Navy Strength **204**
Phoenician juniper 21
phylloxera 33
Phytophthora austrocedri **20–21**
pink gin 111
Plymouth Gin 29, 40, 46, 74, **75**, **163**
pot stills 49, **50–51**, 52
potatoes 67

Q

quince 190
quinine **36–37**

R

Ramsbury Single Estate 44, **196**
raspberries 190
  Clover Club 128
rectification 69, 217
Red Snapper **144**
redberry juniper 21
redistilled gin 14
refills 46, 47
Rock Rose Citrus Coastal
  Edition **213**
Rock Rose Pink Grapefruit
  Old Tom **171**
rock samphire 206
Roku **180**
Romans 18
roots **90–91**
rosemary 174
rosewater: Juliet and Romeo 139
rum 41
Rumfustian 38

S

Sacred Pink Grapefruit **172**
St Germain: Old Friend 143
Salerno 23
salt garnishes **152–53**
Sandy Gray **205**
Santa Ana **189**
Satan's Whiskers **145**
scent libraries **96**

Procera Blue Dot **205**
Procera Green Dot **163**
prohibition 39, 70
Puerto de Indias Strawberry **196**

sea lettuce 206
Second World War (1939–45) **40**
seeds **90–91**
serving gin **110–11**
Seven Hills (VII) Italian
        Dry **180**
shakers 119, 121
shell-and-tube condensers 55
shiso 174
Silent Pool **189**
Silent Pool Rare Citrus **172**
single-estate gin 44
Sipsmith VJOP **164**
sloe gin 14, **76–77**
smell 94, 95
soda water: Gin Fizz 137
    Southside Rickey 146
The Source **197**
Southside Rickey **146**
speakeasies 39
Spice Islands 34
spicy garnishes **152**
spirits: bases 66, **68–69**
    mixing gin with 114
spoons, bar 120
star anise 198
stillage 58, 59, 217
stills: column stills 49, **52–53**
        copper stills **60–61**
        history of 32
        hybrid stills 64
        pot stills 49, **50–51**, 52
strainers and straining 120, 121
sugars **66–67**
supercritical extraction **64–65**
Suze: White Negroni 149
sweet vermouth: Bijou 125
    Bronx 127
    Hanky Panky 138
    Martinez 141
    Negroni 142
    Satan's Whiskers 145
syrup, simple **120**

T

tails 58, 59, 63, 217
Tanqueray Blackcurrant Royale
        Distilled **197**
Tanqueray London Dry **164**
Tanqueray No. Ten **173**
Tarquin's Cornish Dry **165**
taste: gin tasting **98–103**
        glassware and **104–105**
        taste sensation 94, 95, 97
Texas juniper 21
Thomas, Jerry 38
Tippling Act (1751) **28–29**
tomato juice: Red Snapper
        144
tonic syrup 113
tonic water 32, **112–13**
        Gin & Tonic **114–15**
        history of **36–37**
        sugar in **214–15**
transport 46, 47
tumblers **106–107**
20th Century (cocktail) **147**

U

UK 13, 17, 42
        history of gin in **24–31**, 32, 35, 38,
            39, 40
        tonic water 36–37
umami and maritime gins 152–53, **206–13**
US 14, 17
        craft distilleries 42–43
        history of gin 33
        prohibition 39, 70

V

vacuum distillation 64
vapour infusion **56–57**
Vereenigde Oostindische
        Compagnie (VOC) 34

vermouth 111
    Bronx 127
    Dirty Martini 130
    Dry Martini 131
    Gibson 134
    Hanky Panky 138
    Martinez 141
    Negroni 142
    Satan's Whiskers 145
vodka 41, 42
volatility 50, 94

W

Wa Bi **173**
water 45, 49, 110
whey 67
White Lady **148**
White Negroni **149**
William of Orange 15, 24
wine 33
woody garnishes **152**
worm tubs 54

X

Xoriguer Mahón 13, **181**

Y

York Gin Old Tom **165**
yuzu 166

ABOUT THE AUTHOR

Anthony Gladman is a drinks writer from London. He has always been fascinated by flavour; now he gets to write about it for a living. In 2022, he won the Guild of Food Writers Drinks Writing Award, largely because the judges had (almost) as much fun reading his work as he did writing it. He has also won numerous awards from the British Guild of Beer Writers, most recently for articles published on sustainability in brewing. His storytelling is entertaining, precise, rich with hilarity, and fizzing with well-researched information. You can find his work in trade and consumer magazines on both sides of the Atlantic and online at anthonygladman.com.

AUTHOR'S ACKNOWLEDGMENTS

The book you hold in your hands would not have been possible without the support of my agent, Elly James, and the vision of Cara Armstrong at DK for commissioning it. I'm also hugely grateful to Izzy Holton for running the editorial process so smoothly; to Dawn Titmus for her deft and insightful editing; to Vanessa Hamilton for design and illustrations; and to Marta Bescos for contacting the distilleries and collecting all the images. Thanks also to everyone else at DK who helped bring this book to life.

Selecting gins to taste for this book, and actually getting hold of them, was no small task. I am hugely grateful to all the distillers who sent me their gins to taste – and to Anita Ujszaszi and Alison Taffs for helping me find particular gins when my own efforts fell short.

Where I could, I leant on those who know more than me. It's a sound strategy and I heartily recommend it. Big thanks to David T. Smith for sharing his wide-ranging knowledge, especially on gins from further afield; to Susan Boyle for her insights into Irish gins; to Christine Lambert for turning me on to some superb French gins; and to Charlie Thomas at Jensen's for his sound counsel on cocktails. I almost certainly owe Chris Garden at Hepple a Martini or two for answering all my questions on the technical minutiae of distilling with such good grace.

I also owe a debt of gratitude to all those without whom I wouldn't have been in a position to write this book in the first place. Big up Hannah Lanfear from The Mixing Class for filling my head with spirits, being interested/brave/foolish enough to taste neutral spirits with me, and always being up for nerding out about flavour. Thanks also to John McCarthy at Adnams, Nik Fordham at Ramsbury, Ian McCulloch at Silent Pool, Fairfax Hall and Sam Galsworthy at Sipsmith, and Charles Maxwell at Thames Distillers. They have all been generous over the past few years with their time, knowledge, and contacts.

And lastly, thanks to my family for putting up with a house full of gin for months on end. I promise I'll get rid of it soon. I just need to taste a few more first.

PUBLISHER'S ACKNOWLEDGMENTS

DK would like to thank the gin distilleries for their kind permission to reproduce images of their products, Marta Bescos and Niranjan Sathyanarayanan for picture research, Niyran Gill for the cover illustration, John Friend for proofreading, and Vanessa Bird for the index.

p20 Affected Areas: data from www.forestresearch.gov.uk/ tools-and-resources/fthr/pest-and-disease-resources/ phytophthora-austrocedri-disease-of-juniper-and-cypress/ Open Government Licence v3.0, www.nationalarchives.gov.uk/ doc/open-government-licence/version/3/

PICTURE CREDITS

The publisher would like to thank the following for their kind permission to reproduce their photographs:

(Key: a-above; b-below/bottom; c-centre; f-far; l-left; r-right; t-top)

Alamy Stock Photo: Zuri Swimmer 15, British Library/Album 22, Pictorial Press Ltd 23, 25b, Heritage Image Partnership Ltd/ London Metropolitan Archives (City of London) 26, Natthanan Limpornchaicharoen 27, World History Archive 28, 29, Chronicle 30, M&N 31b, Steve Vidler 31t, incamerastock/ICP 32, CPA Media Pte Ltd 34, incamerastock 35, Historic Images 36bl, Science History Images 36tr, History and Art Collection 38, Neil Baylis 40, f8 archive 41, Sunny Celeste 52, Carolyn Eaton 60, Glasshouse Images/JT Vintage 112; © Board of Trustees of the Royal Botanic Gardens, Kew: 37cla; Bridgeman Images: Florilegius/Rowlandson, Thomas (1756–1827)/English 25t; Dà Mhìle Organic Seaweed Gin: Heather Birnie 208bl; Depositphotos Inc: guieriero93.gmail. com 42bc, br; Dreamstime.com: Nicku 24, Rasto Blasko 33cla, Monticelllo 33ca; Dunnet Bay Distillers Ltd: 213bl; Getty Images: Universal Images Group/Werner Forman 18; Holyrood Distillery: Murray Orr 159bl; Kangaroo Island Spirits: 43tc; Melifera: Miguel Ramos photographie 187bl; Shutterstock. com: barinart 43fbl; Southwestern Distillery: 165tl; The Advertising Archives 39.

All other images © Dorling Kindersley.

Project Editor Izzy Holton
Senior Designer Glenda Fisher
Production Editor David Almond
Senior Production Controller Luca Bazzoli
Jacket Designer Eloise Grohs
Jacket Coordinator Abi Gain
Art Director Maxine Pedliham
Editorial Director Cara Armstrong
Publishing Director Katie Cowan

Editorial Dawn Titmus
Design and Illustration Vanessa Hamilton

First published in Great Britain in 2023 by
Dorling Kindersley Limited
DK, One Embassy Gardens, 8 Viaduct Gardens,
London, SW11 7BW

The authorized representative in the EEA is
Dorling Kindersley Verlag GmbH. Arnulfstr. 124,
80636 Munich, Germany

Printed and bound in Slovakia

For the curious
www.dk.com

This book was made with Forest
Stewardship Council™ certified
paper – one small step in DK's
commitment to a sustainable future.
For more information go to
www.dk.com/our-green-pledge